John Ash
cooking
one
on
one

John Ash
cooking
one
on
one

Private Lessons in Simple, Contemporary
Food from a Master Teacher

JOHN ASH with Amy Mintzer

CLARKSON POTTER/PUBLISHERS
NEW YORK

Grateful acknowledgment is made to the following for permission to reprint previously published material:

Alfred A. Knopf: Excerpt from *Home Cooking: A Writer in the Kitchen* by Laurie Colwin. Reprinted by permission of Alfred A. Knopf, a division of Random House, Inc.

Lescher & Lescher, Ltd.: "A Delicate Onion Soup," "A Robust Onion Soup" and excerpts from *A Cordiall Water* by M.F.K. Fisher. Published by North Point Press. Copyright © 1961, 1981 by M.F.K. Fisher. All rights reserved. Reprinted by permission of Lescher & Lescher, Ltd.

Published by Clarkson Potter/Publishers, New York, New York.
Member of the Crown Publishing Group, a division of Random House, Inc.
www.crownpublishing.com

CLARKSON N. POTTER is a trademark and POTTER and colophon are registered trademarks of Random House, Inc.

Printed in United States of America

Design by Maggie Hinders

Library of Congress Cataloging-in-Publication Data
Ash, John
   John Ash: cooking one on one : private lessons in simple, contemporary food
from a master teacher / John Ash with Amy Mintzer.
1. Cookery, American.   I. Mintzer, Amy.   II. Title.
   TX715.A774   2003
   641.5973—dc21   2002153603

ISBN 0-609-60967-X

10 9 8 7 6 5 4 3 2 1

First Edition

acknowledgments

I have to say that I'm one of the luckiest people on earth. I found something in food that continues to sustain me and keep my passions alive. I've had the chance to do all sorts of things, from creating a restaurant to writing, doing a little TV, and doing to what I love to do most: teaching about food, its lore and seductions. This book shares gifts and inspiration that I've gotten from so many talented folks, including four amazing women who I'm so thankful are in my life: first, my "co-conspirator" (as I've referred to her elsewhere in the text) Amy Mintzer, who is an amazing editor and wordsmith; Sarah Jane Freymann, our literary agent, whose gentle and clear vision keeps me centered; Beth Henderson, a great research assistant and techno wiz; and Andrea Koweek, recipe tester, champion, and good friend.

I've had and continue to get inspiration from many cooks and chefs too numerous to mention here (but thank you!). However, two who are in my Northern California "backyard" I must acknowledge: Jeff Madura, who continues to do great work at John Ash & Company restaurant, and Bridget Harrington, who is an inspiration at Fetzer Vineyards Valley Oaks Ranch, where I spend as much time as I possibly can. My continued association with Fetzer has been one of the delights of my career.

For the production of this book, thanks to Pam Krauss, Marysarah Quinn, and Maggie Hinders of Clarkson Potter, and especially thanks to Noel Barnhurst, a photographer I've been lucky enough to work with for a number of years, for his uncluttered vision.

John Ash
SONOMA COUNTY, CALIFORNIA

In addition, I would like to thank Bill, Rose, and Max for generosity, patience, and being good eaters; Ruth Seidler for friendship and a place to work; Carole De Santi for introducing me to John . . . and for a place to work; Janis Allicock for her help and goodwill; Ellen Lourie, Stacey Frisch, Lisa Schroeder, and Susan Varisco, among many friends whose uninhibited questions helped us shape this book; and my brother, Damon, whose transcontinental cell phone calls from the supermarket aisle inspired me to propose such a project to John. As someone who thinks she knows everything, let me just say how grateful I am for the privilege of working with John Ash, who really does know everything and is unfailingly generous and gracious about it. Believe me: If John can teach me, he can teach anyone.

Amy Mintzer

contents

read this introduction

You may or may not consider yourself a cook,

but I know you're an eater. You eat three times a day, or two, or five, and if you didn't like it, you wouldn't be reading this book. So it's as an eater that I'm going to address you. Don't worry about whether you're a "good cook" or a "bad cook." You're a person who likes to eat and needs to eat, maybe a person who likes and needs to feed others, and you've decided for whatever reason to try producing more of what you eat in your own kitchen. At the very least, you'd like some fresh ideas for dinner.

Because here's the rub: You have very high standards for the food you eat—higher in many ways than any previous generation's. You have sophisticated ideas about what constitutes "good food," and you assume it takes time and expertise to produce good food at home. To you, good food has to be fresh, it has to be healthy, and it has to be grilled over a mesquite fire and served in a nest of baby vegetables glazed with reduced balsamic vinegar and garnished with a kumquat and sun-dried tomato compote. Meanwhile, you spend a lot of hours at work, you're overcommitted outside your job, and either you have a family (which means too many people to please at dinner) or you're single (which means there's no one else to please at dinner). Either way, it seems daunting or pointless to cook. I know from teaching that those of you who are accomplished cooks are just as vulnerable to that sinking feeling. So you order take-out. Or you stock your freezer with glamorous-sounding frozen entrées. Or you clean out the prepared-foods counter at your gourmet supermarket where balsamic-glazed baby vegetables and kumquat and sun-dried tomato compote are readily available.

Or you choose a route home from the gym that takes you past McDonald's.

I'm here to tell you there's another way. A way through your own kitchen. A way that will bring pleasure to your table and, yes, your life (and who couldn't use a little more of *that*?), while saving you some money and some calories along the way. And remember: money and calories that you save by skipping the mediocre take-out are money and calories that you can spend in a really good restaurant.

And guess what? You don't need to learn *how* to cook. You just need to learn *what* to cook. That's where this book comes in.

John Ash: Cooking One on One is a series of self-contained lessons. It is not a kitchen primer and it's not "the only cookbook you'll ever need." It is my highly personal take on the very contemporary food that you already love, approached in the most unintimidating way possible. You can work your way through the book from cover to cover, if you feel like it, but you don't need to. On a day when you're relaxed and have a little bit of time, pick a lesson that appeals to you. Read it through—introduction, recipes, and all. Make a shopping list. Go buy what you need. Then make something. It can be a very little something, a vinaigrette, some dried beans, or a little dipping sauce. Then you can add it to the dinner you were already going to have, or you can set it aside and plan a whole meal around it tomorrow. After twenty-five years of teaching, I know that you don't have to perfect all the basic kitchen skills in order to make great food. I also know that even experienced cooks can be surprised at how simple preparing great food can be.

You'll find three kinds of lessons: those based on **flavor-makers,** such as salsas and marinades; those teaching a **technique,** such as oven-drying or soufflé-making; and those offering a fresh look at a familiar **main ingredient,** like chicken or shrimp or dried pasta. Every lesson, no matter how it's structured, opens with a simple discussion about basic procedures, or any issues of interest around buying or cooking the main ingredient—that kind of thing. Though the recipes are self-contained, I do urge you to read the lesson openers. From there, we get right into the kitchen. In some lessons, the recipes are all fairly simple; in others, they progress from simple to more elaborate. Even the simplest may include a few add-ons or variations. Even the most elaborate can be simplified by leaving out a component or two. My goal is to teach you about flavor and to encourage your creativity and sense of the possibilities of the kitchen, even with the most basic of meals. As in my live classes, I've tried to include enough background and tips to keep things interesting, without overwhelming you with information you don't need. If the style of the recipes is a little different from what you're used to, that's my way of trying to be in the kitchen with you, to break it all apart into manageable components and teach as I go. I want to take the mystery out of cooking so that the magic can go back in.

Dialogue is essential to teaching, and when I teach, I try to elicit and answer as many questions as possible. Since I'm not actually in the room with you, I've tried to anticipate your questions and answer them within the lessons. Here are a few that I'm anticipating right now.

I've flipped through the book. If these recipes are supposed to be simple, how come they have seventeen ingredients?

The short answer is: short is not the same as simple. A recipe can have three ingredients and still require four pots, three hands, and a delicate touch with caramelizing sugar. Another recipe with lots of ingredients can be thrown together in one bowl in ten minutes by any well-meaning twelve-year-old. There are certainly wonderful recipes in this book, recipes that will excite your palate and impress your friends, and that use very few ingredients (the Ponzu Sauce on page 72 and the Grilled Salmon with a Lemon-Balsamic Glaze on page 259 are good examples). But in general, interesting flavors, to me, mean lots of flavors, and you can achieve that only by combining a bunch of different things. Don't judge a recipe's degree of difficulty by its length. Now there are some genuinely longer (to make) and more complex (to assemble) recipes here, generally toward the ends of the lessons. Of course, you never have to make one of them. But I hope they'll interest you, I hope they'll inspire you, and I hope you'll give them a try someday.

I never cook with cream or butter or a cup and a half of olive oil. How can this be healthy?

Fat is an essential nutrient, and fat is an incomparable flavor carrier. But that's not going to convince you. Think about this: when you eat out, how often do you actually, really and truly, order the baked fish and steamed vegetables, hold the sauce? Maybe never? The simple truth is that there's almost nothing you're going to prepare at home that contains as much fat as most restaurant food, good or bad. If you're really strict, there are plenty of recipes in this book (probably most of them, in fact) that would pass nutritional muster. But I encourage you to loosen up.

Why do you use so many far-out ingredients, like Asian fish sauce and chipotles in adobo? I don't have this kind of thing in my pantry.

People tell me all the time that they don't have time to cook; I've never had anyone tell me that they don't have time to shop. *Shopping is one of the simplest techniques imaginable for making great food.* Most of the flavors of the world are available in a store near you; this is one of the great pleasures of cooking and eating in America today. If you don't have fish sauce and canned chipotles in your pantry, go out and buy some. Nothing that comes out of a bottle or can is difficult to use, whether or not you can locate its country of origin on a world map. The Glossary and Pantry section at the end of the book will give you all the information you need on unfamiliar ingredients.

Can I skip the parts about organics, chicken farming, and sustainable aquaculture?

Well, I'd rather you didn't. True, a genetically engineered potato grown with pesticides and harvested with herbicides on a corporate "farm" and shipped to you from halfway around the world behaves in much the same way on your cutting board as an organic heirloom potato lovingly raised on the nearest family farm. But it may not taste the same, and it may not treat your body the same, and the planet we live on may be able to tell the difference too. How food is grown, harvested, slaughtered, fumigated, packaged, stored, and handled should be of concern to all of us, as cooks and eaters, and as residents of Earth. As I learn more about specific food production practices, my concern grows, but so does my conviction that individuals can effect change. The choices that each of us make every day as we purchase the food we eat are critical: they affect our personal health and the diversity and quality of what's available, as well as the environment itself. Great ingredients come from great land. I've tried not to overwhelm you with information on ethical agriculture and related topics, because my primary goal in this book is to get you cooking more. Just know that in spite of my restraint, these issues are always on my mind now when I cook and shop and I hope to raise your consciousness too.

So let's get into the kitchen. And by the way: How to make Reduced Balsamic Vinegar is on page 161.

part one

flavor-maker
lessons

1

salsas

America's Favorite Fresh Condiment

In most
of America
today, we take
salsas almost for granted. The news that sales of salsa had passed

ketchup, making it America's number one condiment, was a major side-

bar topic a couple of years ago. It was an indication of both how the

ethnic balance in America was changing and how much more adventur-

ous Americans had become in their eating. (Of course, it's also because no

one eats a jarful of ketchup in one sitting, but, hey, who's counting?)

But while supermarket salsa is a narrowly defined condiment with

limited uses, the wide world of homemade salsas is a great adventure

in flavor and texture. The word *salsa* is Spanish for "sauce" and covers a

wide range of recipes, from fresh, raw, chunky *salsa frescas, salsa crudas,* and

pico de gallos to cooked and sometimes vinegared smooth sauces, includ-

ing mysterious and complex moles of many colors. For most of us, however, salsa has come to mean the chunky, Mexican tomato-based condiment-cum-salad, and that is the focus of this lesson. Salsas are easy to make, can be made ahead, and are the perfect healthy topper to all manner of quickly prepared dishes, enlivening the most unlikely foods—everything from roasted potatoes to seafood cakes, grilled meats, and poultry. They can be used like any relish or served in larger portions like mini-salads. Best of all, salsas give terrific bang for your buck: with minimal effort from you, a salsa can deliver an incredible blend of flavors and sensations—sweet, sour, hot, herbal, cool, crunchy—in one tiny mouthful.

Good salsas are easy to make: generally it's chop, mix, and eat. Great salsas demand little more—the biggest difference between a good salsa and a great one is the quality of the ingredients. A little restaurant that I like puts out the simplest salsa fresca and tortilla chips when they bring the menu. I never leave without having eaten the entire bowl, because they always use the most amazing tomatoes, and the flavor impact of that one ingredient is incredible. Use top-notch raw materials full of flavor at the peak of freshness and you'll have great salsa.

How can I make salsa if chopping onions makes me cry?

If you harvested your own onions, you wouldn't have this problem. "Young" (recently harvested) onions are generally sweeter, with less of the sulfur compounds that make some onions taste funky and set you weeping. Most of us, however, have little control over the age of our onions. You can minimize this problem—and have better tasting salsa—by immediately throwing your chopped onions into a bowl of ice water. Try several changes of water for best results. Unless I've got a Walla Walla or a Vidalia or one of the other super-sweet varieties, I do this soak-drain-repeat process not just for salsas, but whenever the onions are going to be eaten raw.

Is salsa a good "make-ahead" food?

The "freshness factor" means that salsas are at their best soon after they are made, although most benefit from a little sitting time so the flavors can develop. That's not to say that you can't make a salsa today and store it in the fridge for dinner tomorrow or the next day; you can. But long before it goes bad, a salsa will start to wilt, losing that bright, crisp quality that makes it so irresistible. Once you realize how many uses there are for salsa beyond tortilla chips, I doubt it'll hang around your refrigerator long enough for it to be a problem.

basic salsa fresca or cruda

MAKES ABOUT 1¼ CUPS

The simplest of the salsas (and the most familiar to us all) is the classic New World combination of tomatoes, onions, chiles, and garlic, to which other seasonings can be added as desired. The basic recipe follows, along with some suggested additions. You can certainly eat this straight out of the bowl with tortilla chips, but you can also use it to top various cooked foods. I've given some recipes; I hope they'll open up your mind to the possibilities.

2 medium ripe tomatoes, seeded and
   diced (about ¾ pound)
½ cup diced red onion
1 teaspoon minced, seeded serrano
   chile, or to taste
1 tablespoon minced fresh garlic

3 tablespoons chopped fresh cilantro
   leaves
Drops of lime or lemon juice to taste
Pinch of sugar
1 tablespoon olive oil (optional)
Salt and freshly ground pepper to taste

COMBINE ALL THE ingredients in a mixing or serving bowl, and set aside for at least 30 minutes to allow the flavors to blend. Before using the salsa, taste it and add more of any of the seasonings you think are needed. Store covered in the refrigerator. For best flavor, eat within 1 day, but it can be stored for as long as 3. (Use your judgment here.) You can easily multiply the quantities to make more.

NOTE: For more information on serrano, jalapeño, habanero, and other chiles essential to making great salsas, see the Glossary and Pantry.

variations CHARRED SALSA Place a heavy, unoiled skillet over medium heat for a minute or two. Add a whole unpeeled onion, 2 to 3 cloves of garlic, and 1 or 2 chiles, and toast for a few minutes on all sides or until the vegetables have softened a bit and blackened in small spots. Transfer to a plate to cool, then remove the peels from the onion and garlic. Chop these and the chiles following the quantities in the recipe above or adjusting to your taste, and add to the rest of the ingredients.

GREEN AND RED SALSA Substitute 2 to 3 fresh husked tomatillos (see Glossary and Pantry) for one of the tomatoes.

SMOKED SALSA You can lightly smoke the tomatoes, onions, chiles, and garlic before chopping in a stovetop smoker (available at better cookware stores), or on the grill.

HERE ARE two of my favorite ways to use a a simple Salsa Fresca.

grilled marinated shrimp with salsa fresca

SERVES 4 AS A MAIN COURSE

These shrimp can be served right off the grill or at room temperature as part of a summer buffet. You can either peel the shrimp as suggested or grill them with the shell on, which adds a lot of flavor. If you choose to grill with the shell on, snip it along the back with a pair of scissors so that you can remove the sand vein.

I pound large (16–20 size or larger)
   shrimp
½ teaspoon salt

MARINADE
¼ cup olive oil
2 teaspoons finely minced or pressed
   garlic
I tablespoon finely minced green onions
½ teaspoon finely chopped fresh
   oregano (or ¼ teaspoon dried)

¼ teaspoon red pepper flakes
2 tablespoons white wine, preferably a
   dry or off-dry aromatic

Basic Salsa Fresca or Cruda (page 4)

Garnish if you like with avocado slices,
   lime wedges

PEEL AND DEVEIN the shrimp (tail on, tail off—it's up to you). Whisk the marinade ingredients together, toss with the shrimp, and marinate for up to 45 minutes in the refrigerator. Skewer, if desired, to facilitate grilling.

Prepare a charcoal fire or preheat a gas or stovetop grill or broiler. Grill or broil the shrimp quickly, 1 to 2 minutes per side, until they just begin to turn pink. Be careful not to overcook; the shrimp should remain slightly transparent in the middle.

Spoon the salsa onto the middle of each plate and arrange the shrimp around it. Garnish with avocado slices and lime wedges, if desired, and serve. I eat this with my fingers.

NOTE: For a more detailed description of peeling and cleaning shrimp, see page 272. Shrimp headed for the grill really benefit from a little time spent in brine. For that procedure, see page 271.

white bean salad with salsa fresca

SERVES 4 TO 6

This is a delicious, healthy salad that is good both as a stand-alone dish or as a bed for a piece of grilled or broiled chicken or fish.

3 cups cooked white beans, such as cannellini (drained and rinsed if using canned)

2 tablespoons extra virgin olive oil

I cup diced red or green onions

3 tablespoons drained, chopped capers

I tablespoon minced fresh mint leaves

I tablespoon minced fresh parsley leaves

I tablespoon roasted or poached garlic (see Glossary and Pantry)

Salt and freshly ground black pepper to taste

2 cups or so lightly packed tender arugula or watercress leaves

2/3 cup or so **Basic Salsa Fresca or Cruda (page 4)**

Garnish if you like with freshly grated Cotija (aged Mexican cheese) or Pecorino and lemon wedges

COMBINE THE BEANS, olive oil, onions, capers, mint, parsley, garlic, salt, and pepper. Mound the bean mixture on plates and arrange the arugula around it. Make an indentation in the mound of beans and spoon in some salsa. Sprinkle with a little cheese and serve with lemon wedges, if desired, so everyone can add lemon juice to taste.

NOTE: The bean mixture can be made up to 3 days ahead and stored covered in the refrigerator.

NOW THAT you've got a basic fresh salsa down, here are some additional salsa ideas, along with recipes to expand your repertoire.

grilled corn salsa

MAKES ABOUT 3 CUPS

Tomatoes are only one vegetable that can make a delicious salsa. Here grilled corn and peppers, mild and hot, combine for a complex-flavored salsa with great texture and visual appeal. Grilling the corn adds a smoky flavor, but if you are in a hurry you can skip the grilling, especially if the corn is sweet and tender. Other variations could include the addition of finely diced zucchini or jicama, and cooked black beans or black-eyed peas can be substituted for the corn. Use this just like you would use the Salsa Fresca—that is, almost anywhere! I like it so much that I've used it with both salmon and shrimp (page 261). This salsa also can double as a side dish for a summer picnic.

3 large ears sweet corn
I medium red bell pepper, cut in half, with stem, ribs, and seeds removed
I medium poblano pepper, cut in half, with stem, ribs, and seeds removed
I small jalapeño chile
I medium red onion, peeled and halved

4 tablespoons olive oil
Sea salt and freshly ground pepper
2 tablespoons fresh lime or lemon juice, or to taste
I teaspoon honey, or to taste
1/3 cup chopped fresh cilantro or mint leaves, or a combination

PREPARE A CHARCOAL fire or preheat a gas or stovetop grill or broiler. Brush the corn, peppers, chile, and onion with 3 tablespoons of the olive oil and season generously with salt and pepper. Place the vegetables on a medium-hot grill and cook on all sides until they just begin to color. Remove from the grill.

When the vegetables are cool enough to handle, cut the kernels from the cob and place in a bowl. (If you cut or break the ears in half, you'll have a flat surface to hold against the cutting board as you work.) Pull as much of the skin as possible from the peppers, dice them, and add them to the corn. Dice the onion and add it to the corn, along with the lime juice, honey, cilantro or mint, and the remaining tablespoon of olive oil. Set aside for at least 30 minutes before using to allow the flavors to blend. Store covered in the refrigerator for up to 3 days.

pineapple melon salsa

MAKES ABOUT 3 CUPS

Salsas are not only made from tomatoes but often from fruits as well. Any combination of firm ripe fruits can be used. How about mango, cucumber, or even firm banana? I love this recipe as a topper for grilled pork; meaty fish like sea bass, halibut, or tuna; and of course, with chicken done almost any way.

1 cup diced melon
2 cups diced fresh pineapple (from
   1 small pineapple, peeled and cored)
1 teaspoon seeded and minced serrano
   chiles
1/2 cup finely diced red onion
2 tablespoons olive oil

1 teaspoon finely minced garlic
1 tablespoon rice or apple cider vinegar
1 tablespoon fresh lemon or lime juice
1 teaspoon honey, or to taste
Salt and freshly ground pepper to taste
3 tablespoons chopped fresh cilantro or
   mint leaves

COMBINE THE MELON, pineapple, chiles, and onion in a bowl. In a separate bowl, whisk the olive oil, garlic, vinegar, lemon juice, and honey together. Taste the oil mixture and adjust the seasoning with salt, pepper, or additional drops of vinegar, lemon juice, and honey, if needed. Just before serving, drizzle the oil mixture over the fruit and gently toss with the cilantro. Can be made ahead and stored covered in the refrigerator for up to 3 days.

variation For additional flavor, lightly oil and grill or broil the pineapple (round slices are easiest), chile, and onion before chopping them up.

pan-seared sea bass with
pineapple melon salsa

SERVES 6

You could use any fresh meaty fish, such as halibut, tuna, or salmon, for this recipe. Note the technique here of starting the fish on top of the stove and then finishing it in the oven, a practice used widely in restaurants. Pan-searing creates a rich crust that helps seal in the juices; then the oven's more gentle heat cooks the fish through. You could of course do the whole thing on top of the stove. Start the fish on high heat to form the crust, turn to form a crust on the other side, then reduce the heat to medium, partially cover, and finish cooking.

5 tablespoons olive oil
2 tablespoons fresh lime juice
2 teaspoons pure chile powder, such as ancho or chipotle (see Glossary and Pantry)
6 5-ounce fillets of sea bass, cut at least ¾ inch thick

Sea or kosher salt
Pineapple Melon Salsa

Garnish if you like with fresh cilantro or mint sprigs

PREHEAT THE OVEN to 425°F. Whisk together 3 tablespoons of the olive oil, the lime juice, and chile powder until just combined. Place the fish in a single layer on a plate and rub both sides of each fillet with the oil mixture. Marinate for about 10 minutes, then salt the fish lightly on both sides.

Heat the remaining 2 tablespoons of olive oil in a heavy ovenproof skillet over high heat. When the oil is shimmering, add the fish and sear on one side, until it develops a nice golden crust. Turn the fish over and immediately place the pan in the hot oven for about 5 minutes, until just cooked through. Serve immediately on warm plates topped with the salsa and sprigs of cilantro, if desired.

xnipec

No, it's not a typo! I've included this salsa because it has a wonderful history as well as a mysterious name. Pronounced schnee-peek, it is one of the most ancient salsa recipes from the Mayans in the Yucatan area of Mexico, where I first encountered it many years ago. It is traditionally made with a sour orange related to Europe's Seville orange, which has an exotic, wonderful perfume quite distinct from those of other oranges. Chances are you won't find Sevilles in most American markets but they're worth looking for. I've substituted a mixture of lime and orange that approximates the flavor. By the way, xnipec translates to "the dog's nose." Eat too much and your nose will run and be wet like a dog's, according to old friends of mine. In Mexico, they don't remove the chile before serving, as I've done here, but they are tougher than we are. If you are a real "chile head" then you can chop up the chile and leave it in.

1 cup seeded and diced firm ripe
   tomato
¾ cup finely diced white onion
⅓ cup fresh lime juice
⅓ cup fresh orange juice
1 small habanero chile, cut in half, with
   seeds removed

½ cup finely sliced red radishes
2 tablespoons finely chopped fresh
   cilantro or mint leaves, or a
   combination
Salt to taste

COMBINE THE TOMATO, onion, citrus juices, and chile halves in a bowl and stir gently. Set aside for an hour while the heat of the chile develops. Taste carefully, and remove the chiles when the "temperature" is hot enough. Stir in the radishes and cilantro, taste, and season with salt as needed. This is best served the day it is made.

grilled thin pork chops
with xnipec and avocado sauce

SERVES 4

Many supermarkets today offer thin cut pork chops that take just a couple of minutes to cook. Buy them with the bone on if you can, because the bone adds flavor to the meat.

1 small, ripe avocado, peeled and pit removed

1/2 teaspoon finely chopped serrano or jalapeño chile

2 tablespoons chopped fresh cilantro leaves

1/2 cup or so homemade chicken stock or your favorite canned broth, or water

Salt and freshly ground pepper

Drops of fresh lime or lemon juice

1/3 cup finely diced white onion, soaked in ice water for 30 minutes, then drained

8 thin cut pork chops, 3 to 4 ounces each

Olive oil

Xnipec

PREPARE A CHARCOAL fire or preheat a gas or stovetop grill. Combine the avocado, chile, and cilantro in a blender and whir it up, adding enough stock or water to make a smooth sauce. It should be the consistency of heavy cream. Taste and season with salt and pepper and drops of lime juice. Stir in the onion. Set aside.

Brush or rub the chops liberally with olive oil and season lightly with salt and pepper. Cook the chops over medium-high heat on both sides until done to your liking.

Arrange 2 chops on each warm plate. Spoon some avocado sauce over it and top with Xnipec.

cucumber and mint salsa

MAKES ABOUT 2 CUPS

This is a bright, clean salsa that goes well with grilled or smoked fish and meat. It also makes a delicious condiment to serve as part of an antipasto platter or picnic.

2 medium cucumbers (English, Armenian, or Kirby are my favorites), peeled, seeded, and diced (about 2 cups)
1 tablespoon slivered garlic
1 teaspoon finely minced serrano chile
1/4 cup green onions or scallions (white and green parts), cut on the bias

1/3 cup fresh lime juice
2 teaspoons sugar
1/2 cup chopped fresh mint leaves
2 tablespoons olive oil
Salt and freshly ground pepper to taste

COMBINE ALL THE ingredients in a bowl and set aside for at least 30 minutes. This is best eaten the same day, because the color will start to turn.

grilled lamb chops
with cucumber and mint salsa

SERVES 2

Salsa can often serve as both a marinade and a sauce for the finished dish, as this recipe demonstrates. This technique works equally well with pork or chicken.

4 thick-cut loin or double-cut rib lamb chops
Cucumber and Mint Salsa
Olive oil

Salt and freshly ground pepper
3 tablespoons chopped unsalted, dry-roasted peanuts

PLACE THE CHOPS in a shallow dish or resealable plastic bag and pour half of the salsa on top. Marinate in the refrigerator for at least 30 minutes and up to 2 hours.

Prepare a charcoal fire or preheat a gas or stovetop grill or the broiler. Remove the chops from the marinade and brush them off. Rub them lightly with olive oil and season well with salt and pepper. Grill over medium-high heat, or broil in the oven until done to your liking.

Serve topped with the remaining salsa and a sprinkling of peanuts.

roasted lemon salsa

This is an unusual approach that produces a great condiment. Roasting a lemon softens its acidity and adds a toasty note. It's a great topper for broiled or grilled chicken and fish. I also like to stir a little into soups and risottos at the last minute to add brightness. For variation, you can add some finely diced green or black olives or chopped herbs, such as parsley or chives. It's simple to put together, but the lemons need to be roasted and cooled first, and the mixture should sit for several hours before serving, so make this one ahead of time.

2 large lemons (about 1/2 pound), scrubbed (see Note)
2/3 cup extra virgin olive oil
1/4 cup finely chopped shallots or green onion (white part only)

1 tablespoon sugar, or to taste
2 teaspoons kosher or sea salt, or to taste
Freshly ground pepper
1/4 cup fresh lemon juice, or to taste

PREHEAT THE OVEN to 400°F. Cut the lemons in half and pick out the seeds. Lightly coat the lemons with a tablespoon of the olive oil. Place the lemons cut side down in a baking dish and roast uncovered for 25 minutes. Remove, cool, and cut the lemons into 1/4-inch dice.

In a bowl, combine the lemons, the remaining olive oil, shallots, sugar, and salt and stir gently. Cover and set aside for at least 3 hours so the flavors can marry and mellow. Initially, the lemons may seem a little harsh or bitter but as they sit the flavor changes markedly. Taste it a couple of times throughout the rest period and you'll see. Adjust the seasonings with additional salt, pepper, and lemon juice. Store covered in the refrigerator for up to a week.

NOTE: Commercially grown citrus is coated with a wax that gives it a nice shine and also helps extend its shelf life—fruits don't dry out as quickly when waxed. Although it's "food-grade" wax, none of us needs to consume it. The best way to remove it is to use a mild detergent solution and a clean pot-scrubber sponge. Rinse thoroughly, of course.

fresh cranberry and tangerine salsa

MAKES ABOUT 1 QUART

Now here's a pan—North American twist on our chunky salsa—Mexico to Maine! It's fresh and uncooked and is an excellent accompaniment to roast turkey. Try it at Thanksgiving, when fresh cranberries and tangerines are widely available in the market. You'll find it terrific with ham, pork, and game, and it's also nice with smoked meats and sausages.

3 cups (12 ounces) fresh or frozen cranberries (that's the size of the bags sold nationwide)
2 tangerines, scrubbed
1/2 cup chopped fresh cilantro or mint leaves, or a combination

1 cup sugar, or to taste
2 tablespoons fresh lemon juice
Drops of your favorite hot sauce to taste
3/4 cup finely chopped, lightly toasted walnuts or pecans

WASH AND PICK over the cranberries. Cut the tangerines into eighths, peel and all, and pick out all the seeds. Place the cranberries, tangerines, cilantro or mint, sugar, lemon juice, and hot sauce in a food processor and chop in short bursts until relatively fine. Be careful not to over-process; you still want some texture. Taste for sweetness and add more sugar if desired. Allow to sit for at least 2 hours while the flavors develop. Stir in the nuts just before serving so they don't get soggy. Store the salsa (without nuts) covered in the refrigerator for up to 3 days, or in the freezer for up to 2 months.

2   vinaigrettes

Everyone
knows what a
vinaigrette is,
but you may not realize how much this simple little sauce has

evolved since the days in which it was relegated to splashing on some

greens for a salad. Today vinaigrette has become one of the most impor-

tant flavor-makers around. You'll find it used not only tossed with salad

greens but also as a sauce for meats, fish, vegetables, and even desserts. The

great joy of vinaigrettes is that they are easily and quickly made and can

bring brightness, flavor, and interest to very simply cooked foods. When I

don't have a lot of time to cook, whisking together a fast vinaigrette to top

a grilled or broiled piece of fish, chicken, or vegetable is not only deli-

cious but also healthy. If I make enough to save some, I can have a differ-

ent meal the next night with even less effort.

As the name suggests, a vinaigrette is a mixture that usually includes vinegar for flavor. Traditionally, it is made by whisking together vinegar and oil until the mixture is slightly thickened, or emulsified. Emulsions are basically combinations of fat (in this case, the oil) and water (vinegar is 95 percent water), beaten together to form a thickened, relatively homogeneous mass. Examples of other emulsion sauces are mayonnaise and the hollandaise family, in which fats like egg yolks, butter, and oil are blended with watery acids like lemon juice to make a smooth sauce.

Unlike mayonnaise, a vinaigrette is an "unstable" emulsion. This only means that it will not stay emulsified for very long. If you make your vinaigrette ahead, you may have to whisk or blend it again at serving time. When you use a blender or food processor to make a vinaigrette, it will be thicker and stay emulsified longer than the same version whisked by hand. (If you want to learn more about emulsions and indeed the whole fascinating world of the science of food and cooking I recommend Harold McGee's book *On Food and Cooking: The Science and Lore of the Kitchen* and Shirley Corriher's more recent book *Cookwise*.)

How much oil and how much vinegar make a vinaigrette?

The traditional recipe for vinaigrette was 2 to 3 parts olive oil to one part wine or cider vinegar. This made for a pretty tart, acidic dressing that was nice on most salad greens and made a refreshing palate cleanser that, when consumed after the rich main course, as they traditionally did in France, also aided in digestion. Today, however, we don't follow the traditional "order of courses." Americans typically serve salad either before the main course or, as it often happens in my house, *as* the main course. A super-tart vinegary dressing may not be appealing at that point in the meal, and the traditional ratio of oil to vinegar may end up being too aggressively acidic. At the same time, there is pressure to lower the amount of fat in our diets, which often leads people to reduce the amount of oil in a dressing or to replace it with something utterly unsuitable. (Look at the ingredients list on a bottled low-fat salad dressing some time. The high-quality brands use water and various gum thickeners; the low-quality brands use much worse. Either way, it's no way to dress a great salad.) I'm not going to be able to single-handedly change the country's attitude toward fat, but let me try this:

~ We need fats and the nutrients they contain in our diet; the key is to pick the right kind, such as olive oil.
~ Just because you make a vinaigrette with a lot of oil doesn't mean you have to use a lot of vinaigrette on your food. A salad doesn't benefit from swimming in its dressing.
~ Cook something healthy, and dress it up with a little of something rich and delicious. Nutritionally speaking, you can't really go wrong.

As you try the vinaigrette recipes that follow, let your tastebuds guide the proportions of acid and oil. Sometimes a tart mixture will seem right, sometimes a more unctuous one will please your palate.

A note about oils and vinegars, the basic components of most vinaigrettes. Part of the versatility of vinaigrettes is the wide range of options available for these two basic ingredients. In fact, the variety in a store that stocks a good range

of oils and vinegars can be a little overwhelming, to say the least. To help ease the situation but still give you lots of options, I suggest you stock your pantry with the following:

VINEGARS There are vinegars out there in hundreds of flavors but here are my four picks for a basic pantry:

~ **Wine Vinegar**—either red or white or both. Many, many brands are available in even an ordinary supermarket. If you've got a brand that you like, stick with it. If you're not sure, buy a couple (they're cheap) and taste-test them (yep—just sip a little from a spoon). Keep the winners, give away the losers. Now you've got a favorite brand too.

~ **Balsamic Vinegar:** To buy a good one, you need to taste-test and to read the label. Some mass-produced brands contain caramel coloring and sugar, some are blended with other kinds of vinegar—I'd stay away. The other piece of information you can get from the label is how long the vinegar has been aged, which will account, at least in part, for its price. You can get a fine balsamic for around ten dollars for a 10- to 12-ounce bottle. Even cheaper ones are fine for uses like marinating. Taste them and pick one that you like. Some tend to be sweeter, some woodier, some thinner, some more syrupy. The balsamic that sells for a hundred dollars a bottle and is treated like a miracle elixir by connoisseurs is a sublime substance on its own, but it does not concern us here. If you are lucky enough to possess some, do *not* use it to mix a salad dressing.

~ **Rice Vinegar:** You'll likely find this in the "ethnic" or Asian foods section of your market. It is sold plain and seasoned (the label will say), which means basically that it's been sweetened and salted. I was going to suggest that you buy only unseasoned so that you can season your dishes to taste, but then I realized that many of my recipes use the seasoned kind—so I must like something about it. Buy both.

~ **Sherry Vinegar** comes from Spain, as does true sherry, and is aged in old sherry wine barrels. It has a woody, nutty flavor unlike that of any other vinegar.

Cider and malt vinegars also offer unique flavors, and in recent years I've been using a lot of Chinese black vinegar, which you can find at any well-stocked Asian market. Beyond these is a whole world of flavored, infused vinegars: raspberry, basil, hot chile, and the like. If you've been given some or if you can't resist a beautiful bottle in the gourmet store, by all means try them.

OILS The subject of oils could be the basis for a book in itself (maybe I'll do one!). Most vegetable oils are refined to make them more shelf-stable. Neutral in every way, they impart no flavor of their own. These are the oils—corn, vegetable (generally made from soybeans), sunflower—that many of us knew growing up as "salad oil"; safflower and canola are recent additions to this list. Certainly you need one on your shelf for basic kitchen duty. They are best used for cooking or frying. But in a vinaigrette, because of the mixture's simplicity, the oil needs to contribute flavor and balance the acid. For this reason, I look for oils that are unrefined and cold- or expeller-pressed; these have the best flavor. And, as with the rest of my pantry, I buy oils from organic sources when possible. Here are my three choices for oils to have on hand beyond basic cooking oil:

~ **Two Olive Oils,** one extra virgin and one ordinary virgin. Flavorful extra virgin—made from the first pressing of raw olives—is an essential ingredient in so many recipes and a delicious condiment on its own. The finest come from Italy, California, and Spain, and their flavors can be fruity, herbaceous, and even peppery. What's important is to find one that you like, and the only way to do that is by tasting. So buy a couple of bottles of olive oil and taste them. Pour a little bit into a dish, and give it a good sniff. The aroma is a major component of its taste. Go ahead and taste it, either off your finger or by dipping in a crust of bread. If you try a few side by side, you'll see (and smell and taste) how really varied extra virgin olive oils can be. In addition, you should have a neutral (and less expensive) "ordinary virgin" olive oil—made from subsequent pressings of the crushed olives and generally less flavorful. Sometimes you might not want the strong flavor and aroma of extra virgin. It's up to you.

~ A **Nut Oil** or two, such as walnut or hazelnut. The most flavorful are made from toasted nuts. If you find you like nut oil flavors, then expand your pantry to include a pecan or pumpkin seed oil.

~ Also a good **Toasted Sesame Oil.** Look at the label and pick one that is 100 percent sesame. (See Glossary and Pantry for more information.) Some brands blend sesame with a neutral oil such as canola, because many people find pure sesame oil pretty overpowering, which it can be if you use too much. So don't use too much.

You don't have to stop there. A broad range of organic, cold- and expeller-pressed oils is available from Spectrum Naturals, a producer of which I'm especially fond. One of my favorites is their true corn oil, with the flavor and color of *real corn*. I've used it in the Wild Mushroom Salad recipe (page 34).

It's sensible to buy only as much oil as you think you can use up in six months. Opened oils, especially those that are natural, cold-pressed, and free of additives, will go rancid after that. To extend their life, store your oils in the refrigerator. Refrigeration won't keep them from going rancid forever, but it does slow down the process. If a refrigerated oil looks a little cloudy and pours sluggishly, don't worry; it will liquefy and become clear again when it comes to room temperature.

What follows are some recipes for vinaigrettes, starting with the most basic, and ideas for how to use them. I hope you make a lot of these recipes, and of course I hope you like them. It's equally important to me, however, that you use this lesson as a jumping-off place. One of the reasons I like teaching vinaigrettes is that they are a great building block, a simple formula with which anyone can experiment. If you are inexperienced in the kitchen or experienced but very recipe-bound, try inventing a vinaigrette of your own. All you have to do is combine some oil, some vinegar, and some seasonings, and you're on your way.

WITH THE recipes that follow (unless otherwise specified) you can decide whether to use extra virgin olive oil with its more pronounced aromatic flavors or more subdued virgin olive oil. It's all to your taste! Any of these would make cooked vegetables stellar.

basic vinaigrette and some variations

MAKES I CUP

This is the classic vinaigrette that the French have used for as long as anyone can remember. There are all kinds of variations on this theme, and you should feel free to experiment with different oils and vinegars or other acids. If you are serving wine alongside a dish that uses a vinaigrette, you might try using citrus juices instead of vinegar. The acidity of citrus juice is not as pronounced, which makes a citrus vinaigrette much more "wine friendly." The key is to make sure that the acidity in the vinaigrette is in balance with the acidity in the wine. Milder vinegars such as rice, balsamic, sherry, and fruit-infused vinegars generally work better with wine for the same reason.

3 to 4 tablespoons red or white wine vinegar
2 teaspoons finely minced shallots or I teaspoon finely minced garlic
1/2 teaspoon dry mustard
Sea salt and freshly ground pepper to taste
3/4 cup olive oil

IN A MIXING BOWL, whisk together the vinegar, shallots, mustard, and some salt and pepper. Continue to whisk vigorously as you slowly add the oil in a thin stream. This will form an emulsion and the sauce will thicken. Alternatively, you can put all the ingredients in a jar with a tight-fitting lid and shake vigorously. The emulsion won't be quite as thick or stable but it's another way to combine the ingredients.

Vinaigrettes are best served within a couple of hours or so and at room temperature for maximum flavor. Whisk or shake again if it has stood for more than a few minutes.

variations ROASTED GARLIC AND MUSTARD VINAIGRETTE Whisk in 1 to 2 tablespoons Dijon mustard and 1 tablespoon roasted garlic that has been mashed to a paste. This is great on spicy greens such as arugula or watercress and delicious as a marinade for plain broiled or grilled chicken. Rub it on and allow the meat to sit in the refrigerator for at least 30 minutes before cooking.

FRESH HERB AND LEMON VINAIGRETTE Use extra virgin olive oil, replace the vinegar with ¼ cup fresh lemon juice, and add 2 tablespoons finely chopped fresh herbs, such as chives, parsley, basil, tarragon, or a combination. I love this on seared delicate seafood such as scallops. It also makes a great marinade for chicken.

BALSAMIC VINAIGRETTE Use extra virgin olive oil and replace the wine vinegar with balsamic vinegar. The deep, sweet flavor of the balsamic goes great with roasted or grilled mushrooms and meats.

NUT OIL VINAIGRETTE Replace half or all of the olive oil with fragrant walnut or hazelnut oil. Replace the wine vinegar with sherry vinegar. The toasty, nutty flavor that comes from both the oil and the sherry vinegar complements a lot of different foods, but I especially like this in a savory salad with crisp greens and shavings of a nutty cheese like Parmigiano-Reggiano or Vella Dry Jack.

CAPER DILL VINAIGRETTE Add 1 tablespoon chopped fresh dill, 1 tablespoon chopped drained capers, and ½ teaspoon finely grated lemon zest. This is great with poached or grilled salmon—just drizzle some on.

asparagus with vinaigrette

SERVES 6 OR SO AS A SIDE COURSE

1½ pounds fresh asparagus	Grated hard-boiled eggs or grated aged
One of the vinaigrettes above	goat cheese, such as French Crottin

IF THE ASPARAGUS are large, peel them just shy of the tip. If they are small (pencil size), no peeling is necessary. Blanch (boil in lightly salted water) or steam the asparagus until crisp-tender. Immediately plunge into an ice-water bath to stop the cooking. Drain and arrange on plates.

Spoon the vinaigrette of your choice over the center of the asparagus and garnish with egg or goat cheese, if desired.

NOW THAT you've had a chance to try the basic versions, here are a couple of "New Wave" vinaigrettes; their structure is the same, but they break the flavor mold. I think vinaigrettes, more than any other thing in the cook's repertoire, encourage and even demand experimentation.

blue cheese and mustard vinaigrette

MAKES ¾ CUP

This creamy vinaigrette has all kinds of uses, both as a dressing and as a dip. Choose a rich, creamy blue like Cambazola, Saga, or, my favorite, Point Reyes Original Blue. I've decided not to worry about eating raw egg, but if it concerns you, you can coddle or even hard-boil the egg before using the yolk.

3 tablespoons homemade chicken or vegetable stock or your favorite canned broth

3 ounces crumbled creamy blue cheese (½ cup or so)

I egg yolk

I½ tablespoons Dijon mustard

I tablespoon white wine vinegar or cider vinegar

I teaspoon packed light or dark brown sugar

¼ cup olive oil or ⅛ cup olive oil and ⅛ cup toasted walnut oil

I tablespoon chopped chives

Salt and freshly ground pepper

STIR THE STOCK and cheese together to form a smooth paste (if you give the stock a quick zap in the microwave first, it may blend with the cheese more easily). Place the mixture in a blender, and add the egg, mustard, vinegar, and sugar. Blend and, while the motor is running, slowly add the olive oil in a thin stream. Pour the mixture into a bowl and stir in the chives, then taste and add salt and pepper if you think it needs it. If the dressing seems too thick, you can thin it with additional stock. Store covered in the refrigerator for up to 5 days.

suggestions ~ This is my favorite dip for buffalo wings.
~ For a more elegant dish, drizzle it on a carpaccio of beef (thinly sliced raw fillet) topped with a little arugula salad.
~ It's fantastic on roasted asparagus.

grapefruit vinaigrette

Here is a vinaigrette that uses citrus juice in place of vinegar. The acidic grapefruit and sweet honey make for a lively combination of flavors. I love it on a salad of spicy young greens—arugula, mustard, cress. Add grilled shrimp and you've got a tasty main dish.

1/2 cup fresh grapefruit juice
2 teaspoons finely minced shallots
2 teaspoons soy sauce

2 teaspoons honey, or to taste
1/2 cup olive oil
Freshly ground pepper

WHISK TOGETHER THE grapefruit juice, shallots, soy sauce, and honey. Continue to whisk vigorously as you slowly add the olive oil in a thin stream. Add pepper to your taste. Store covered in the refrigerator for up to 3 days.

miso vinaigrette

Miso, a rich paste made from fermented soybeans and often other grains, is a common ingredient in Japanese cooking. Lighter-colored misos are usually sweeter and more delicate. Miso is available in most natural foods stores and also in Asian markets. (See page 301 for more discussion about miso.) I love this vinaigrette as a dressing for ripe tomatoes and cucumbers or as a dip for crisp raw vegetables.

1/2 cup seasoned rice vinegar
2 teaspoons peeled and finely chopped
  fresh ginger
1 tablespoon chopped fresh garlic
4 tablespoons white ("shiro") miso
  paste
1/2 teaspoon toasted sesame oil

1 teaspoon packed palm or light brown
  sugar, or to taste
2 tablespoons homemade chicken or
  vegetable stock or your favorite
  canned broth, or water
2 tablespoons olive oil

COMBINE ALL THE ingredients in a blender and blend until smooth. Store covered in the refrigerator for up to 3 days.

orange nut oil vinaigrette

MAKES A GENEROUS 1/2 CUP

This simple blend is delicious not only on spicy greens like arugula and cress but also on grilled greens like radicchio and endive and crisp cooked vegetables like green beans and asparagus. It's also a nice marinade or finishing sauce for simply cooked chicken, pork, and shrimp. I guess I'd say it's one of those all-purpose sauces. I return to it again and again, and you will too.

2 tablespoons soy sauce
1 tablespoon honey
5 tablespoons fresh orange juice
2 teaspoons finely grated orange zest

6 tablespoons toasted walnut oil or other nut oil
2 teaspoons sherry vinegar
Salt and freshly ground pepper to taste

VIGOROUSLY WHISK ALL the ingredients together until combined or combine in a glass jar and shake. Store in the refrigerator for up to 3 days.

spicy sesame ginger vinaigrette

MAKES ABOUT 1 1/4 CUPS

This delicious sauce makes an excellent dressing for a cold Asian noodle salad and a delicious marinade for fish, chicken, or pork. Next time you make a batch, use some to marinate meat or fish, grill or sauté it, then serve it on a bed of noodles dressed with more vinaigrette.

3 tablespoons peanut oil
3 tablespoons toasted sesame oil
1 teaspoon crushed red chile flakes
2 tablespoons peeled and coarsely chopped fresh ginger
1/4 cup coarsely chopped scallions (white and green parts)

1/2 cup soy sauce
3 tablespoons unseasoned rice vinegar
2 tablespoons balsamic vinegar
3 tablespoons sugar
1 tablespoon finely chopped fresh cilantro or mint leaves (optional)

IN A SMALL saucepan, heat the oils together until just smoking and add the chile flakes, ginger, and scallions. Remove from the heat, cover, and set aside at room temperature for 1 hour.

Strain the oil and discard the seasonings. Whisk in the soy sauce, vinegars, and sugar, whisking until the sugar is dissolved. Store covered in the refrigerator for up to 3 days, and add the cilantro or mint, if desired, just before serving.

grilled tuna with
spicy sesame ginger greens

SERVES 4

This uses the Spicy Sesame Ginger Vinaigrette above, so you'll want to make that first. It's a very simple recipe, and the thing that will make it memorable is your seeking out special young tender savory greens, like cress (of which there are many varieties), arugula, and mizuna, to name a few, and also some savory sprouts, like sunflower and daikon. The idea is to grill the tuna so that it is still beautifully pink inside, top it with your amazing salad mixture, and then spoon over the vinaigrette.

**4 thick-cut (2 inches) absolutely fresh
tuna steaks, about 6 ounces each
Spicy Sesame Ginger Vinaigrette**

**3 cups lightly packed mixture of savory
greens and sprouts**

PREPARE A CHARCOAL fire or preheat a stovetop grill. Brush the steaks with a couple of tablespoons of the vinaigrette and grill on both sides until they are to your liking but hopefully no more than medium-rare. Place on warm plates, arrange greens and sprouts attractively on top, and spoon over some of the vinaigrette. Serve immediately.

dried fig vinaigrette

MAKES ABOUT 2 CUPS

This has a delicious sweet-tart flavor that is great with grilled or roasted meats, especially pork. And a salad of spicy greens and rich blue cheeses topped with this vinaigrette is downright exciting.

½ cup coarsely chopped dried figs plus
   3 tablespoons finely diced dried figs
½ cup apple juice or cider
2 teaspoons minced fresh thyme leaves
2 teaspoons toasted black or yellow
   mustard seeds

1½ tablespoons minced shallots
6 tablespoons sherry vinegar
1 cup olive oil
Salt and freshly ground pepper to taste

COMBINE THE ½ cup of chopped dried figs with 1 cup of water in a saucepan over high heat and bring to a boil. Reduce the heat and simmer until the liquid is reduced by half, about 7 minutes. Transfer to a blender or food processor and puree until smooth.

Pour the fig puree into a mixing bowl. Whisk in the juice or cider, thyme, mustard, shallots, vinegar, olive oil, and the 3 tablespoons of diced figs. Taste and season with salt and pepper. If the dressing seems too thick, you can thin it with additional juice or cider. Store covered in the refrigerator for up to 5 days.

WITH THE suggestions accompanying the vinaigrette recipes in this chapter, I've encouraged you to see vinaigrette as a sauce that can dress—or dress up—all kinds of simple foods. The recipes that follow are dishes where the vinaigrette is an integral part and the flavors play off one another in wonderful ways.

charred tomato vinaigrette

MAKES ABOUT 2 CUPS

I'm not suggesting that you go to the trouble of preparing a charcoal fire just to grill the tomatoes for this vinaigrette—there are several alternatives that are just fine. But if you have the grill fired up for something else, go ahead and cook the tomatoes; you can refrigerate them overnight and make the dressing the next day.

1 1/2 pounds firm ripe tomatoes
1/3 cup extra virgin olive oil, plus extra for oiling the vegetables for grilling
3 large garlic cloves
1/4 cup balsamic vinegar
1/4 cup or so homemade vegetable or chicken stock or your favorite canned broth

1 tablespoon fresh lemon juice, or to taste
2 tablespoons chopped fresh basil leaves
2 teaspoons chopped fresh mint leaves
1 tablespoon finely chopped black olives (oil-cured are best here)
Salt and freshly ground black pepper to taste

PREHEAT A BROILER or stovetop grill or prepare a charcoal fire. Cut out the stem ends of the tomatoes. Lightly oil the tomatoes and the garlic (just rub it on with your fingers). Grill the tomatoes and garlic, turning frequently, until they are browned and charred in spots, about 4 minutes. (You may need to use a basket or fine mesh grate if you're cooking over charcoal.) Set a strainer over a bowl. Cut the tomatoes in half over the strainer and then gently squeeze out the juice and seeds into the strainer. Reserve the juice and discard the seeds.

Chop the tomato flesh and skin and add to the juice. Peel the garlic and chop finely, then add it to the tomato. In a separate bowl, whisk together the vinegar, stock, 1/3 cup of the olive oil, lemon juice, basil, mint, and olives, and add the tomato mixture. Taste, and season with salt, pepper, and additional lemon juice. If it seems too thick, thin it by adding a little stock, water, or tomato juice. Store covered in the refrigerator for up to 3 days.

roasted eggplant salad
with charred tomato vinaigrette

I call this a salad, but for me it's a main course. Because it's so flavorful at room temperature, it works well as a buffet dish and is portable enough for a picnic.

2 medium eggplants, each cut into
   6 slices, ends discarded
2 tablespoons olive oil
Salt and freshly ground pepper
8 ounces fresh goat cheese
¼ cup mixed chopped fresh herbs, such
   as basil, chervil, tarragon, and chives
Charred Tomato Vinaigrette

4 cups loosely packed, savory young
   greens, such as arugula, mizuna, red
   mustard, cress, mâche, young spinach,
   or a combination

Garnish if you like with toasted pine
   nuts

PREHEAT THE OVEN to 425°F. Lightly brush the eggplant slices with the olive oil, season with salt and pepper, and arrange in a single layer on a baking sheet. Roast until lightly browned and tender, about 15 minutes. Remove from the baking sheet, and when cool enough to handle, top each eggplant slice with ⅔ ounce of cheese and a sprinkle of the chopped herbs, and roll them into tube shapes.

Place the eggplant rolls in a shallow bowl or small baking dish and pour the vinaigrette over them. Marinate for 1 to 2 hours.

Arrange the greens on plates. Place 2 eggplant rolls on top of each serving and drizzle each serving with a tablespoon or two of the vinaigrette marinade. Top with toasted pine nuts, if desired.

wild mushroom salad with two vinaigrettes

SERVES 6

This recipe is a vinaigrette extravaganza, using not one but two of these snappy blends—one as a dressing, the other as a sauce. It's a pretty straightforward salad—sautéed mushrooms on a bed of greens—but it is dependent on a few special ingredients to make it great. First, good mushrooms. Use the best selection that you can find. The second essential in this recipe is the corn oil. It's not the run-of-the-mill corn oil found in supermarkets, but a very special oil made by Spectrum Naturals: a pure, expeller-extracted oil that uses no solvents or preservatives and tastes and smells exactly like corn (what a concept!). You can find it at natural food stores.

1 ½ **pounds fresh wild mushrooms, such as oyster, chanterelle, alba, or the best available, cleaned**
3 tablespoons olive oil
Sea salt and freshly ground pepper
8 cups loosely packed, savory young greens

Honey Lemon Vinaigrette
Corn Mustard Dressing

Garnish if you like with fried capers and shaved Parmesan or dry Jack cheese

IF THE MUSHROOMS are large, halve them; otherwise, leave them whole. (They are so beautiful on the salad.) In a large sauté pan, heat the olive oil and sauté the mushrooms until they are barely tender, 3 to 4 minutes. Season with salt and pepper, set aside, and keep warm.

Lightly toss the greens with some of the Honey Lemon Vinaigrette and arrange on plates, then top with the mushrooms. Spoon a little of the Corn Mustard Dressing around the edge of the plate. That way, as you drag your fork through, each bite will be a little different. Garnish with fried capers and cheese, if desired. Serve immediately.

honey lemon vinaigrette

2 tablespoons finely chopped shallots
6 tablespoons seasoned rice vinegar
2 tablespoons honey

4 tablespoons fresh lemon juice
4 tablespoons olive oil

Whisk all the ingredients together. Store covered in the refrigerator for up to 5 days. MAKES 1 GENEROUS CUP

corn mustard dressing

2 tablespoons finely chopped shallots
2 teaspoons poached or roasted garlic
¼ cup double strength, unsalted homemade chicken or vegetable stock or your favorite canned broth
1 tablespoon Dijon mustard, or to taste

½ cup Spectrum Naturals unrefined corn oil
1 teaspoon fresh lemon juice
Sea salt and freshly ground pepper to taste

Combine the shallots, garlic, and stock in a blender or food processor and blend until smooth. Add the mustard. With the motor running, slowly add the oil in a thin stream and blend until the dressing is smooth and thickened. Stir in the lemon juice, taste, and season with salt and pepper. Store covered in the refrigerator for up to 3 days.
MAKES ABOUT 1 CUP

agrodolce dressing

MAKES ABOUT 1 CUP

This dressing is based on the Italian sweet and sour sauce agrodolce, which is basically a mixture of caramelized sugar and vinegar or wine. Unlike an ordinary vinaigrette, which tastes best soon after it's made, agrodolce needs to sit awhile for its flavor to develop, so be sure to start well ahead of when you want to use the dressing.

¼ cup sugar
¼ cup balsamic vinegar
1 cup full-bodied red wine
1 tablespoon chopped garlic
1 teaspoon mixed whole peppercorns

1 teaspoon coarsely chopped fresh
   rosemary leaves
½ teaspoon salt
¼ cup or so olive oil
1 to 2 teaspoons fresh lime juice

COMBINE THE SUGAR and ¼ cup of water in a small saucepan and stir over low heat until the sugar dissolves. Raise the heat and bring to a boil. Cook without stirring until the mixture is golden and caramelized, 4 to 5 minutes. Remove from the heat and carefully add the vinegar and wine (the mixture will sputter). Place back on medium heat and stir in the garlic, peppercorns, rosemary, and salt. Stir for a minute or two until all the caramel has melted. Remove from the heat, cool, cover, and set aside for at least 3 hours or overnight. Whisk in the olive oil and lime juice to taste. Store covered in the refrigerator for up to 5 days.

melon and goat cheese salad with agrodolce dressing

SERVES 4

This is a very easy summer salad. Agrodolce is a nice counterpoint to the sweet fruit and tart goat cheese, and the spicy greens and tannic walnuts round it out. For different flavor counterpoints, try grilled fresh figs or pears wrapped in prosciutto for the melon.

1 ripe 2- to 2½- pound Crane melon,
   muskmelon, or cantaloupe
4 cups lightly packed arugula
1 cup fresh blueberries

Agrodolce Dressing
8 ounces fresh goat cheese, crumbled
½ cup toasted walnut halves
Freshly ground black pepper to taste

CUT THE MELON in half, remove the seeds, and cut off the rind. Cut the flesh into attractive shapes (don't go crazy—I just mean small slices or something that works on a salad plate). Arrange the greens on plates with the melon and berries. Drizzle a tablespoon or two of the agrodolce on each serving and top with the goat cheese, walnuts, and a grind or two of black pepper. Serve immediately.

3 pestos

Most Versatile of Flavor-Makers

Most
Americans
are now
familiar with pesto, that fragrant herb mixture often served as a

quick sauce for pasta. The cooks of Genoa, Italy, are credited with invent-

ing the traditional version, which is a simple combination of fresh basil,

garlic, cheese, and olive oil pounded in a mortar and pestle. Contempo-

rary recipes often call for the addition of pine nuts or walnuts.

Pestos are easy to make, and they have many applications beyond pasta.

Spread pesto on lightly toasted bread or crostini, drizzle some on a pizza,

fold a spoonful into an omelet. Pesto makes a great stuffing for baked

tomatoes and mushrooms and a tasty topper for baked potatoes. You can

swirl some into mashed potatoes or cooked rice (it will color them beau-

tifully) or into hot and cold soups (whether or not they're homemade!).

Pestos can contribute wonderful flavor pushed up under the skin of chicken prior to roasting or tucked into a pocket cut in a thick pork chop on its way to the grill. Pesto can be thinned with a little vegetable or chicken stock to make a delicious quick sauce or dressing for almost anything.

If you have leftover pesto of any kind—and you can ensure leftover pesto by doubling the recipe—I'd suggest freezing at least some of it in tiny portions: an ice cube tray is ideal. Keep the frozen "pesto cubes" in a resealable plastic bag and use them to jazz up any needy food at a minute's notice.

Here are two tips that have made a big difference to my pestos:

~ Blanch the basil (or other herb) first to keep the beautiful green color.
~ Use poached, toasted, or roasted garlic instead of raw for a mellower flavor.

The benefits of blanching green herbs are cosmetic, but I always blanch. Blanching means plunging the leaves into lightly salted boiling water for just a second then scooping them out and plunging them into ice water to stop the cooking. If you use unblanched basil, as many recipes instruct, invariably the mixture begins to darken from oxidation before you can finish pureeing it. Blanching deactivates the enzymes that cause the basil to discolor when it's chopped. Blanched basil will make a pesto that stays bright green for up to 5 days in the refrigerator and up to 3 months in the freezer.

I also never use raw garlic in pesto, though this is a matter of taste. When cut, raw garlic will also oxidize quickly, becoming strong, funky, hot, and often overpowering. None of that happens with garlic that's been toasted, poached, or roasted (see Glossary and Pantry for a description of those procedures). I'd rather be sure that the garlic flavor and intensity remain stable in my pesto, especially if I'm not going to use it right away or if I'm making a big batch to freeze for later use.

If you've made pesto before I encourage you to try it "my way" and see if you prefer the results. But if all this talk about blanching and poaching makes the whole process sound like too much trouble, then skip the extra steps. Funky, dark-colored, homemade pesto is much, much better than no pesto at all.

To pound or to process, or what was that you said about a mortar and pestle?

Traditionally, pesto (or *pistou*, as the French call it) was made by gradually pounding ingredients together in a heavy mortar and pestle. In fact, pesto gets its name from the Italian verb *pestare*, which means "to pound." Purists still think this is the best way to make pesto, and although it does take more time, the resulting sauce has a silkiness and texture that machine pesto lacks. I was always a little skeptical, but when I finally took the time to try the old-fashioned way, the texture really was different and I loved it. The added advantage, of course, is that you get a good workout in the process!

But let's be real: I find the blender or food processor gives a perfectly acceptable result. If you're down to choosing between the blender and the food processor, I recommend the blender because it gives a smoother, silkier, more consistently textured sauce. A properly made pesto is not soupy: it should be thick enough to mound on a spoon. You can always add a little olive oil, stock, or water, if you want or need it to be thinner.

A final comment on the ubiquitous word *pesto* before we hit the recipes: we Americans often use culinary terms liberally and inventively (especially on restaurant menus!). There are all kind of mixtures labeled "pesto" that don't have much in common with the authentic stuff. In a quick tour through a local shop I spotted "sun-dried tomato pesto" and "black olive pesto," neither of which contained a drop of any of the basic pesto ingredients, except for olive oil. So I guess anything goes. But for the purposes of this lesson, *pesto* means a paste made from fresh herbs, garlic, and oil with flavorings.

Can I freeze pesto?

Pesto freezes beautifully, but cheese doesn't freeze particularly well—it loses something in both flavor and texture. If you are making pesto in order to freeze it, I suggest you leave out the cheese and then beat some into the defrosted pesto when you're ready to use it. If you've already made pesto with cheese and end up with some left over, by all means go ahead and freeze it; it'll be fine.

basic basil pesto or pistou

MAKES ABOUT 1 CUP

3 cups firmly packed fresh basil leaves
2 tablespoons chopped poached or
  toasted garlic
3 tablespoons lightly toasted and
  chopped pine nuts or almonds
  (preferably blanched or skinned)

⅓ cup extra virgin olive oil
⅓ cup freshly grated Parmesan or
  Asiago cheese
Salt and freshly ground pepper

DROP BASIL INTO a pot of boiling water for 5 to 10 seconds. Immediately drain and plunge into a bowl of ice water to stop the cooking and set the bright green color. Drain the basil and squeeze out as much water as you can. Chop the basil coarsely and place in a food processor or blender, and add the garlic, nuts, and olive oil. Puree until smooth. Transfer to a bowl and stir in the cheese. Taste and season with salt and pepper. Store covered in the refrigerator for up to 5 days or in the freezer (see note on page 41) for up to 3 months.

variations

Pesto is open to improvisation. During the winter, when good basil is impossible to get, I love to make parsley pesto. But don't stop with the herbs; you can also play around with any of the four basic ingredients:

GREEN HERBS Substitute parsley, cilantro, arugula, spinach, chard, watercress, or scallion tops for the basil, singly or in combination.

NUTS Substitute walnuts, pecans, cashews, pistachios, macadamias, pepitas (pumpkin seeds), sesame seeds, or peanuts for the pine nuts and almonds.

OILS Substitute flavored olive oils, such as lemon or orange, or nut oils, such as walnut, hazelnut, pecan, pistachio, or pumpkin seed, for some or all of the olive oil.

CHEESE Substitute any dry grating cheese for the Parmesan, such as aged Crottin (a dry goat cheese), Queso Anejo (dry Mexican grating cheese), or whatever else you like.

asian pesto

To complete the transformation from Mediterranean to Asian, substitute a teaspoon or two of Asian chili-garlic sauce for the serrano chile. Toss with some fresh or dried Chinese noodles for a new take on pasta al pesto.

3 cups packed fresh basil leaves

3 cups packed fresh cilantro leaves

1 cup packed fresh mint leaves

2 tablespoons peeled and finely chopped fresh ginger

3 tablespoons chopped poached or toasted garlic

1 teaspoon seeded and finely chopped serrano chile, or to taste

Zest and juice of 1 medium lime

1 tablespoon toasted sesame oil, or to taste

1/4 cup chopped dry-roasted unsalted peanuts or cashews

1/2 cup or so peanut or olive oil

Salt and freshly ground pepper to taste

DROP THE BASIL, cilantro, and mint into a pot of lightly salted boiling water for 5 seconds. Drain and immediately plunge into ice water to stop the cooking and set the color. Drain, squeeze dry, and chop the herbs. Transfer to a blender or food processor, and add the ginger, garlic, chile, lime zest and juice, sesame oil, and peanuts. Pulse a few times to chop and then, with the motor running, slowly add the peanut or olive oil in a thin stream, stopping a few times to scrape down the sides. Taste and season with salt and pepper. Store covered in the refrigerator for up to 5 days or in the freezer for up to 3 months.

cilantro pesto

MAKES ABOUT 1 CUP

This pesto uses ingredients from the Mexican larder. I've cut back on the oil and substituted a little stock to reduce the fat and make the mixture easier to puree.

3 cups packed fresh cilantro leaves
1 tablespoon chopped poached or roasted garlic
⅓ cup toasted pepita seeds (see Note)
⅓ cup crumbled Mexican cheese such as Queso Fresco or Queso Anejo
½ teaspoon minced jalapeño chile, or to taste

2 tablespoons chopped fresh tomatillos (optional but very desirable)
¼ cup olive oil
2 to 3 tablespoons or so homemade vegetable or chicken stock or your favorite canned broth
Salt and freshly ground pepper to taste

DROP THE CILANTRO into a pot of boiling water for 5 to 10 seconds. Immediately drain and plunge into a bowl of ice water to stop the cooking and set the color. Drain well, pat dry, and chop coarsely. Transfer to a food processor or blender and add the garlic, pepitas, cheese, chile, tomatillos, and olive oil. Process in short bursts until combined but not completely smooth. Add the stock a bit at a time until the sauce is as thin as you like. Taste and season with salt and pepper. Store covered in the refrigerator for up to 5 days or in the freezer for up to 3 months.

NOTE: Pepitas are the seed of a pumpkin grown for the seeds rather than the flesh. They are widely available in Mexican markets as well as stores that sell nuts and seeds in bulk.

pistachio pesto

MAKES ABOUT ¾ CUP

Nuts play a larger role in this combination than in the basic basil version. You can add up to ¼ cup of a grating cheese such as Parmesan or Asiago, but I prefer it without the cheese. This is one recipe that violates my rule about always blanching the herbs. Since they're such a small component of the pesto, blanching isn't necessary.

½ cup unsalted, lightly toasted
  pistachios, chopped
½ cup packed fresh basil leaves
¾ cup extra virgin olive oil
1 tablespoon poached or toasted garlic

2 tablespoons chopped fresh mint leaves
1 tablespoon fresh lemon juice
Finely grated zest of 1 large lemon
¼ cup chopped chives
Salt and freshly ground pepper to taste

COMBINE ALL THE ingredients except the salt and pepper in a blender or food processor and puree until smooth, stopping a few times to scrape down the sides. Taste and season with salt and pepper. Store covered in the refrigerator for up to 5 days or in the freezer for up to 6 months.

basil-mint pesto

MAKES ABOUT 1 CUP

2 cups packed fresh basil leaves
½ cup packed fresh mint leaves
2 tablespoons chopped poached or
  toasted garlic
3 tablespoons lightly toasted pine nuts
  or chopped almonds

⅓ cup extra virgin olive oil
⅓ cup freshly grated Parmesan or
  Asiago cheese
Salt and freshly ground pepper

DROP THE BASIL and mint into a pot of boiling water for 5 seconds. Immediately drain the herbs and plunge them into a bowl of ice water to stop the cooking and set the bright green color. Drain and squeeze out excess water. Combine the herbs, garlic, nuts, and olive oil in a blender or food processor and puree until smooth. Transfer to a bowl and stir in the cheese. The mixture should be thick and not runny. Taste and season with salt and pepper. Store covered in the refrigerator for up to 5 days or in the freezer for up to 3 months.

HERE ARE a trio of soups "au pistou." Vegetable soup with a swirl of pesto or "pistou," as it's called in local dialect, is a Provençal classic. The many variations usually include both dried and fresh beans, tiny pasta, root vegetables, and whatever other fresh vegetables are available. It's a quick-cooked soup—all the vegetables stay bright and fresh-tasting—and you stir a spoonful of pesto into your own bowl at the table. The aroma released is fantastic; it's a heady experience. What follows is a traditional French version, then one based on Asian ingredients and one built from Mexican ingredients. Each soup uses a complementary pesto. I hope you'll try making them. But even just by reading them, you'll see something about the versatility of pesto; and together, they demonstrate nicely how easy it is to invent your own soup.

asian vegetable soup with asian pesto

SERVES 8 OR SO

3 tablespoons olive oil

4 cups thickly sliced shiitake mushrooms, stems removed

7 cups homemade chicken or vegetable stock (see pages 90–91 and 94) or Dashi (page 98)

2 tablespoons Asian fish sauce (see Glossary and Pantry), or to taste

1 tablespoon Asian chile-garlic sauce (see Glossary and Pantry), or to taste

2 cups canned diced tomatoes in juice

3 cups coarsely chopped baby bok choy or cabbage

6 ounces firm tofu cut into 1/2-inch cubes

Salt and freshly ground pepper

1/2 cup green onions sliced on the diagonal

Asian Pesto (page 43)

HEAT THE OIL in a deep soup pot over moderately high heat, add the mushrooms, and sauté and stir for 3 or 4 minutes, or until they just begin to brown. Add the stock, fish sauce, chile-garlic sauce, and tomatoes and bring to a boil. Add the bok choy and bring back to a boil again. Reduce heat and simmer for 2 to 3 minutes, then add the tofu and simmer for a couple of minutes longer to heat the tofu through. Taste and season with salt and pepper. Add the green onions. Ladle into warm bowls, swirl in a tablespoon or two of the pesto, and serve.

provençal vegetable soup with basil pesto

SERVES 8 OR SO

Don't let the long list of ingredients deter you. The soup cooks quickly, and the pesto's already made, right? My little secret ingredient is a piece of Parmesan cheese rind, which simmers along with the vegetables and adds great flavor. You remove it at serving time and can reuse it till it's gone. Store wrapped in the freezer. The rind of Parmesan and related hard cheeses like Asiago or Pecorino are amazing flavor boosters. Of course, if you don't have any rind, the soup will still be delicious.

4 tablespoons olive oil

2 cups chopped onions

2 cups leeks, including white and tender green parts, cut into rings

4 large garlic cloves, peeled and sliced

I large red or white boiling potato, scrubbed and diced

2 medium carrots, peeled and coarsely chopped

2 bay leaves

I teaspoon fennel seed

2 teaspoons whole thyme

2 quarts homemade chicken or vegetable stock or your favorite canned broth or water

3- or 4-inch chunk of Parmesan rind (optional)

I cup seeded and diced fresh tomatoes, or drained, canned diced tomatoes

½ cup small dry pasta such as riso

2 cups cooked dried beans of your choice such as navy, flageolet, or garbanzo, drained and rinsed if canned

2 cups fresh green beans or zucchini cut in ½-inch pieces

Basic Basil Pesto (page 42)

HEAT THE OLIVE OIL in a deep soup pot over moderate heat and add the onions, leeks, garlic, potatoes, and carrots. Sauté and stir for 3 or 4 minutes, until the vegetables begin to soften and just begin to brown. Add the bay leaves, fennel seed, thyme, stock, Parmesan rind, if using, and tomatoes to the pot and bring to a boil. Reduce the heat and slowly simmer for 10 minutes, or until the vegetables are almost tender. Add the pasta, cooked dried beans, and green beans and simmer for 5 minutes more, or until all is tender to your taste. Remove the rind and bay leaves and season to taste with salt and pepper.

Ladle into warm bowls, swirl in a heaping tablespoon or two of basil pesto, and serve. Actually, it's nice to let the soup eaters swirl in their own pesto at the table; that way, everyone gets the full experience of the aroma as it hits the soup.

spicy mexican vegetable soup
with cilantro pesto

SERVES 8 OR SO

This spicy soup uses hominy, or posole, as the Mexicans call it, to balance the heat. Canned hominy is readily available, but cooking your own dry hominy is worth doing if you have time—both the corn flavor and the texture are much more intense. You can buy dried posole in Mexican markets or by mail order from Indian Harvest (800-346-7032). You can also add your favorite meats, sausages, or fishes to make this a meal in a bowl.

3 tablespoons olive oil
I pound sliced white onions
I to 2 stemmed and seeded chopped
    dried chipotle chiles or 2 teaspoons
    chopped canned chipotles in adobo
I tablespoon finely slivered garlic
2 cups husked and quartered fresh
    tomatillos or 2 16-ounce cans,
    drained
I teaspoon crushed fennel seeds
I teaspoon crushed cumin seeds
I teaspoon crushed coriander seeds

2 teaspoons dried oregano (Mexican
    preferably)
¼ teaspoon ground cinnamon
2 cups diced and seeded tomatoes,
    drained if canned
7 cups homemade chicken, corn, or
    vegetable stock or your favorite
    canned broth
2 cups cooked white hominy (posole),
    drained and rinsed if canned
Salt and freshly ground black pepper
Cilantro Pesto (page 44)

HEAT THE OLIVE OIL in a deep soup pot over moderate heat. Add the onions, chipotles, and garlic. Sauté until soft but not brown, about 5 minutes. Add the tomatillos, fennel, cumin, coriander, oregano, cinnamon, tomatoes, and stock. Bring to a boil, then reduce heat and simmer gently for 15 minutes. Add the hominy and simmer to heat through. Taste and season with salt and pepper. Ladle into warm soup bowls, swirl in a tablespoon or so of pesto, and serve.

HERE ARE several of my favorite recipes using pesto. The first two are really methods more than recipes, and you'll see that even though I've suggested a specific pesto for each, any of the pestos in the lesson—or any pesto that you improvise—would work just as well and be delicious in a different way.

roast lobster with basil pesto

SERVES 4

Here is one of my favorite recipes using basic pesto. Lobsters are elegant, of course, but lately not so expensive. You can also use this same approach with any fish or shellfish. Before splitting, a lobster can be humanely killed by inserting a knife decisively between its eyes. Alternatively, it can be killed by plunging it into lightly salted boiling water for 2 to 3 minutes. Unfortunately, we don't know which is preferable to the lobster.

4 whole lobsters (1 ¼ to 1 ½ pounds each)
Basic Basil Pesto (page 42)

2 cups coarse dry bread crumbs (I like panko)
2 teaspoons finely grated lemon zest
3 tablespoons extra virgin olive oil

PREHEAT THE OVEN to 450°F. Split the lobsters in half lengthwise and gently crack the claws. Remove and discard the long thin intestinal tract that runs the length of the lobster tail and also the lumpy head sac that is located near the eyes. Remove and reserve the pale green liver, called the tomalley, from the body cavity. Also remove and reserve the dark green coral (lobster roe) if present in the female.

Combine the pesto with the tomalley and coral in a blender or food processor and process. (Some people avoid the tomalley because of their concern over environmental toxins, which concentrate in the liver. If you are among those, just discard the tomalley.) In a bowl, stir the bread crumbs, zest, and pesto together to make a light, crumbly mixture. It should not be soggy or pasty; add more bread crumbs if necessary. Divide and top each of the lobster halves with the pesto–bread crumb mixture and drizzle with the olive oil. Roast for 12 to 14 minutes or until the lobsters are just cooked through and the topping is golden brown. The meat should be moist and still very slightly translucent in the center. Serve immediately.

mussels baked with asian pesto

SERVES 6 AS AN APPETIZER

This is a fun little appetizer or hors d'oeuvre. It can be assembled as much as a day ahead, refrigerated, and then baked at the last minute. Be sure to serve with little cocktail forks or spoons so that you can get every bit of the pesto out of the shell. (Actually, the best tool for this job is your tongue.) And of course, feel free to substitute any pesto you like for the Asian Pesto. The bonus in this recipe is that you also get the mussel stock, which is a delicious base for seafood soups and sauces. Strain it through a fine sieve and freeze for use later on.

3 pounds fresh mussels
1 cup dry white wine
2 tablespoons butter

3 tablespoons chopped fresh parsley
Asian Pesto (page 43)

WASH THE MUSSELS thoroughly and pull off the "beards" (the little bit of seaweed that might be clamped in the shell). Transfer the mussels to a large saucepan or pot and add the wine, butter, and parsley. Cover tightly and cook over high heat, stirring a couple times, until the mussels open, about 4 minutes. Drain the mussels, reserving the broth for another use, and discard any mussels that don't open.

When they are cool enough to handle, remove the top shell from each mussel. Loosen the meat with your fingers or a fork (to make it easier to eat) and arrange the mussels in their half shells on a baking sheet lined with a loosely crumpled sheet of foil or on a bed of coarse salt. (This will help keep the mussels upright.) Lift each mussel and place a teaspoon or two of the pesto in the shell and lightly press the meat back in place. If not baking immediately, cover the entire sheet with plastic wrap and refrigerate.

At serving time, preheat the oven to 400°F. Bake the mussels (plastic wrap removed of course!) just until the pesto begins to bubble and the mussels are heated through, 4 to 6 minutes. Serve immediately.

basil-mint pesto halibut sautéed in rice paper with citrus salad

SERVES 6

Edible rice paper is used extensively in Southeast Asian cooking and is a very versatile way to wrap up almost anything. (And it's much easier to use than the instructions make it appear.) It can be eaten raw (after softening); sautéed, as it is in this recipe; or baked. Look for it in Asian markets and in large supermarkets that serve a Southeast Asian population. If you can't find rice paper or if the whole idea makes you nervous, just grill the fish or bake it with a little of the pesto spread on top and serve it with the salad. Delicious. You can substitute a variety of fishes: fresh tuna, sea bass, and salmon all work well.

6 halibut fillets, about 4 ounces each, skin removed
Salt and freshly ground pepper
6 8-inch rice paper rounds
Basil-Mint Pesto (page 45)
2 tablespoons olive oil

1 to 2 cups young, tender, savory greens, such as arugula, cress, mustard, mizuna, or a combination
Citrus Salad

Garnish if you like with fresh mint sprigs and basil oil (available in gourmet stores)

LIGHTLY SEASON THE halibut with salt and pepper. Dip a rice paper round completely in tepid water and wet it thoroughly. Transfer the paper to a dry tea towel and then lay a piece of fish on the lower third. Top the halibut with about a tablespoon of Basil-Mint Pesto and spread it out to coat the fish evenly. Fold the sides of the rice paper over the fish and then fold the bottom edge up and the top part down (like closing an envelope) to enclose completely. Repeat with the remaining fillets.

In a nonstick sauté pan heat the olive oil over medium heat. When the oil is hot and shimmering, add the fish packets. Sauté, turning once, until the rice paper is golden brown on both sides and the halibut is opaque, 4 to 5 minutes total. Drain the packets on paper towels. (If you can't fit them all at once, you can sauté in batches, keeping the cooked packets warm in a low oven.)

Combine the greens with the Citrus Salad and arrange on serving plates. Top with the sautéed halibut packet. Garnish with mint sprigs and sprinkle with basil oil, if desired. Serve immediately.

citrus salad

2 cups fresh orange sections

2 cups fresh grapefruit sections

2 limes or lemons, peeled, seeded, and
    sectioned

1 tablespoon sherry vinegar, or to taste

3 tablespoons fresh orange or grapefruit
    juice (collected from sections above)

1 teaspoon peeled and finely minced
    fresh ginger

Pinch of cayenne pepper

Salt and freshly ground pepper to taste

1 tablespoon finely minced fresh mint
    leaves

1 tablespoon extra virgin olive oil

Drops of honey to taste

COMBINE THE CITRUS sections in a mixing bowl. In a separate small bowl, combine the vinegar, the 3 tablespoons of reserved citrus juice, ginger, cayenne, salt and pepper, and mint. Whisk in the olive oil and add drops of honey as necessary to balance the tartness of the fruit. Pour the dressing over the citrus and stir gently to combine. MAKES ABOUT 4 CUPS

4 marinades of the world

An interesting marinade is pretty much the simplest way there is to add flavor notes to all kinds of meat, as well as fish, chicken, tofu, and vegetables, especially those vegetables that take well to grilling, broiling, or roasting. I think eggplant, zucchini, potatoes, cauliflower, broccoli, and asparagus are particularly good.

A marinade can be as simple as olive oil flavored with a little garlic and some fresh herbs or it can be a fancier, more complex, cooked concoction. Vinaigrettes (see page 18) often make very good marinades also. Every cuisine has its own special marinades. We could fill several books with all the possibilities! Here, I'll share my own interpretations of some marinades from several cultures to get you started.

Why marinate?

For me, there's only one reason, and that's to add flavor. You may think of marinating as a way to tenderize meat, but in my opinion, that's a bad idea. Marinades "tenderize" by using some sort of acid, such as vinegar, wine, citrus juice, or buttermilk, which breaks down the protein in meat, softening its connective tissue, but an acid marinade actually diminishes meat's ability to retain moisture, thereby drying it out. Bad trade-off. Commercial meat tenderizers contain enzymes that can turn meat to mush, hardly a better choice. If you've got a truly tough piece of meat, you are much better off making it tender and succulent by using a slow, moist cooking method, such as braising or stewing (see Pot-Roasting lesson, page 130). Alternatively, you can tenderize tough cuts by pounding them with a meat hammer or even with the bottom of a heavy skillet.

TWO QUICK CAUTIONARY NOTES

1. Always refrigerate meats, chicken, and fish as they marinate. Bacteria can grow very quickly on meats at room temperature. Students often ask about reusing marinades, and I don't usually recommend it. However, if you've got a big batch of used marinade that you can't bear to throw away, be sure to bring it to a rolling boil and then immediately refrigerate it. Plan to reuse it within a day or two.

2. If you are going to use some of your marinade as a dipping sauce or drizzle (great idea!), make sure you set aside that quantity before the meat or fish goes in.

These precautions are not necessary with vegetables.

to marinate and to cook marinated foods

All of the recipes that follow make enough to marinate at least a couple of pounds of meat, fish, or vegetables. I've suggested some combinations—a marinade I love with swordfish, another that's great with flank steak—but try any marinade with any food that sounds appealing to you.

In a pinch, it's perfectly acceptable to use bottled marinades, as well as other commercially made products such as teriyaki or Worcestershire sauce. Just make sure to taste them first. If the flavor isn't appealing straight out of the bottle, it's not likely to improve the taste of your dinner.

You can marinate food in any container except one made of uncoated cast iron or aluminum, which can react with acids and develop off-flavors. Remember that the goal is to have every food surface bathed in the marinade. Perhaps the easiest way to marinate is to put everything into a resealable plastic bag and seal it securely. You can then turn the bag and food easily, and it won't take up much room in the fridge.

As with most things, the principle of diminishing returns also applies to marinating; left in a marinade too long, the proteins will begin to break down. It's also possible to add too much flavor. You'll see a few exceptions in the recipes ahead and elsewhere in the book, but as general guidelines:

~ Marinate seafood (except whole fish) and vegetables a maximum of 45 minutes.
~ Marinate individual portions of meat and chicken parts up to 2 hours.
~ Marinate tofu or tempeh at least 1 hour and up to 6 hours if using a whole block.
~ Marinate whole chickens, whole fish, and large cuts of meat up to 6 hours.

When you are ready to cook, remove the food from the marinade and gently pat it dry. Typically, marinated food is grilled or broiled, but most of these marinades will also work if you prefer to pan-roast or sauté. Give special cooking attention to marinades that have sugar, honey, or other natural sweeteners in them. Sugar burns quickly, so moderate the heat accordingly. Let's start with some simple, all-purpose marinades.

a simple balsamic vinegar marinade

MAKES I GENEROUS CUP

This delicious marinade can be used on almost anything. It's especially nice with grilled or broiled steaks and rich fish like tuna or swordfish. Because of the acidity, it's also fast acting; you can be ready to go in as little as 15 minutes after the meats have been coated. Regular balsamic vinegar is very dark. The so-called white balsamics on the market are ideal for chicken or white fish since they won't color the meat. (See page 21 for a discussion of balsamic vinegars.)

2/3 cup balsamic vinegar

1/3 cup olive oil

2 tablespoons finely chopped fresh
   rosemary leaves

4 garlic cloves, peeled and thinly sliced

2 teaspoons kosher or sea salt

I teaspoon freshly ground black pepper

WHISK ALL THE ingredients together. Can be made ahead and stored covered in the refrigerator for up to 3 days.

mustard and tarragon marinade

MAKES ABOUT I 1/4 CUPS

Mustard and tarragon are a classic French combination of flavors. Use this to marinate and baste grilled or roasted chicken, pork, or fish. This is enough marinade for up to 2 pounds of boneless chicken, meat, or fish.

1/2 cup smooth Dijon mustard

1/2 cup apple juice or cider

2 tablespoons olive oil

2 tablespoons honey

1/3 cup (or more) chopped fresh
   tarragon

WHISK ALL THE ingredients together. Store covered in the refrigerator for up to 3 days.

a simple olive oil and fresh herb marinade

MAKES ABOUT 1 CUP

This Mediterranean-inspired marinade really benefits from a good, flavorful extra virgin olive oil (see pages 22–23 for a discussion of olive oils). My favorite use of this is with chicken breasts, thinly cut pork loin chops, or on fish like sea bass, salmon, or shrimp.

**3 tablespoons chopped mixed fresh
   herbs, such as parsley, rosemary, and
   chives**
2 teaspoons finely chopped fresh garlic
**Juice and finely grated zest of 1 large
   lemon**

**1 tablespoon grainy Dijon mustard
   (optional)**
²/₃ cup extra virgin olive oil

WHISK ALL THE ingredients together. Store covered in the refrigerator for up to 3 days.

miso marinade

MAKES ABOUT 1 CUP

Fish, chicken, or pork really shine after a miso marinade. It's one of my favorite marinades for grilled salmon, and it's excellent on eggplant. Miso is highly nutritious and a great ingredient to have on hand in the pantry to make a wide variety of stocks, salad dressings, or sauces.

¼ cup white ("shiro") miso paste
¼ cup mirin (see Glossary and Pantry)
2 tablespoons unseasoned rice vinegar
2 teaspoons toasted sesame oil

**2 tablespoons minced scallions (white
   and green parts)**
**1 ½ tablespoons peeled and minced
   fresh ginger**

STIR ALL THE ingredients together until smooth. Add enough water, about ¼ cup or so, so that the mixture is about as thick as heavy cream. Store covered in the refrigerator for up to 1 week.

miso grilled salmon

SERVES 6

Miso is a delicious marinade for rich salmon. Be careful that the fire is not so hot as to burn the sugar in the marinade. The idea is to get a tasty crust. You can also cook the salmon under a broiler or pan-roast it, starting it skin side up in a heavy ovenproof skillet until it's nicely lacquered. Then turn it over and finish in a hot 425°F. oven.

6 5-ounce fillets of salmon, skin on
Miso Marinade

Garnish if you like with toasted sesame seeds, daikon sprouts, and slivered nori (toasted seaweed)

REMOVE ANY PIN bones from the salmon. Coat the salmon with the marinade, cover, and refrigerate for at least 30 minutes, and up to 2 hours, turning occasionally.

Prepare a charcoal fire or preheat the broiler. Wipe the excess marinade off the salmon with your fingers and grill or broil the salmon on both sides until just cooked through. The fish should still be translucent in the very middle. Place on warm plates, skin side down. Sprinkle with sesame seeds, daikon sprouts, and nori strips, if using, and serve immediately.

asian marinade

½ cup tamari or soy sauce

½ cup sake or Shaoxing (rice wine)

1 tablespoon finely minced garlic

2 teaspoons peeled and finely minced
   fresh ginger

½ cup mirin (sweet rice wine)

1 tablespoon honey

2 teaspoons toasted sesame oil

2 tablespoons hoisin sauce

½ teaspoon five-spice powder

WHISK ALL THE ingredients together. Can be made 1 day ahead and stored covered in the refrigerator.

roast pork tenderloin with asian marinade

SERVES 4 TO 6

Tenderloins vary in size. If you get little ones, they'll cook more quickly than a larger one. This is also a delicious way to serve a pork loin, which of course is larger, and will need to cook longer. It's ready at 155°F. internal temperature.

If you love to grill, you can prepare the tenderloin that way, but be careful because the marinade has sugar, which tends to burn and become bitter, so use the indirect heat method (see page 152 for a discussion of grilling techniques).

2 pounds fresh pork tenderloin

Asian Marinade

COMBINE THE PORK with the marinade and refrigerate covered for up to 6 hours. Turn a few times while marinating.

Preheat the oven to 375°F. Add 1 cup of water to a roasting pan fitted with a rack. Reserving the marinade, remove the tenderloins, pat them dry, and place them on the rack. Roast in the oven for 25 to 30 minutes; brush the pork with some of the reserved marinade several times while it is roasting. The meat is done when an instant-read thermometer inserted in the center reaches 155°F. Let the tenderloins rest at least 5 minutes before slicing. While the tenderloins are cooking or resting, put the remaining marinade in a small saucepan and bring it to a boil over high heat. Boil uncovered for 3 to 4 minutes; this will kill any unwanted bacteria and reduce the marinade slightly to make a better sauce consistency. Strain the sauce through a sieve and drizzle over the sliced meat.

mojo marinade

Mojo, a Caribbean-inspired marinade and sauce popularized by chefs working in the pan-Latin arena, adds bright flavor notes to almost anything you grill. Since the citrus gives it lots of acidity, do not overmarinate meats or fish. I love this for grilled asparagus.

1 ½ cups fresh orange juice
⅓ cup fresh lime juice
⅓ cup olive oil
¼ cup minced fresh parsley leaves
2 teaspoons chopped fresh garlic

1 tablespoon chopped fresh mint leaves
1 tablespoon chopped fresh oregano
   leaves
1 teaspoon ground ginger
2 teaspoons salt

COMBINE ALL THE ingredients in a blender or food processor and pulse to form a smooth mixture. Store covered in the refrigerator for up to 3 days.

mojo-marinated skewered beef

SERVES 4

You can add all manner of things to the skewers—tropical fruits, cherry tomatoes, mushrooms, etc. Reduce the marinade over high heat for a few minutes to thicken it for a good drizzling or dipping sauce.

1 ½ pounds beef sirloin cut into
   ¼-inch-thick slices
Mojo Marinade

Red onion wedges; large pineapple
   cubes; crimini mushroom halves;
   thick zucchini rounds—any fruits and
   vegetables of your choice in any
   quantity

PREPARE A CHARCOAL fire or preheat a gas or stovetop grill.

About 20 minutes before you plan to grill the beef, combine the meat and about two-thirds of the Mojo Marinade in a shallow dish or resealable plastic bag. Turn the beef occasionally to make sure all sides come in contact with the marinade.

Thread the beef onto skewers with the additional ingredients. You may have a few skewers that are mostly meat or lots of mixed skewers. Grill over high heat until the meat is rare or medium-rare or to your taste. Serve immediately with the reserved Mojo Marinade on the side.

yogurt and mint marinade

MAKES ABOUT 1¼ CUPS

The only marinades that actually seem to work to tenderize meats are those made from yogurt or buttermilk. It's not entirely clear why they work, but the lactic acid in dairy seems to activate enzymes in meats that help to gently break down muscle fiber. It's similar to the way that aging tenderizes meats. Because yogurt marinades are only mildly acidic, they also don't dry out meat the way strong acid marinades do.

This Indian-inspired marinade can be used with any meat (it's delicious with lamb), bird, or fish. When you are ready to cook, wipe off the excess marinade with your fingers, as it has a tendency to burn when grilled, sautéed, or broiled. Depending on how much marinade I need, I often set some aside to combine with diced cucumbers or other chopped raw vegetables. The Indians call this a raita and it's a delicious accompaniment.

**2 teaspoons toasted and ground cumin
seeds**
½ teaspoon crushed red pepper flakes
1 tablespoon minced or pressed garlic
**¼ cup minced green onions (white and
green parts)**

1¼ cups plain yogurt
2 tablespoons sweet paprika
**¼ cup loosely packed, finely chopped
fresh mint leaves**

MIX ALL THE ingredients together. Store covered in the refrigerator for up to 2 days.

suggestion   Use half the marinade to make chicken for 2 (or chicken for 1 plus leftovers), saving the rest of the yogurt mixture. The next night, combine the yogurt with diced cucumbers or other raw vegetables and eat it on top of some grilled fish.

grilled yogurt and mint chicken

SERVES 4

This is similar to the tandoori chicken served at Indian restaurants. The traditional tandoor oven is shaped like a large clay urn with very hot coals at the bottom. The chicken (or other meats or vegetables) is skewered and placed point down in the center of the oven. The chicken cooks very quickly, developing a tasty crust as the juices drip down onto the coals, giving the meat a unique and sweet fragrance. I've adapted the technique to the grill, but you could also make this in a preheated 500°F. oven, placing the chicken pieces on a rack. Boneless breasts or thighs will cook through in just 6 to 8 minutes.

**4 large boneless chicken breasts or
    8 chicken thighs**
4 tablespoons fresh lemon or lime juice

2 teaspoons kosher or sea salt
Yogurt and Mint Marinade

WASH THE CHICKEN, remove the skin, and pat dry. With the point of a sharp knife, cut several short, shallow (about ¼ inch deep) slashes on one side of the meat, about 1 inch apart. Rub the chicken with the lemon juice and the salt.

Coat the chicken with the yogurt marinade and refrigerate covered for at least 2 hours and up to 12 (see Note). Turn occasionally. Prepare a charcoal fire with medium-hot coals and brush the grill with oil. Remove the chicken from the marinade and wipe clean with your fingers. Grill slashed side up until richly colored. Turn and grill on the other side until cooked through.

NOTE: This is an exception to what I said earlier about the length of time for marinating. We do it longer here because the yogurt is a more gentle acid and therefore won't "damage" the meat like stronger acids such as wine or citrus would. In the process, it develops great flavor!

moroccan marinade

Freshly ground spices are stunningly more flavorful than commercial powders. Toast whole seeds in a dry sauté pan, stirring over moderate heat just until the seeds are fragrant. Turn them immediately out of the pan (be careful not to burn them) and grind them in your electric coffee grinder or handy mortar and pestle. If you can't get hold of whole spices, ground ones are an adequate substitute. I love this bouquet of fragrant spices on almost anything.

2 teaspoons toasted coriander seeds, ground

2 teaspoons toasted cumin seeds, ground

¾ cup coarsely chopped fresh mint leaves

1½ tablespoons peeled and chopped fresh ginger

1 tablespoon chopped garlic

2 teaspoons sweet paprika

2 teaspoons ground turmeric

¼ cup fresh lemon juice

¼ cup olive oil

2 teaspoons salt

1 tablespoon sugar

1 teaspoon bottled hot pepper sauce

PLACE ALL THE ingredients in a food processor or blender and pulse until fairly smooth. Store covered in the refrigerator for up to 3 days.

roast moroccan marinated game hens

SERVES 2 TO 4 DEPENDING ON REST OF MEAL

2 large game hens (about 20 ounces each)

Moroccan Marinade

PLACE THE GAME hens in a shallow glass dish or in a large resealable plastic bag and cover with the marinade. Marinate in the refrigerator for up to 6 hours, turning occasionally.

Preheat the oven to 425°F. Remove the hens and pat dry, reserving the marinade, and set them on a rack in a roasting pan. Roast in the oven for 30 minutes, brushing a few times with the reserved marinade. You can tell the birds are cooked through when the joint where the leg joins the body is no longer pink. Remove from the oven, let the hens rest for 5 minutes, then split lengthwise and serve.

teriyaki marinade

Americans are familiar with teriyaki. It's served everywhere, and "teriyaki" sauces and marinades are readily available in all supermarkets. Unfortunately, most of what you find there is not very good. Teriyaki really is a very simple mixture, but to be its best, it requires the best ingredients. For more on sake, mirin, and soy sauce, see Glossary and Pantry.

Teriyaki is actually the name for a grilling technique. Teri translates to "glossy" and yaki to "grilling." The method involves constantly brushing marinade on skewered foods (fish, meats, and vegetables) cooked over hot coals. The grilled food attains a rich lacquered color and a delicious sweet-salty flavor. Basic teriyaki includes just 4 ingredients, but you can add all sorts of additional flavorings, such as fresh ginger, citrus juices like lime or orange, honey in place of the sugar, hot chiles or chile pastes. . . . Grilling with teriyaki is a bit of an art because the sugar in the marinade can easily burn if the coals are too hot. Pan-roasting, as in Teriyaki Sea Bass on Spinach (recipe follows), simplifies things and tastes just as good.

⅓ cup sake (rice wine)
½ cup mirin (sweet rice wine)

⅓ cup soy sauce (I like Japanese soy sauce, called shoyu, or tamari for this)
2 tablespoons sugar

COMBINE THE SAKE and mirin in a small saucepan and bring to a simmer over medium heat. Stir in the soy sauce and sugar and continue to cook until the sugar is dissolved, about 5 minutes. Cool and store in the refrigerator for up to 1 month.

NOTE: If using to baste rather than marinate, continue to cook the sauce over medium heat until it thickens and lightly coats a wooden spoon, about 15 minutes more. This will help it cling better and prevent flare-ups.

teriyaki sea bass on spinach

SERVES 4

Teriyaki Marinade (page 65)
2 teaspoons ginger juice (see Note)
¼ cup fresh orange juice
4 5-ounce fillets of Chilean or other sea
   bass
5 tablespoons olive oil
2 large bunches of spinach, well washed
   and stems removed

Drops of toasted sesame oil
Salt and freshly ground pepper

Garnish if you like with fresh lemon or
   lime wedges

STIR TOGETHER THE Teriyaki Marinade and the ginger and orange juices.
Place the sea bass fillets in a flat bowl just large enough to hold them
in one layer and cover with the marinade (or alternatively, use the
resealable plastic bag approach). Marinate, refrigerated, for 30 minutes,
turning the fish a couple of times. Remove and wipe relatively clean.
Heat 2 tablespoons of the olive oil in a nonstick skillet and sauté the
fillets over medium-high heat until nicely "lacquered" on the bottom.
Flip the fillets, reduce the heat to medium, and continue to cook on the
other side until just cooked through. Keep an eye out here because the
sugar in the marinade tends to burn if the heat is too high.

In a separate skillet, heat the remaining oil and quickly cook the
spinach over high heat until just wilted, about a minute. Season with
sesame oil, salt, and pepper and place on warm plates. Place the fish on
top and serve with citrus wedges, if desired.

NOTE: To make ginger juice, chop ¼ cup of ginger (washed, but you
can leave the skin on) in a mini-processor or by hand and squeeze with
a garlic press or potato ricer to extract juice. Strain before using to
remove any bits of skin.

chipotle marinade

I love this spicy Mexican marinade with grilled flank steak, grilled or broiled chicken breasts, or shrimp. I'd suggest saving a little of the marinade to serve on the side; it also makes a great little sauce for dipping or to spoon on rice.

1/3 cup red wine vinegar
2 teaspoons dried oregano
2 tablespoons chopped fresh cilantro
1 to 2 tablespoons chopped chipotle chiles in adobo (see Glossary and Pantry)

1 tablespoon chopped garlic
1 tablespoon packed light or dark brown sugar
1/2 cup olive oil
Salt to taste

COMBINE THE VINEGAR, oregano, cilantro, chipotle, garlic, and brown sugar in a blender or food processor and blend until smooth. Add the olive oil and pulse to combine and thicken slightly. Add salt to taste. Store covered in the refrigerator for up to 5 days.

jerk marinade

A marinade that comes from the Caribbean, jerk incorporates flavors of both Africa and the New World. Its name is a reference to the way the marinated meat is chopped or shredded after cooking. It is quite spicy, so add or subtract chiles to suit your own taste. This recipe makes enough for 6 chicken breasts or 5 pounds of pork shoulder or ribs.

1 tablespoon ground allspice
1 1/2 teaspoons ground cinnamon
1 teaspoon freshly grated nutmeg
1 tablespoon freshly ground black pepper
1 tablespoon salt
2 tablespoons minced fresh thyme
2 cups finely chopped green onions (white and green parts)

3 tablespoons finely chopped garlic
2 to 6 seeded and finely chopped serrano chiles
2 tablespoons packed light or dark brown sugar
3 tablespoons cider or sherry vinegar
Juice and finely grated zest of 3 large limes
1/2 cup olive oil

COMBINE ALL THE ingredients in a food processor and pulse a few times to combine. Store covered in the refrigerator for up to 2 days.

jerked pork shoulder

SERVES 8 TO 10

This is not a last-minute dish. The large piece of meat needs to marinate for at least 4 hours, and is best if allowed to marinate longer. It takes a couple of hours on the grill, but it's really worth cooking it that way. Read the grilling lesson (page 148) for an explanation of the indirect heat method and grilling tips. Oven-roasting instructions are included as well. Jerk is great served with grilled or roasted onions, sweet peppers, and a crisp cabbage slaw.

5 pounds boneless pork shoulder or butt
Jerk Marinade

2 cups low-sodium homemade chicken stock or your favorite canned broth

TRIM THE PORK of excess fat and any gristle. Place in a bowl and coat with the marinade. Cover and refrigerate for at least 4 hours or up to 12.

TO GRILL: Prepare a charcoal fire or preheat a gas grill. Remove the meat from the marinade, reserving the marinade, and grill over medium heat using the indirect heat method and a drip pan (page 152) for 2 hours or until the meat is very tender. Brush the meat occasionally with the reserved marinade. Remove the pork from the grill, and when it is cool enough to handle, chop or shred the meat.

TO ROAST IN THE OVEN: Preheat the oven to 325°F. Remove the meat from the marinade, reserving marinade, and wrap completely in foil. Place on a rack in a roasting pan and roast in the oven for 4 hours or until the meat is very tender. Open the top of the foil and cook for another 30 minutes or until the meat is lightly browned and caramelized. Remove the pork from the oven, and when it is cool enough to handle, chop or shred the meat.

In a small saucepan, combine the stock and the remaining marinade and bring to a boil over high heat. Reduce the heat and simmer uncovered for 5 to 7 minutes to reduce and lightly thicken. Strain the sauce and keep warm, skimming off as much fat as possible. Spoon the warm sauce over the shredded meat and serve.

5   simple savory sauces that go with (almost) anything

For many home cooks (including me!) some easy grilling, sautéing, or broiling is about all we are up to after a busy day. But hardly anyone wants to eat a plain pork chop or piece of baked chicken anymore. If it seems too boring to eat something totally plain, and too hard or too time-consuming to cook something interesting, all too often we end up opting for take-out again.

The addition of a simple and flavorful sauce can make the difference between something ordinary and a memorable dish. Many feel that sauce-making is complicated and beyond the scope of the average cook. Well, it's not. Several years ago I participated in the revision of the *Joy of Cooking* and one section that I took on was sauces. Lots had changed since 1974, the last time the book was updated. Italian cooking had replaced French as our European touchstone. Ethnic flavors and techniques from Asia and Latin America had become an integral part of American cuisine. And the identification of "sauce" with butter and cream, elaborate stocks, long reductions, and the technical demands of something like hollandaise, had been severed. The lightening, brightening, and expansion of our idea of sauces is one of the best culinary developments of recent decades; take advantage and see how sauces can enliven a meal without a lot of additional effort.

A point I want to make fits in nicely here: home cooking is not an all or nothing proposition. If you have a take-out place that makes a good rotisserie chicken, of course you're going to fall back on it sometimes (it would be silly not to). But you can make it sparkle with one of these sauces, a vinaigrette, or with a couple spoonfuls of homemade salsa, and you'll have a better meal than you would have had otherwise. Buying a rotisserie chicken can even give you the ten minutes to make the sauce you didn't think you had time for; trying different sauces with the same chicken lets you experiment with the effects of different flavors and textures without a huge kitchen commitment.

Sauce used to go on top of food; now every restaurant lays the food on top of the sauce. Who changed the rules and which do I follow at home?

The changes in restaurant presentation in the last couple of decades are not just affectations, and those of us cooking at home for ourselves can take a tip. Sauce can be served on top, on the side, pooled underneath; it can completely blanket what's beneath or be drizzled on artfully, or it can be presented in a separate little dish for dipping. There are "reasons" for the old ways as well as the new, but the important thing is this: food and sauce can be arranged in a variety of ways, and each arrangement will give you a different effect—visually and on the palate. This is true for all of the components of the meal, not just the sauce and the sauced. Try it and see.

HERE, THEN, are some of my favorite sauces that I bet will become some of your standards too. They are drawn from several cuisines, and I've organized them into three categories that I hope will help you sort through the possibilities. The first group is sauces that don't require any cooking at all; it doesn't get much easier than that. The second group is pan sauces, which are prepared in the same pan as the food. This is a classic technique that really should be in your repertoire if it's not already. The third group is a random collection of my favorites.

UNCOOKED SAUCES Some of the classic uncooked sauces
are vinaigrettes (see page 18) and pestos (see page 38). Here are some of my favorites that don't fall into one or the other of those categories but that still require no cooking at all.

ponzu sauce

Ponzu makes a delicious dipping sauce or drizzle for grilled and deep-fried fish, poultry, and vegetables. In Japan, true ponzu is made with the juice of a small, aromatic citrus fruit called yuzu, rarely seen in this country. See Glossary and Pantry for information on mirin and Asian fish sauce.

1/2 cup fresh lime and/or lemon juice
2 tablespoons rice vinegar
1/3 cup soy sauce

2 tablespoons mirin
2 tablespoons packed light brown sugar
1/2 teaspoon Asian fish sauce

WHISK ALL THE ingredients together or combine in a jar and shake. Set aside for at least 1 hour before serving to allow the flavors to blend. Store covered in the refrigerator for up to 1 week.

mango mustard seed sauce

MAKES ABOUT 2 CUPS

This delicious fresh sauce is great with grilled white meats or fish. Thinned with additional juice or stock, it can become a dressing for savory salad greens. Fresh mango puree is my first choice, but you might find frozen puree if your market carries Hispanic foods, and canned puree is available in Indian groceries.

2 tablespoons yellow or black
   mustard seeds
1 cup fresh mango puree (from 2 ripe
   mangoes)
2 teaspoons minced fresh ginger
1 teaspoon finely minced garlic
1/2 teaspoon fragrant curry powder

1/2 cup or so fresh grapefruit juice
2 teaspoons sherry vinegar
1 1/2 teaspoons hot pepper sesame oil
1/3 cup chopped ripe banana (optional)
1 teaspoon honey, or to taste
Salt and freshly ground white pepper
   to taste

IN A SMALL, dry sauté pan over medium heat, toast the mustard seeds until they just begin to pop. Immediately cover the pan (so they don't pop out) and remove from the heat. Combine all the ingredients except the salt and pepper in a blender or food processor and blend to produce a smooth sauce. Taste and season with salt and pepper. Store covered in the refrigerator for up to 3 days.

salsa verde

This is a quick little sauce that has its origins in both Italy and Spain and is traditionally served with grilled meats, especially beef. It is also delicious on all kinds of grilled, pan-seared, or roasted meats, fish, and vegetables. Note that I've used poached or roasted garlic rather than raw. I think this is especially important if you are going to make the sauce ahead. Within an hour, raw garlic can become harsh and hot. Poached or roasted garlic maintains its more subtle and sweet flavor and doesn't overpower the sauce as it sits. (I know I'm repeating myself, but it really makes a difference in this recipe.)

1 cup coarsely chopped fresh parsley leaves
4 anchovy fillets, rinsed
2 tablespoons drained capers
2 tablespoons poached or roasted garlic (see Glossary and Pantry)

2 tablespoons chopped fresh basil or mint leaves or 1 tablespoon chopped fresh tarragon leaves
1 tablespoon finely grated lemon zest
2/3 cup or so extra virgin olive oil
Salt and freshly ground black pepper

COMBINE THE PARSLEY, anchovies, capers, garlic, herbs, and zest in a food processor or blender. With the motor running, slowly add the olive oil in a thin stream until everything is just blended. The sauce should still have a little texture. Taste it and season with salt and pepper. Store covered in the refrigerator for up to 2 days.

suggestion Try tossing this sauce with some cooked chickpeas or other beans. This makes a great side dish, or you could serve the beans as a bed for grilled or roasted fish, meat, or vegetables.

uncooked tomato sauce

MAKES ABOUT 3 CUPS

This is a standard for me. Easy to put together, it can be made a day ahead and used on everything from pasta and rice to anything grilled, broiled, or sautéed. If you're stuck with feeble winter tomatoes, try oven-drying them a bit first to concentrate their flavor (see page 115).

2½ pounds ripe Roma tomatoes (or whatever type is best in the market)

3 tablespoons chopped toasted or poached garlic (see Glossary and Pantry)

½ cup coarsely chopped mixed fresh leafy herbs, such as parsley, basil, or mint

1 tablespoon chopped mixed fresh woody herbs, such as rosemary, oregano, marjoram, or thyme

4 anchovy fillets, rinsed and chopped, or 3 tablespoons rinsed and chopped oil-cured black olives

1 tablespoon or so rinsed and chopped capers

2 teaspoons finely grated lemon zest

½ cup or so fragrant extra virgin olive oil

Salt and freshly ground pepper to taste

CUT THE CORES from the tomatoes, cut them in half crosswise, and gently squeeze out the seeds (don't worry about getting them all out). Coarsely chop the tomatoes and combine with the garlic, herbs, anchovies or olives, capers, zest, and olive oil. Set the mixture aside at room temperature for at least 1 hour before using to allow flavors to develop and marry. Before serving, taste the sauce and season it with salt and pepper, if you think it needs it. Store covered in the refrigerator for 1 day. Allow to return to room temperature before using.

fresh carrot jus or sauce

MAKES 1¼ CUPS

Electric juicer gathering dust on your counter? I've come to love my old juicer because I use it to make colorful delicious sauces in an instant.

This sauce is delicious at room temperature, but if you're going to serve it with a warm dish, you can heat it gently; if it begins to "break" (separate), simply return it to the blender and buzz it up. I especially like champagne vinegar because it's a little more piquant, so try it if you have some (no reason to go out and buy it just for this). I love this sauce with pan-seared white fish or chicken breasts.

1 cup homemade or other fresh carrot juice, preferably organic
¾ teaspoon chopped chipotle in adobo, or to taste (see Glossary and Pantry)
¼ to ⅓ cup extra virgin olive oil
2 teaspoons champagne or white wine vinegar, or to taste
Salt and freshly ground white pepper

PLACE THE JUICE and chipotle in a blender or food processor. With the motor running, gradually add the olive oil in a thin stream. The sauce should have a velvety texture. Stir in vinegar, salt, and pepper to taste.

PAN SAUCES A pan sauce is probably the quickest and simplest cooked sauce you can make. There are two categories. Some are thickened with flour, generally in the form of a roux, which is a mixture of flour and fat. We usually refer to these sauces as "gravies." The other category is true pan sauces, which don't use any flour or starch to thicken them, but are simply a reduction of *liquids* (stocks, juices, and/or wine), *flavorings* (aromatics like shallots and whatever else you like), and *enrichments* (like butter or cream) to blend and mellow the flavors and also to add a little body. The best and simplest pan sauces are made to accompany a quick sauté of meats, fish, or vegetables, and are cooked in the same pan. When you sauté any food, you leave brown bits sticking in the pan, and you probably know that the brown stuff, which is caramelized sugars, has great flavor. A pan sauce uses the brown bits to build flavor. Even if you haven't sautéed something first, you can make a great pan sauce by starting with some chopped shallots or green onions. (For a quick lesson in sautéing, see page 330.)

What follows are two very basic recipes to get you started. You can then experiment by varying the three components endlessly. Remember that if you start with a pan in which you sautéed something first and you've got flavorful little bits in the bottom—so much the better. You'll have more flavor, and making the sauce in that pan will help you clean it at the same time!

basic herb pan sauce for chicken or fish

MAKES ABOUT ¹/₂ CUP, ENOUGH TO SAUCE 4 CHICKEN BREASTS OR FISH STEAKS OR FILLETS

4 tablespoons cold butter
¹/₄ cup finely chopped shallots or green onions (white parts only)
1 cup homemade chicken stock or your favorite canned broth
2 tablespoons fresh lemon juice, or to taste

3 tablespoons finely chopped fresh herbs, such as parsley, dill, chives, or preferably a combination
Salt and freshly ground pepper

HEAT 2 TABLESPOONS of the butter in a sauté pan over medium heat (preferably the same pan you used to cook the chicken or fish you are saucing), and sauté the shallots or onions until softened but not brown, about 2 minutes. Add the stock and lemon juice, and bring to a boil over high heat, stirring regularly and making sure to scrape up all the brown bits. Continue to cook until the liquid is reduced by half and lightly thickened, 3 to 5 minutes. Remove the pan from the heat, whisk in the remaining 2 tablespoons of butter a bit at a time to thicken the sauce, and then the herbs. Taste and season with salt and pepper if you think it needs it. Serve immediately, spooned over chicken or fish.

basic red wine pan sauce
for hamburgers or steaks

MAKES ABOUT ½ CUP, OR ENOUGH FOR 4 SERVINGS

4 tablespoons cold butter
¼ cup finely chopped shallots or green onions (white parts only)
1 cup homemade beef or chicken stock or your favorite canned broth

¾ cup hearty, full-bodied red wine
1 tablespoon balsamic vinegar
2 teaspoons Dijon mustard, preferably grainy
Salt and freshly ground pepper

HEAT 2 TABLESPOONS of the butter in a sauté pan over medium heat (preferably the same pan you used to cook the meat you are saucing), and sauté the shallots or onions until softened but not brown, about 2 minutes. Add the stock, wine, vinegar, and mustard and bring to a boil over high heat, stirring regularly and making sure to scrape up all the

brown bits. Continue to cook until the liquid is reduced by half and lightly thickened, 3 to 5 minutes. Remove the pan from the heat, and whisk in the remaining 2 tablespoons of butter a bit at a time to thicken. Taste and season with salt and pepper. Serve immediately, spooned over hamburgers (call it *steak haché,* in the French manner) or steaks.

roasted red bell pepper sauce

MAKES ABOUT 2 CUPS, DEPENDING ON THE SIZE OF THE VEGETABLES

Oven-roasting or grilling some vegetables concentrates their flavor and caramelizes their natural sugar. Pureed with some stock and strained, they make lovely savory sauces that are smooth and rich without any butter or cream. It couldn't be simpler. If you like the effect, you can try it with almost any vegetable.

Olive oil
3 large red bell peppers
3 medium Roma or other plum tomatoes
1 small red onion, peeled and quartered
1 tablespoon roasted garlic

½ cup or so homemade chicken or vegetable stock or your favorite canned broth
Drops of your favorite hot sauce
Salt and freshly ground pepper
2 tablespoons butter, softened (optional)

PREHEAT THE OVEN to 450°F. (You can also prepare the vegetables under a broiler or on a gas or charcoal grill.) Lightly oil the peppers, tomatoes, and onion, arrange on a baking sheet, and roast until the skins are blistered (do not blacken the tomatoes). Place the peppers in a bowl, cover with a lid or plastic wrap, and allow to steam for a few minutes. Scrape the skins off the peppers (do not rinse) and discard the skin, stems, and seeds. Peel the onions and chop them along with the peppers and tomatoes, being sure to save all the juices.

Transfer the chopped vegetables to a blender or food processor, add the garlic, and puree until smooth. Add stock to thin the sauce to the desired consistency. Strain through a medium strainer to remove any remaining seeds and skin. Taste and season with hot sauce, salt, and pepper. Serve warm. If using butter, whisk it in just before serving. Can be made up to 3 days ahead; store covered in the refrigerator and reheat before serving.

variation   For a sauce with even smokier notes, substitute ½ teaspoon or so of chopped chipotle in adobo in place of the hot sauce.

corn cream

MAKES ABOUT 2 CUPS

This is another good example of how vegetable purees can be turned into worthy sauces, though this time, I go for the cream. You can use the same approach with sweet peas, roasted butternut squash, or carrots. I serve this with delicate fish or chicken dishes; one of my favorite pairings for this sauce is bacon-wrapped scallops. The complete recipe follows.

2 tablespoons butter or olive oil

1 cup chopped onions

1/2 teaspoon medium-hot pure chile powder, such as Chimayo or chipotle (see Glossary and Pantry)

2 cups homemade chicken or vegetable stock or your favorite canned broth

1 1/2 cups sweet corn kernels, fresh or frozen and thawed

2/3 cup heavy cream

1 teaspoon dry sherry (optional)

Salt

WARM THE BUTTER or olive oil in a deep saucepan over medium heat. Add the onions and chile powder and sauté until the onions are soft but not brown. Add the stock and the corn, cover, and simmer until the vegetables are very soft, about 10 minutes. Add the cream and sherry, if desired, and bring to a simmer. Pour the mixture into a blender or food processor (you can let it cool slightly first, for safety) and puree until very smooth. Strain through a fine mesh strainer, pressing down on the solids. Discard the solids, and return the sauce to the pan and keep warm. (Depending on the corn, the sauce can appear a little "grainy" even after straining. If you want a velvety smooth sauce, you can puree and strain again.) Taste and season with salt and additional chile powder, if you think it needs it. The sauce can be made a day or two ahead and stored covered in the refrigerator.

seared scallops with corn cream

SERVES 6

I love this combination of rich scallop, salty pancetta, peppery cress, and sweet Corn Cream sauce. Dry-pack scallops are those that are never put in seawater or brine and are much firmer and meatier as a result. You'll probably have to ask your fishmonger to order these ahead of time for you. If scallops are unavailable, substitute firm white fish, such as halibut or sea bass. You can also certainly do the recipe without the pancetta wrap, if desired.

12 thinly sliced rounds of pancetta
12 large dry-pack fresh scallops (about
   1 1/2 pounds)
3 tablespoons olive oil

2 cups young watercress leaves with
   tender stems (discard woody stems)
Corn Cream
Freshly ground black pepper

GENTLY UNWIND THE pancetta and then wrap it around each scallop. Secure with a toothpick, if necessary. Heat the olive oil in a large heavy-bottomed sauté pan over medium-high heat until very hot and just beginning to smoke. Using tongs, carefully place the scallops flat side down and cook until golden brown, about 2 minutes. Turn and cook the other side until browned, about 1 minute. Resist the temptation to move the scallops around so that they can brown quickly and evenly.

Arrange the watercress leaves in the center of warm plates (a nice touch) and place the scallops on top. Spoon the Corn Cream around and garnish with a grinding or two of black pepper. Serve.

grapefruit sauce

This tart-sweet reduction sauce is delicious with all kind of grilled and roasted meats. Note the addition of the bit of fresh grapefruit juice at the end. This "brightens" the rich sauce and reestablishes the aromas of the fruit that cooked off in the reduction process.

1 ¹/₂ tablespoons balsamic vinegar
2 tablespoons sugar
2 cups homemade chicken or duck stock or your favorite canned broth

1 cup plus 2 tablespoons fresh grapefruit juice
³/₄ cup heavy cream
Salt and freshly ground pepper

IN A SAUCEPAN over high heat, cook the balsamic vinegar and sugar until the sugar is melted and the mixture is reduced to a syrupy consistency, about 2 minutes. Add the stock and 1 cup of the grapefruit juice and reduce over high heat to ³/₄ cup or so, 15 to 18 minutes. (You can learn to eyeball this. Pour ³/₄ cup water into the empty pan before you start and memorize what it looks like.) Whisk in the cream and continue to simmer until the sauce is slightly reduced and thickened, 3 to 4 minutes. Remove the pan from the heat, stir in the remaining grapefruit juice, then taste and season with salt and pepper. Serve immediately or keep warm. Can be made a day or two ahead, stored covered in the refrigerator, and gently reheated before serving.

roast duck breasts with grapefruit sauce

SERVES 4

This has been a signature dish of mine over the years. To make the sauce and the duck, you'll need a total of 4 grapefruits. Don't hesitate to substitute chicken breasts or pork loin or tenderloin if you're not a duck fan. You can also prepare the meat on the grill rather than roasting. My favorite grapefruits are the Texas pinks or reds that come to the market in late fall.

1 tablespoon honey

3 tablespoons fresh grapefruit juice

½ teaspoon ground allspice or juniper berry

4 duck breast halves (6 to 7 ounces each)

Salt and freshly ground pepper

2 grapefruits, peeled and sectioned

2 cups young watercress leaves with tender stems (woody stems discarded)

Grapefruit Sauce

PREHEAT THE OVEN to 425°F. Whisk the honey, grapefruit juice, and allspice together in a small bowl. Trim the duck breasts of excess fat and score the skin in a cross-hatch pattern, cutting almost but not quite through to the meat. Brush the breasts with the honey mixture, season with salt and pepper, and set aside for at least 15 minutes.

Heat an ovenproof sauté pan over medium-high heat. Place the duck breasts in the dry pan skin side down and sear until golden brown, about 4 minutes. Turn them over and place the pan in the oven for 3 to 4 minutes more, or until the meat is medium rare. Be careful not to overcook. Remove the pan from the oven and then remove the breasts to a cutting board and allow to rest for at least 3 minutes. Cover loosely with foil to keep warm.

To serve, arrange the grapefruit sections and watercress on plates. Thinly slice the duck breasts and arrange on top, spoon warm Grapefruit Sauce over the duck, and serve.

NOTE: If you want to go all the way, garnish with something crispy like thinly sliced parsnips or julienned leeks, which have been quickly fried in ¼ inch or so of vegetable oil.

part two

technique
lessons

6　　soup basics

Soup is an important part of every culture's cuisine; its variations could fill several books (and have! Two good books on soups are *Splendid Soups* by James Peterson and *Soup, A Way of Life* by Barbara Kafka). Soup is the most basic of dishes. When meat, fish, vegetables, or grains are cooked in plenty of water, much of the flavor ends up in the water—which is why boiling is rarely a first-choice cooking method. But food's loss is water's gain—that flavorful liquid is broth, or stock, the simplest of soups. Originally the word *soupe* or *sops* described a hot broth poured on or combined with bread—the bread being the sopping vehicle. *Soupe* and *sops* are also the root of the word *supper*. When I was growing up on a ranch in Colorado, the big meal of the day was lunch. Supper, which was the last meal of the day before bed, was often something "soupy" or "stewy," a simple one-dish meal that was easily digested. Amy Mintzer, who is my collaborator and confidant on this book, recalls that when she went to summer camp as a girl they also served the big meal at lunch with some kind of soup for dinner. The unimpressed campers called the dinner soup "cream of lunch"!

Soups run the gamut of flavor, texture, and temperature. They can be clear, thick, light, hearty, creamy. Most soups are served hot but there are many delicious cold soups besides the familiar gazpacho and vichyssoise. A soup can be perfectly smooth or it can derive some of its interest from contrasting textures in the same bowl. The soup world encompasses the spicy soups of Asia, Africa, and South America and the sweet fruit soups of Scandinavia. We've adopted names from different cuisines to describe various soup types—chowder, bisque, consommé, gumbo—but we're not going to concern ourselves with those distinctions here.

For me, soup is a basic comfort food: it's easy to put together, it's satisfying, and it can be made ahead. If that weren't enough, soup is also generally healthy and economical. An old Spanish proverb claims, "Of soup and love, the first is best." We've all been through times when that seemed accurate, but even if you're lucky in love, you can still learn to love making soup.

At its most basic, soup-making is a three-step process: add water or stock to a pot, add food on hand, and cook till tender. If you end up with something more liquid than solid, and you can eat the liquid, then it's soup. For whatever reason, however, many Americans seem mystified by soup-making. Maybe soup has come out of a can for so long that we've been convinced it must be beyond us. It isn't! There are three parts to this lesson. First we'll start with the liquids or stocks. Next I'll give you some simple recipes that take those stocks and make them into soup with a few tasty additions. Finally I'll give you some full-fledged recipes that have become my favorites and which I know you'll improve upon; all these recipes teach basic methods and techniques that you can use to create soups of your own.

basic stocks and broths

I'm sure you've noticed that chicken or vegetable stock appears as an ingredient in as many as half the recipes in this book; it is a wildly versatile ingredient across the board. But most important, stock is *the* building block of soup-making. It is soup at its most basic: water flavored by long contact with various foodstuffs. Some of the classic soups are nothing more than broths. So stock can *be* soup or it can be the basis for soup. For the beginning home soup-maker, there are really only two stocks you need to learn. First is a good **chicken stock** (which can be turned into a great fish stock using shrimp shells—see page 272). *And yes—it's okay to use canned chicken stock if you need to!* I recommend choosing one that is defatted and salt-reduced. Beyond that, read the ingredients list and use your own tastebuds to pick a favorite brand. I've included a quick tip for adding more flavor to canned stock (page 91). The other stock that you should feel comfortable with is a good **vegetable stock** and I've included my favorite all-purpose version below. I've yet to find a good commercial vegetable stock. They all seem to taste too strongly of a single vegetable.

Beyond that, there are worlds of other stocks and broths and I've included three more just to give you a sense of the possibilities: Fresh Juice Stock, Japanese Stock or Dashi, and Green Tea Stock.

STORING STOCKS

The recipes for the Vegetable and Chicken Stocks yield about 1 gallon. These stocks freeze well, and you should keep any surplus in your freezer. Because I use stock in so many different ways, I freeze a single batch of stock in various-sized containers: some in quart containers, some in 1-cup containers, some in ice-cube trays. That way it's easy to defrost the exact amount I need.

If you don't have that kind of space in your freezer, you don't have to reduce the recipe. Instead you can reduce the stock—just boil it down. Either while it's cooking or after you've chilled and defatted it, bring the stock to a boil and let it boil away uncovered until there's only half as much left in the pot. What you've got now is concentrated stock. If you like the intensity, you can use it at full strength. Otherwise you can add water when you're ready to use it.

What's the difference between stock and broth?

Traditionally, "stock" suggested something richer and stronger in flavor, whereas "broth" was basically the edible by-product of cooking meat in water. Today, beyond the confines of professional cooking schools, the two terms are used interchangeably.

basic chicken stock

There are two "geographical" approaches to making chicken stock. The traditional European approach, codified for most of us as the "French" approach, is to use aromatic vegetables—onions, carrots, celery, and garlic—along with the chicken. In Asia, the stocks are often simpler and rely on just the meat and bones, sometimes with ginger and scallion, as they do in China. I'm going to give recipes for both, and you can decide which you like.

The key to good chicken stock is to use all parts of the chicken, including dark meat if possible, bones, skin, and—if you can get them—the feet, which contribute not only flavor but also texture to the stock. And don't season the stock with salt or pepper yet. You may decide to reduce the stock (boil it down to concentrate it) for a sauce and if you season it to a pleasing level now, it will be over-seasoned when reduced.

the european approach

6 to 8 pounds meaty chicken parts, including legs, wings, backs, etc.
2 tablespoons olive oil
3 cups chopped onions
1 cup chopped carrots
1 cup chopped celery
6 large garlic cloves, crushed
1 1/2 gallons water
3 cups dry white wine

RINSE THE CHICKEN parts and set aside. Heat the olive oil in a large, deep pot over medium-high heat, then add the onions, carrots, celery, and garlic and sauté until the vegetables just begin to color. Add the chicken, water, and wine and bring just to a boil. Immediately reduce the heat and simmer, without boiling, partially covered for 2 to 3 hours, skimming any foam or "scum" from the surface. (The reason we don't want to boil the stock at this stage is that it will become cloudy. It will still taste good but a clearer stock is prettier, especially if it's going to be used in a clear soup or sauce.) Remove the pot from the heat, allow the stock to cool (for safety in pouring), and strain through a fine mesh strainer. Discard the solids. Refrigerate overnight or until the fat has congealed. Remove and discard the fat. Divide the stock into storage containers, and store covered in the refrigerator for up to 5 days or in the freezer for up to 6 months. MAKES ABOUT I GALLON

the asian or chinese approach

6 to 8 pounds meaty chicken parts, including legs, wings, backs, etc.

6 half-dollar-size slices of fresh ginger, smashed with the side of a cleaver or knife

6 whole scallions or green onions, smashed with the side of a cleaver or knife

1½ gallons or so of water

RINSE THE CHICKEN parts and place in a large, deep pot. Add the ginger, scallions or onions, and water, and bring just to a boil. Immediately reduce the heat and gently simmer, without boiling, partially covered for 2 to 3 hours, skimming any foam from the surface. Remove the pot from the heat, allow the stock to cool (for safety in pouring), and strain through a fine mesh strainer. Discard the solids. Refrigerate overnight or until the fat has congealed on top (it's the yellow blobs or yellow solid layer on top). Remove and discard the fat. After straining and defatting, return the stock to a clean pot and bring to a boil. Continue to boil uncovered until it is reduced by at least a third. Divide the stock into storage containers, and store covered in the refrigerator for up to 5 days or in the freezer for up to 6 months. MAKES ABOUT 3 QUARTS

NOTE: For an additional stock recipe, see Ginger-Poached Chicken (page 214).

improving canned chicken stock

BASICALLY WHAT I do is take aromatic vegetables (onions, carrots, celery, garlic), sauté them until they are lightly browned, and add them, along with a bay leaf and one whole clove, to the canned stock. Figure on about 2 cups of raw vegetables to 6 cups of stock. Bring this to a boil, reduce the heat, simmer covered for 20 to 30 minutes, and you've added a lot of flavor to the stock.

parmesan-pepper egg drop soup

SERVES 6 TO 8

If you've got a rich, tasty chicken stock, one of the simplest and quickest recipes that I can think of is Egg Drop Soup. Interestingly, the technique appears in the cuisines of both China and the northern Mediterranean. It's one of those simple peasant dishes to which you add anything you have on hand. I'm doing an Italian-style version here, but I've suggested some variations as well.

4 eggs

½ cup freshly grated Parmesan or Pecorino cheese

2 teaspoons freshly ground black pepper

8 cups homemade chicken or vegetable stock or your favorite canned broth

1 tablespoon finely grated lemon zest

4 cups lightly packed fresh young spinach or watercress leaves, stems removed

Garnish if you like with tiny toasted croutons

IN A SMALL bowl, beat the eggs with the cheese and pepper until well mixed and set aside.

Heat the stock to a boil in a deep saucepan over high heat. Reduce the heat and simmer, then stir in the zest. With a large spoon, gently swirl the broth in a circle. Gradually pour in the egg mixture in a thin stream. The egg will cook instantly as it hits the hot stock, and the swirling motion will make it form little shreds.

Divide the spinach among warm bowls and spoon the soup over the top. Serve immediately, garnished with little croutons, if desired.

variations

CHINESE EGG DROP SOUP Leave out the cheese and add a teaspoon of hot pepper sesame oil to the eggs.

JAPANESE EGG DROP SOUP Leave out the cheese and add 2 teaspoons of mirin (see Glossary and Pantry) and 2 teaspoons of soy sauce to the eggs. Add thinly sliced shiitake mushrooms to the stock and simmer for 2 to 3 minutes before adding the eggs.

YOUR VERSION Go ahead. Make something up.

vegetable stock

MAKES ABOUT 1 GALLON

There are two keys to making good vegetable stocks. The first is to stick with the basic aromatic vegetables and maybe mushrooms and tomatoes if you like them. Unless you really want a specific flavor, I'd avoid using cruciferous vegetables (cabbage, broccoli, etc.) or other strongly flavored vegetables such as asparagus or artichokes. What you're shooting for here is a basic stock that can go with anything. The other key is to be sure to lightly brown or caramelize the vegetables before adding liquid. As with the chicken stock, I don't add salt or pepper at this point in case I want to reduce the stock for a sauce.

⅓ cup olive or other light vegetable oil
10 cups chopped onions or leeks or a
    combination
4 cups chopped carrots
2 cups chopped celery including tops
¼ cup chopped garlic
4 cups chopped fresh mushrooms
    (crimini or portabella work well)

1½ gallons water
3 cups dry white wine
4 cups chopped tomatoes, fresh or
    canned
2 teaspoons whole black peppercorns
3 bay leaves
2 cups roughly chopped fresh parsley
    leaves and stems

HEAT THE OLIVE oil in a large, deep pot and add the onions, carrots, celery, garlic, and mushrooms. Cook over medium-high heat, stirring occasionally, until the vegetables are lightly browned. Alternatively, you can toss the vegetables with the oil, spread them out in a single layer on a couple of baking sheets, and roast in a preheated 400°F. oven until lightly browned, about 40 minutes. Be sure to turn the vegetables occasionally. When they are browned, transfer the vegetables to a large, deep pot.

Add the water, wine, tomatoes, peppercorns, bay leaves, and parsley, bring to a boil, then immediately reduce the heat and simmer partially covered for 1½ hours. Allow the stock to cool slightly (for safety while pouring), and then carefully strain through a fine mesh strainer. Divide the stock into storage containers and store covered in the refrigerator for up to 5 days or in the freezer for up to 6 months.

variation   If you want your vegetable stock to have a little more body, add a cup or two of chopped white potatoes. The potato starch adds texture and mouth feel, but will make your stock a bit cloudy.

carrot, orange, and ginger soup

SERVES 4

This brightly colored soup is delicious either hot or chilled. And if you're not a vegetarian, it's delicious made with chicken stock too. I'm suggesting white pepper for aesthetic reasons only; as always, use what you have on hand.

2 tablespoons olive oil

I cup chopped onions

I pound carrots, grated (about 6 cups)

2 tablespoons peeled and finely chopped fresh ginger

2 tablespoons finely grated orange zest

4 cups homemade vegetable stock or your favorite canned broth

$1/2$ cup or so fresh orange juice

I teaspoon freshly grated nutmeg or cinnamon

Salt and freshly ground white pepper

Garnish if you like with toasted pecan or walnut oil (see Glossary and Pantry)

HEAT THE OLIVE oil in a deep saucepan or pot and add the onions, carrots, ginger, and orange zest. Sauté until the onions are translucent. Add the stock and bring to a boil. Reduce the heat and simmer covered until the vegetables are tender, about 8 minutes.

Transfer the mixture to a blender or food processor or use an immersion blender, and puree the mixture until very smooth. Return the puree to the pot. Add the orange juice a bit at a time until the soup is the consistency you desire, and return to a simmer. Stir in the nutmeg, taste, and season with salt and pepper. Ladle into bowls and drizzle with nut oil, if desired. Serve immediately.

fresh juice stock

Fresh fruit and vegetable juices make wonderful stocks (and sauces too, as discussed on page 76). Their bright color and fresh taste are delicious, and you can't argue with their nutritional benefits. When cooking with juices, the objective is not to boil them but to just heat them through. There are no hard-and-fast rules for substituting juices for some or all of the stock in a recipe. Let your imagination and tastebuds guide you.

Electric juicers vary in terms of how much pulp they remove, but I like the kind that capture most of the pulp and provide a clear, sparkling juice. You don't have to spend a fortune for a juicer. I have used versions from Braun, Juiceman, KitchenAid, and others that all cost less than a hundred dollars on sale.

YIELDS, OF COURSE, vary depending on the fruit, herb, or vegetable used and the type of juicer, but I usually figure on approximately 1 cup of juice for each pound of produce.

suggestions

HERE ARE SOME ideas for using juices:

~ Use a combination of chicken stock and fresh fennel juice to poach chicken breasts for salads.
~ Use fresh carrot or sweet red pepper juice as a beautiful garnish to ladle around a risotto.
~ Use fresh juices as a basis for vinaigrettes or marinades.
~ Reduce juices (boil them uncovered in a saucepan) until they become syrupy, and drizzle over grilled or roasted meats, cooked vegetables, or fresh fruits.

cold cream of red bell pepper soup from the juicer

SERVES 4

This soup is a simple, vibrant illustration of how fresh juice can serve wonderfully as a stock. It is a very flexible base; any number of additions can be made. I often throw in shrimp just off the grill, for example.

And make sure to try this both cold and warm. Starch from potato juice thickens the warm version—and both are extremely tasty.

I cup carrot juice (from about 4 large peeled carrots)
2 cups red bell pepper juice (from about 3 large, stemmed peppers)
½ cup cucumber juice (from about ½ small cucumber, peeled if skin is waxed)
I tablespoon fresh lime or lemon juice
½ cup potato juice (from I small, peeled potato), if making warm soup

I cup heavy cream
Salt and drops of hot pepper sauce to taste

Garnish if you like with finely slivered fresh basil leaves or basil olive oil

FOR COLD SOUP: Skim any foam from the vegetable juices and discard. Combine the juices with the cream and season with salt and hot pepper sauce to your taste. Chill and garnish with the basil or basil oil, if desired. This soup is best consumed the day it's made.

FOR WARM SOUP: Gently heat up the juices including the fresh potato juice. The juices might separate and look curdled if the heat is too high; if this happens, use a regular or an immersion blender, and whir them back to a smooth consistency. Add the cream and warm through, making sure the soup doesn't boil. Season with cold and hot pepper sauce, to your taste. Serve with the basil garnish, if desired.

variation

For a low-fat version, substitute good-quality buttermilk for the heavy cream.

japanese stock or dashi

This is the basic stock in Japanese cooking. Classically, it has only 3 ingredients: seaweed, dried tuna flakes, and water. Contemporary cooks might also add a little piece of ginger or cilantro stems but I think the simple classic stock is best. In the United States, the ingredients are generally available in natural foods stores and, of course, Japanese markets. There is a perfectly acceptable instant granule dashi called dashi-no-moto or hon-dashi, which comes in small jars or packets. A teaspoon or two to a quart of water makes a surprisingly good stock (it's very concentrated, but you can adjust it to your taste). Look for this also in natural foods stores and Asian-Japanese markets.

One 4 × 6 inch piece kombu seaweed (dried kelp)
5 cups cold water

1 ounce (1½ cups) shaved dried bonito tuna (katsuo-bushi)

WIPE THE KOMBU clean with a damp cloth. Don't wash or rinse, because its speckled surface is where the flavor is. Combine the kombu and water in a saucepan and set aside for 30 minutes. Place over medium heat and gently bring just to a simmer. Don't boil; the Japanese believe that this will cause off-flavors.

Turn off the heat, remove the kombu from the pot, and add the bonito. Allow the bonito to settle to the bottom (this will take about 3 minutes). Carefully strain the broth through a fine mesh strainer or cheesecloth and discard the bonito. Reserve the kombu for another round of stock-making. (Fish it out of the pot, pat it dry with paper towels, and store it in a clean, dry place.)

NOTE: Dashi is best used the same day it is made. Its subtle flavors fade after that.

miso soup

SERVES 4

Miso is to Japanese cooking what olive oil is to Mediterranean cooking. It appears everywhere, a universal seasoning. Miso is highly nutritious and comes in a wide range of flavors and colors. Miso Soup is quick and easy to prepare and a perfect complement to any fresh seasonal ingredient. Here I've used white miso, which is traditional, but you could also use red, which has a deeper, saltier flavor. I also sometimes blend the two. See the Soy Foods lesson (page 286) for more recipes using miso and for more information about buying and draining tofu.

3 to 4 tablespoons white ("shiro") miso

4 cups Dashi

2 ounces (about 6 medium) fresh shiitake mushrooms, stems removed and sliced

1/2 cake of drained firm tofu (silken or regular) (5 to 6 ounces), diced

1/3 cup loosely packed sliced green onions (white and green parts) or watercress (leaves and tender stems)

Garnish if you like with hot pepper sesame oil

IN A SMALL bowl, soften the miso by stirring in about 1/3 cup of warm dashi. The mixture should be very smooth, with the consistency of a thick sauce. In a deep saucepan, gradually stir the softened miso into the remaining dashi and bring to a simmer over medium heat. Do not boil. The Japanese believe that it will lose flavor.

Add the mushrooms and tofu and simmer gently until the mushrooms are just tender. Again, be careful not to boil the soup. Add the onions or watercress, ladle into warm bowls, and serve. Place a drop or two of hot pepper sesame oil in each bowl, if desired.

japanese soup with dashi, noodles, and vegetables

SERVES 4

This is a very fast soup, especially if you use the instant dashi granules. You can add whatever seasonal vegetables you like, of course. Soba noodles are very thin Japanese noodles made from buckwheat. If you can't find them, use any very thin noodle available.

4 large dried shiitake mushrooms
6 cups Dashi (page 98)
1/3 cup mirin (sweet rice wine)
1/4 cup soy sauce
6 ounces dried soba noodles
1/2 cup finely julienned carrots
2/3 cup celery thinly sliced on the diagonal

1/2 cup silken tofu cut into 1/4-inch dice (optional)
2 cups loosely packed young watercress (leaves and tender stems) or spinach leaves
2 green onions, thinly sliced (white and green parts)

RINSE THE DRIED mushrooms and then cover them with boiling water and allow to soak for 10 minutes. Drain, cut off and discard the stems, slice thinly, and set aside.

In a deep saucepan over medium heat, bring the dashi to a simmer, and add the mirin and soy sauce. Simmer for 3 or 4 minutes to evaporate the alcohol from the mirin.

In a separate saucepan, cook the noodles in boiling salted water until just tender, 3 to 4 minutes. Drain and rinse with cold water.

Add the mushrooms to the dashi mixture and simmer for 2 to 3 minutes. Add the carrots, celery, and tofu and simmer for a minute or two until the vegetables are crisp-tender. Divide the noodles and watercress among warm bowls and ladle the hot soup over them. Garnish with the green onions and serve.

green tea stock

MAKES 6 TO 7 CUPS

This is a broth that I learned in Japan at a Buddhist temple restaurant. It's a little "out there" for those who don't know Japanese food, but I like it because it's vegetarian, which dashi is not, and a perfect broth for delicate vegetables, like young spinach, accompanied by a little tofu and some soba noodles. It's also a little more complicated than dashi stock, but there's nothing tricky about it. I use a special green tea, called Genmai Cha, that has roasted rice added to it. It's an intriguing blend. Some of the rice "pops" like popcorn. Green tea by itself has a somewhat bitter flavor, and the roasted rice softens and rounds it out. You can find Genmai Cha at Asian and Japanese markets and in the surprising number of new specialty tea shops that are springing up around the country in response to the latest information about the health benefits of tea. A clear glass pitcher or large, empty juice bottle is useful here.

4 tablespoons Genmai Cha (green tea with roasted rice)
1½ tablespoons peeled and chopped fresh ginger

8 cups boiling water
4 tablespoons red miso
3 tablespoons soy sauce, or to taste
Drops of toasted sesame oil (optional)

PLACE THE TEA and ginger in a nonreactive pot (stainless steel or enamel are fine, but uncoated cast iron or aluminum are not) and pour the boiling water over them. Steep for 2 or 3 minutes, then stir in the miso and soy sauce. Steep for about another 3 minutes, then strain through a fine mesh strainer. Transfer the mixture to a tall, narrow glass container and refrigerate for at least 3 hours or overnight. Miso solids will fall to the bottom and you'll have a bright, clear liquid on top. (That's why you need a tall, narrow, clear glass container; it's practical, not mystical.) Carefully pour off the liquid, leaving the solids behind. Store covered in the refrigerator for up to 5 days. To use, reheat and add drops of sesame oil to taste, if desired.

soba and chicken in green tea broth

SERVES 4

Soba noodles are one of Japan's treasures and are made of buckwheat, which is very nutritious. They are fairly readily available, and you can also substitute any other fine pasta, like angel hair. Soba noodles cook quickly, and the Japanese believe that the cooking should be very gentle since buckwheat is lower in gluten and starchier than regular wheat flour and has a tendency to become mushy. In this recipe, I've included their interesting cooking technique for soba, which specifies adding cold water at a couple of intervals to ensure that the cooking will be gentle. I think it does make a difference, but you can also cook them straight away if you're in a hurry.

8 ounces soba or other thin noodles
Toasted sesame oil
6 cups or so Green Tea Stock
   (page 101)
1 tablespoon sugar
3 cups lightly packed young spinach
   leaves, stems removed

1 pound poached or grilled boned and
   skinless chicken breast, sliced thinly
4 green onions, sliced on the bias
Japanese pepper blend *shichimi toragashi*
   (available in Asian markets) or
   cayenne pepper
Soy sauce

IN A LARGE pot, bring 6 quarts of lightly salted water to a boil over high heat. Drop in the soba noodles and stir to make sure they separate. When the water begins to boil and foam, add 1 cup of cold water. Return to a boil, and repeat the addition of cold water. Bring them back to the boil and test: the noodles should be cooked through but still firm. If not, repeat the process. When the noodles are cooked, immediately drain and rinse them with cold water. Gently rub the noodles to remove the surface starch. Toss with a few drops of sesame oil to keep the noodles from sticking together, and set aside.

Combine the Green Tea Stock and the sugar in a saucepan and heat to a simmer. Add the spinach and simmer for a minute or two more. Place the noodles in deep bowls and ladle the hot broth over them. Top with the chicken and green onions. Pass the pepper and soy sauce for each person to season to taste.

EXPLORING THE WORLD OF SOUPS The some-what random collection of soup recipes that follows includes some of my favorites, and I've chosen them to show some additional techniques and also encourage your creativity. We start with my new favorite version of chicken noodle soup, followed by two onion soups, and then a few others round out the selection. They are hearty, main-dish offerings that, along with a simple salad, make a full meal.

chicken noodle soup with laksa

SERVES 4 TO 6

On a recent trip to Australia, I noticed that the word laksa appeared almost universally on menus. A Malaysian word, it usually referred to a spicy noodle soup containing coconut milk. It also was used to describe a spicy coconut milk–based sauce flavored with shrimp. The basis for the laksa is a spice paste that can be made days ahead and refrigerated or frozen.

1 pound boneless, skinless chicken breasts
2 tablespoons soy sauce
2 tablespoons rice wine or sake
3 cups homemade chicken stock or your favorite canned broth
3 1/2 cups coconut milk, well stirred
1 cup Laksa Paste, or to taste
2 cups peeled and diced butternut or other hard winter squash
2 tablespoons olive oil

2 small zucchini, cut in long julienne
4 ounces cooked somen (a thin Japanese wheat flour noodle) or thin rice vermicelli, soaked in warm water for 30 minutes
Fresh lime juice to taste
Salt and freshly ground pepper

Garnish if you like with fresh cilantro leaves and green onions, sliced on the bias

TRIM THE CHICKEN breasts of any fat, cut in half lengthwise, and then, at a steep angle, cut crosswise into slices about 1/8 inch thick. Stir the soy sauce and rice wine together and toss with the chicken to lightly coat. Set aside to marinate for up to 30 minutes.

Heat the stock and coconut milk in a deep saucepan over medium heat and whisk in the Laksa Paste. Add the butternut squash and simmer for 5 minutes or until the squash is just tender. Meanwhile, coat a wok or large skillet with the olive oil and heat over high heat. Add the chicken and fry until the meat is just cooked through and the slices separate. Remove the chicken and set aside.

Place the zucchini and noodles in warm bowls. Top with the chicken. Taste the stock mixture and add lime juice, salt, and pepper to taste. Ladle hot stock into the bowls and serve immediately, garnishing with cilantro leaves and green onions, if desired.

laksa paste

2 tablespoons Asian chili-garlic sauce, or
  to taste (see Glossary and Pantry)
1/3 cup chopped shallots
1/3 cup chopped and toasted macadamia
  nuts or blanched almonds
1/4 cup peeled and finely chopped
  ginger
2 tablespoons coriander seeds, crushed

1 teaspoon shrimp paste or
  2 tablespoons Asian fish sauce, or to
  taste (see Glossary and Pantry)
Juice and zest from 2 limes
2 teaspoons sugar
2 tablespoons vegetable oil
1 teaspoon toasted sesame oil
1/2 cup or so coconut milk

PLACE THE CHILI-GARLIC sauce, shallots, nuts, ginger, coriander, shrimp paste, lime juice and zest, sugar, vegetable oil, and sesame oil in a blender or food processor and process for a minute or two, until very smooth. Transfer the mixture to a small saucepan and cook over medium heat for 4 to 5 minutes, stirring constantly. It should be very fragrant. Stir in the coconut milk and cook for 2 to 3 minutes more. You may need to add more coconut milk to achieve a smooth paste. Store covered in the refrigerator for up to 1 week or in the freezer for up to 3 months.
MAKES 1 GENEROUS CUP

NOTE: Asian chili-garlic sauce is available in Asian markets and the Asian section of some supermarkets. Lee Kum Kee from Hong Kong is a widely distributed brand. Other brands may be labeled "chile sauce" or "chile-garlic sauce": flavor will vary by brand and country of origin, but the names are interchangeable.

ONE OF my favorite writers on food (and if you don't know about her, immediately go out and get anything of hers you can lay your hands on!) is M. F. K. Fisher. In her little book *A Cordiall Water*, which explored odd and old "receipts" that cured ills, she described two simple soups that had been prescribed to her for both colds and hangovers. She noted that these ". . . soups are in the main delicious, and like anything potable which is even directly connected with the cure of our universal malady, they are most efficacious when drunk in a warm bed." The first was A Delicate Onion Soup: "Peel and very thinly slice one large mild onion, put it in a pan where 1 tablespoon butter will wilt it without browning. Add 1 cup hot milk and strain. Serve at once in a bowl or cup." The second, A Robust Onion Soup: "Slice one large peeled onion and brown it in 1 tablespoon butter. Add 1 cup strong broth and simmer until the onion is soft. Serve unstrained." What could be simpler!

basic french onion soup

SERVES 6 TO 8

Any onion can make a great soup; I prefer whites because they hold their texture better. The real secret is to take the time to caramelize the onions slowly. Make a double batch and freeze the extra—it lends itself to interesting additions and accompaniments. This soup originated at Les Halles, the huge original food market in Paris. It was a working-man's soup with rich sweet flavors and bubbling fat cheese to fill the stomach and take the chill off.

4 quarts peeled and sliced onions
   (about 4 pounds)
1 tablespoon slivered garlic
2 teaspoons fresh thyme leaves or
   1 teaspoon dried
3 tablespoons butter
3 tablespoons olive oil
1 cup light-bodied white wine
7 cups homemade chicken stock or
   your favorite canned broth

2 large bay leaves
Salt and freshly ground pepper
1/3 cup good cognac or brandy
   (optional)

Accompaniments: French bread croûtes
   (toasted slices), one per serving,
   grated Parmesan or Gruyère cheese,
   or a mixture (2 to 3 cups for 6 to
   8 servings)

IN A HEAVY soup pot over low heat, slowly sauté the onions, garlic, and thyme with the butter and olive oil until they are deep golden brown. Stir regularly to make sure they don't burn. This may take 20 to 30 minutes or more, but be patient—the results are worth it!

Add the wine, stock, and bay leaves and simmer partially covered for another 45 to 50 minutes. Remove the bay leaves and discard. Correct seasoning with salt and pepper and add the cognac, if using.

Ladle into warm bowls and top with a toasted croûte and about $1/3$ cup of cheese. Place the bowls under a hot broiler for a minute or less to melt and lightly brown the cheese. Dig in.

new world onion soup

SERVES 6 TO 8

To explore how this basic soup can take on flavors of another cuisine try this Mexican version. If you want to go "all the way," then drizzle on a little Cilantro Pesto (page 44).

4 quarts peeled and sliced onions
  (about 4 pounds)
2 tablespoons slivered garlic
4 tablespoons olive oil
2 teaspoons crushed cumin seeds
2 teaspoons crushed coriander seeds
2 teaspoons oregano (preferably
  Mexican)
3 tablespoons pure chile powder, such as
  ancho, Chimayo, or California (see
  Glossary and Pantry)

1 cup hearty, full-bodied red wine
7 cups homemade chicken or vegetable
  stock or your favorite canned broth
$1/4$ cup masa flour (see Note)

Garnish if you like with very thinly
  sliced fried tortilla strips, chopped
  fresh cilantro leaves, and grated
  pepper Jack cheese

IN A HEAVY soup pot over low heat, slowly sauté the onions and garlic in the olive oil until they are golden brown. Stir regularly to make sure they don't burn. Add the cumin, coriander, oregano, and chile powder and sauté for 2 to 3 minutes longer, until fragrant. Add the wine and stock and bring to a simmer. Whisk in the masa and continue to simmer for another 15 minutes or so, stirring often. Serve garnished with fried tortilla strips, chopped cilantro, and grated pepper Jack cheese.

NOTE: Masa flour (*masa harina*), is available at most specialty food stores, many supermarkets, and in all Hispanic markets. It is not the same as common cornmeal or cornstarch.

curried tomato soup with riso

SERVES 4 TO 6

This is a simple recipe, easily put together at the last moment. If possible, use white onions rather than yellow, because they provide a better texture. Also, curry powders vary greatly in strength, so add a tablespoon and then taste to decide if you want more. The riso pasta suggested here is pasta shaped like rice. Orzo or any other grain-shaped soup pasta can be used. To turn this into a main course soup, you can add shellfish, such as shrimp or scallops; smoked chicken; or even grilled portabella mushrooms.

3 cups onions, cut in ¼-inch dice

1 tablespoon chopped garlic

1 tablespoon or more good curry
  powder, such as Madras

1 tablespoon olive oil

1 32-ounce can diced tomatoes in juice
  (I like Muir Glen brand)

4 cups homemade chicken or vegetable
  stock or your favorite canned broth

1 cup dry white wine

1 tablespoon peeled and finely minced
  fresh ginger

1 teaspoon whole fennel seeds

¼ teaspoon crushed red chile flakes, or
  to taste

Salt and freshly ground pepper to taste

⅓ cup dried riso pasta, cooked al dente

Garnish if you like with **Basil-Mint Pesto**
  (page 45)

PLACE THE ONIONS, garlic, curry powder, and olive oil in a stockpot and cook over medium heat until the vegetables just begin to color. Add the tomatoes, stock, wine, ginger, fennel, and red chile flakes, and simmer for 10 minutes. Correct the seasoning with salt and pepper. Just before serving, add the pasta and warm through. Serve in warm soup bowls, and swirl in a dollop of pesto, if desired.

cold zucchini soup with cinnamon, cumin, and buttermilk

SERVES 4

This is a quick and simple soup. It's a wonderful base to which you can add all manner of things, including cooked shrimp, sautéed mushrooms, or spring peas, to name a few. I often will drizzle on a little fragrant nut oil as a garnish. Serve the soup chilled or at room temperature. We don't always think about serving soup at room temperature, but it's a nice variation on a warm day.

The buttermilk commercially available today is not a by-product of butter-making, as it was in the old days, but is just cultured skim milk. It's very low in fat, but also quite bland. If you can find good-quality buttermilk, such as Russian or Bulgarian or one from a specialty producer, the soup will be that much tastier.

2½ cups homemade chicken or vegetable stock or your favorite canned broth

1 pound zucchini, ends trimmed, chopped into large chunks

1 tablespoon olive oil

1 cup chopped yellow or white onion

½ teaspoon seeded and minced serrano chiles, or to taste

½ teaspoon whole fennel seeds

½ teaspoon ground cinnamon

1 teaspoon ground cumin

1½ cups good quality buttermilk

Sea salt and freshly ground pepper

Garnish if you like with chopped fresh cilantro or mint leaves and lime or lemon wedges

IN A SOUP pot over high heat, bring the stock to a boil and add the zucchini. Reduce the heat and simmer, covered, for 4 to 5 minutes, or until the zucchini is barely tender but still bright green. Remove the pot from the heat and let cool.

Meanwhile, heat the olive oil in a small, nonstick frying pan. Add the onion, chile, fennel, cinnamon, and cumin, and sauté until the onion is soft but not brown and the spices are fragrant.

Combine both mixtures together in a blender or food processor, and pulse until well chopped but still with some texture (of course, you can puree it completely if you want, but I prefer mine a little rough). Pour into a bowl, stir in the buttermilk, then season with salt and pepper. Chill for at least 2 hours. Taste again at serving time, adding more salt and pepper if you think it needs it. Serve garnished with a sprinkling of cilantro or mint and wedges of lemon or lime, if desired.

rice porridge or congee

SERVES 4

Anyone who has traveled in China, or in any part of Asia for that matter, will recognize this dish. Congee or jook is generally served as the morning meal and is believed to be an important restorative. Big bowls are dished up to which all manner of condiments may be added at the diner's discretion, including soy sauce, chopped green onions, cilantro leaves, finely shredded cabbage, crisp fried slices of garlic or shallot, roasted peanuts, Chinese (Sichuan) pickled vegetables, pickled ginger, poached or roasted chicken or other meats, cooked and dried shrimp, and on and on. It definitely has become one of my comfort foods.

**1 quart homemade chicken stock or
   your favorite canned broth, or water**
2/3 cup long-grain white rice

2 half-dollar-size slices of fresh ginger
Salt and freshly ground white pepper

BRING THE STOCK to a boil in a deep saucepan. Rinse the rice 2 or 3 times in cold water, and stir into the stock along with the ginger. Bring back to a boil, then reduce the heat to a simmer, cover, and gently simmer for 1 hour or until the rice is very soft, porridge-like, and almost smooth. You can adjust the cooking time to create the texture you like. Stir occasionally to prevent the rice from sticking to the bottom. Remove from the heat, season with salt and pepper, and serve with additions of your choice. Thin if desired with additional stock.

cold shrimp and buttermilk soup

SERVES 4

This is a soup my grandmother used to make on those hot days when she didn't want to go anywhere near the stove. At that time, the only shrimp she had available were canned, which were fine (and certainly better than no shrimp at all).

If the red onion is very sweet, then you can omit the soaking step. Otherwise, soaking helps remove some of the "hot," sulfury notes that older onions often have.

This is a very simple recipe, and it can be delicious or it can be bland. Follow the directions, but then use your own tastebuds to guide the final seasoning. You can add more mustard, Tabasco, salt, sugar, or herbs, as you please.

I quart good quality buttermilk

I tablespoon dry mustard, such as Colman's

2 teaspoons salt

2 teaspoons sugar

I teaspoon bottled hot pepper sauce, such as Tabasco

½ pound cooked bay shrimp, or any chopped cooked shrimp

2 cups peeled, seeded, and finely diced cucumber

⅓ cup finely diced red onion, soaked for a few minutes in ice water then drained

2 tablespoons finely chopped chives

2 tablespoons finely chopped fresh dill

Garnish if you like with thin slices of cucumber and ripe avocado

WHISK THE BUTTERMILK, mustard, salt, sugar, and hot pepper sauce together in a bowl. Add the shrimp, cucumber, red onion, chives, and dill, and chill covered for at least 2 hours for the flavors to develop. When food is cold, flavors become more muted, so before serving, taste and adjust the seasoning with salt, hot pepper sauce, and sugar, if you think it needs it. Garnish with slices of cucumber and avocado, if desired.

cold strawberry ginger soup

Summer fruits make great bases for soups. Here, I've combined strawberries and fresh ginger juice for a sweet-tart-spicy soup. Almost any berry or combination can be used, so take advantage of what's in season. If you don't have a juicer you can make ginger juice by using a garlic press or pureeing fresh ginger in a blender and then straining it through a fine mesh strainer or squeezing it through cheesecloth. If you start with all the ingredients right out of the refrigerator, you won't need to chill the soup long, but it will still benefit from time to allow the flavors to blend.

2½ cups strawberry puree (from about 3 pints strawberries), strained
1 ripe banana
1 to 2 tablespoons ginger juice
1 cup or so sparkling apple cider

4 tablespoons plain yogurt
1 cup mixed blueberries and red raspberries
Fresh mint sprigs

COMBINE THE STRAWBERRY PUREE and banana in a blender (or use an immersion blender), and blend until smooth. Add ginger juice to taste, and enough sparkling cider to attain your desired consistency. Chill for at least 2 hours. Ladle into chilled soup bowls. Serve with a dollop of yogurt, a scattering of fresh berries, and a mint sprig or two.

7   oven-drying

A Great Way to Concentrate the Flavors
of Fruits and Vegetables

In this lesson I want to introduce

you to the intense flavor and texture that can be developed by *partially* drying fruits and vegetables. It's a simple technique that I think should be in everyone's bag of culinary tools. Drying is one of the oldest methods for food preservation. For thousands of years, fruits, vegetables, meats, and herbs have been preserved by drying. When most of the moisture (80 to 90 percent) has been removed from almost any food, bacteria, molds, and yeasts that cause spoilage can't grow. Air and sun were the drying methods of choice throughout most of history. With the advent of electricity, the oven became a workable tool for the purpose, and now electric dehydrators of all sorts are available.

Our objective in this lesson is not to dry foods to the point that they can be stored unrefrigerated (that is, when 90 percent or so of the moisture has been removed). Rather, it is to remove 40 to 50 percent of the water content, concentrating the flavor but leaving the food still soft and succulent. Partially dried fruits and vegetables need to be refrigerated if not used right away, since there still is enough moisture for microorganisms to grow.

This lesson includes several full-scale recipes in which one or more of the ingredients is an oven-dried fruit or vegetable. I've also included a chart to guide you through oven-drying any fruit or vegetable that interests you. I urge you to try this sometime, without any "recipe" in mind. Just follow the instructions to oven-dry some mushrooms, some tomatoes, some plums. Then taste the result and see where it leads you.

One of the most dramatic examples of how a familiar food can be transformed by oven-drying is the tomato. Unfortunately, most of the tomatoes we get in our markets today (even in the middle of summer in most places) are really awful. They've been hybridized for shipability, not taste, and chemically "ripened" with ethylene gas. They are usually tasteless, often "cardboardy" in texture (which is the result of getting refrigerated somewhere along the way—you do know, don't you, that you must never, never refrigerate fresh tomatoes!) and without any of a great tomato's intoxicating fragrance. As consumers and cooks, we shouldn't have to take this. But as long as large-scale commercial agriculture continues to hold the reins of our food economy, we can at least try to eke some character out of these bland excuses for tomatoes by oven-drying them. And oven-dried locally produced heirloom tomatoes are out of this world!

The following tables give some guidelines for some of my favorite oven-dried products. As you experiment with this technique, you'll develop your own timetable. One recommendation before you begin: *check your oven with an accurate thermometer so that you'll know what the actual temperature is.* Most home ovens are notoriously inaccurate, especially at very low temperatures. All of the items are dried at 250°F. or so. Roasting at a higher temperature (such as 425°F.) is also a great technique. It takes less time, of course, but it gives you a completely different final result—the flavors are more "toasted" and caramelized. When cutting the produce, try to make the pieces an even thickness. And use a layer of parchment, waxed paper, or a silicone mat (a terrific baking tool sold under the brand name Silpat) on the baking sheet before you put the produce on it. This is especially necessary with fruits whose acids can react with bare metal, which sometimes results in strange flavors. In order to better preserve the color of oven-dried fruits, you may want to use one of the optional pretreatment techniques outlined below. Brushing the vegetables with oil is not optional; without it they will get over-dry. You might try one of the many wonderful nut oils available instead of olive oil. A final note: I don't find microwave ovens suitable for drying. The food ends up being cooked (with attendant cooked flavor) before it can dry.

FRUITS			
	PREPARATION	PRETREATMENT	TIME
APPLE*	Peel, core, slice, or wedge	Citrus or ascorbic dip	2 to 3 hours
APRICOTS*	Halve and pit; skin can be removed after drying	Citrus or ascorbic dip	2 to 3 hours
BANANAS*	Peel, cut lengthwise, or slice into ½-inch-thick rounds	Citrus or ascorbic dip	1 to 2 hours
BLUEBERRIES	Leave whole	None required	1 to 2 hours
FIGS	Remove stem and halve	None required	2 to 3 hours
GRAPES	Remove stem and halve. Seedless types work best	None required	2 hours
MANGO	Peel and slice, discarding seed	None required	2 to 3 hours
PAPAYA	Peel and slice, discarding seeds	None required	2 to 3 hours
PEACHES and NECTARINES*	Remove pit and slice or wedge. Remove skin after drying, if desired	Citrus or ascorbic dip	1 to 2 hours
PLUMS	Remove pit and slice or wedge	None required	1 to 3 hours
STRAWBERRIES	Remove hull and cut in half	None required	2 to 3 hours
* Be sure that fruit is firm ripe. If it's too ripe it will tend to brown.			

PRETREATMENT TECHNIQUES

These are basically methods to keep the produce from oxidizing and losing its color. They can also help add flavor.

~ **Citrus Dip:** Combine 1 cup fresh pineapple or orange juice, 1 cup water, 1 tablespoon honey, and 1 tablespoon fresh lemon juice and stir thoroughly. Toss with produce before drying.

~ **Ascorbic Dip:** 1 tablespoon ascorbic acid crystals or 2 to 3 1-gram vitamin C tablets, crushed and added to 2 cups water. Stir until dissolved. Toss with produce before drying.

VEGETABLES

Partially oven-dried vegetables have textural and taste interest beyond what you might imagine. Tomatoes and mushrooms are obvious choices but corn, cauliflower, and cabbage all yield some interesting results too.

	PREPARATION	PRETREATMENT	TIME
CABBAGE	Core and cut into thick wedges	Brush with olive oil, salt and pepper or brine	2 to 3 hours
CAULIFLOWER	Slice thickly, at least 1/4 inch or so, or break apart into florets	Brush with olive oil, salt and pepper or brine	2 to 4 hours
CORN	Remove husk and silk, cut off cob after drying	Brush with olive oil, salt and pepper	2 to 3 hours
MUSHROOMS	Wipe clean with a damp cloth or wash (see page 237), leave whole or slice thickly	Brush with olive oil, salt and pepper	2 to 4 hours
TOMATOES	Core, halve, and gently squeeze out seeds and juice	Brush with olive oil, salt and pepper	3 to 5 hours
TOMATOES, CHERRY	Halve and gently squeeze out seeds	Brush with olive oil, salt and pepper	30 to 90 minutes
ZUCCHINI	Slice 1/4 inch thick in rounds or lengthwise	Brush with olive oil, salt and pepper	1 to 2 hours

HERE ARE some simple and quick ideas for using oven-dried fruits and vegetables:

~ Add oven-dried mushrooms, tomatoes, zucchini, or a combination to omelets, frittatas, or freshly cooked pasta or rice and top with some freshly grated Parmesan or other cheese of your choice.

~ Place any combination of oven-dried vegetables, including garlic, in a jar with fresh herbs, cover with fruity olive oil, and refrigerate for up to 10 days. These are great used in salads, to top grilled or broiled meats and fish, or as part of an antipasto platter.

~ Add oven-dried grapes, apples, and pears to a salad of arugula, watercress, or other savory greens, along with a nice blue cheese and toasted walnuts.

~ Use any oven-dried fruits in quick breads, pancakes, waffles, or puddings. They are also terrific as an accompaniment to cheese.

~ Oven-dried tomatoes and mushrooms combined with fresh basil and fresh mozzarella make a great sandwich.

~ To make a fast, flavorful, and satisfying soup, add any combination of oven-dried vegetables to simmering chicken or vegetable stock and top with a crouton toasted with a little cheese topping.

~ Finely chopped oven-dried vegetables are a great filling for crepes or filled pastas like raviolis, or even steamed dumplings.

~ Any combination of oven-dried fruits can be served as is drizzled with a flavorful honey (see photo, below).

The following recipes show how oven-dried fruits and vegetables can be used in more complex dishes. The oven-drying obviously needs to be done ahead, but with the goods on hand, the dishes come together quickly. If you've prepared vegetables or fruits other than the ones called for in the recipes, don't hesitate to substitute them. You'll get different but equally tasty results.

crostini with oven-dried tomatoes and garlic

SERVES 6

These are simple, delicious little bites that will give you a starting point for using oven-dried vegetables.

12 slices of good quality baguette or
    Italian bread
Extra virgin olive oil
6 oven-dried unpeeled garlic cloves
6 oven-dried Roma or plum-type
    tomatoes

Salt and freshly ground pepper
2 tablespoons finely chopped olives,
    such as Niçoise, Kalamata, or Gaeta
2 tablespoons mixed chopped fresh
    herbs, such as chives and mint leaves

PREHEAT THE OVEN to 375°F. or preheat the broiler. Liberally brush the bread with olive oil and toast in the oven for 10 to 12 minutes (or a few minutes under a broiler), browning on both sides. Squeeze the garlic from its skins and mash into a paste along with any juices from the tomatoes. Season to your taste with salt and pepper.

Spread the garlic mixture on the toasts, sprinkle with the olives, and top each with a tomato, cut side up. Sprinkle with herbs and serve.

warm spinach salad with bacon, apple cider dressing, and *oven-dried grapes*

SERVES 4

I love warm spinach salads. Here, the grapes add a sweet note that brings balance to the whole dish.

¼ pound good quality bacon, cut into
    ¼-inch dice
3 tablespoons finely sliced shallots or
    green onions (green and white parts)
Apple Cider Dressing

12 ounces young spinach leaves, any
    coarse stems discarded
1 cup oven-dried grapes (about 4 cups
    fresh)

IN A LARGE sauté pan, cook the bacon until crisp. Transfer it to paper towels to drain and pour off all but 2 tablespoons of the fat from the pan. Add the shallots and cook over medium-high heat until lightly browned, 3 to 4 minutes. Add the Apple Cider Dressing to the pan and bring it to a simmer. Remove from the heat, add the spinach and grapes, and toss for a few seconds or until the spinach just begins to wilt. Serve on warm plates, topped with bacon.

apple cider dressing

2 cups apple cider, preferably unfiltered
3 tablespoons apple cider vinegar
2 teaspoons Dijon mustard

1 tablespoon olive oil
Salt and freshly ground black pepper
    to taste

IN A SMALL SAUCEPAN, combine the cider and vinegar and bring to a boil. Continue to boil until the liquid is reduced to a little more than ½ cup; this will take 10 to 12 minutes. (Put ½ cup water in the pan before you start so you can eyeball the quantity you're aiming for.) Remove the pan from the heat, and whisk in the Dijon mustard and olive oil. Taste and season with salt and pepper. Store covered in the refrigerator for up to 1 week. MAKES ABOUT ½ CUP

oven-dried cauliflower, corn, and red pepper risotto

SERVES 6 TO 8

Roasted cauliflower was an epiphany to me the first time I had it—so much better than boiled. You can get different results with the cauliflower by oven-drying it slowly at low temperature (250°F.) or roasting quickly under high heat (425°F.). Slow roasting seems to bring out the sweetness in the vegetable, while hot roasting adds a toastiness.

4 medium ears oven-dried corn

1 small (1 pound) oven-dried cauliflower

2 medium oven-dried red peppers

3 tablespoons extra virgin olive oil

1 cup finely minced white onions

1 tablespoon minced garlic

2 cups Arborio rice

1 cup dry white wine

5 to 6 cups homemade chicken or vegetable stock or your favorite canned broth

1/2 cup pitted and sliced green or black olives

1 tablespoon finely grated lemon zest

1/2 cup loosely packed fresh basil leaves, chopped

2 tablespoons chopped fresh parsley leaves

1 cup freshly grated Parmesan or Pecorino cheese, plus extra for serving

Garnish if you like with basil oil (available in gourmet stores)

CUT THE CORN off the ears, and chop the cauliflower and peppers into small pieces. Set aside. Heat the olive oil in a large deep saucepan and add the onions and garlic. Sauté over medium heat until softened, about 3 minutes. Add the rice and stir, coating the rice grains with the oil, and sauté for another couple of minutes. The grains will turn opaque and "click" against the side of the pan.

Add the wine and cook, stirring, until it is absorbed. Add the hot stock in 1/2-cup increments, stirring until the liquid is almost all absorbed. Continue until the rice is done—that is, each grain is soft and creamy on the outside but still has a little firmness or "bite" in the center. This will take 15 to 18 minutes. Stir the oven-dried vegetables into the rice, along with the olives, zest, basil, and parsley, and warm through. Stir in the cheese and serve. Shallow warm bowls work nicely topped with additional cheese and a drizzle of basil oil, if you have some.

oven-dried mediterranean salad

SERVES 4

1¼ cups oven-dried zucchini, sliced or diced (from about 1 pound fresh)

1½ cups oven-dried cherry tomatoes (from about 1½ pounds fresh)

¼ cup pitted and sliced Kalamata or other olives

1 tablespoon mixed chopped fresh herbs, such as chives, parsley, and chervil

1 teaspoon finely grated lemon zest

Drops of fresh lemon juice to taste

Salt and freshly ground pepper

IN A BOWL, combine the zucchini, tomatoes, olives, herbs, zest, and juice. Season to taste with salt and pepper.

crisp fried polenta with oven-dried mediterranean salad

SERVES 4 AS A MAIN COURSE

This is a template for a neat main course that is infinitely variable. Polenta, the Italian "grits," or cornmeal mush," is cooked ahead, then chilled until firm. At serving time, it's sliced into portions, sautéed, and topped with an intensely flavorful mélange (that means mixture) featuring oven-dried vegetables.

I like my polenta with a little texture, so I cook it for a much shorter period than is traditionally called for. For a smoother, traditional polenta, cook it in a double boiler over simmering water for an hour or so, stirring every 10 minutes.

2 tablespoons butter

¼ cup finely chopped shallots or green onions (white parts only)

½ cup dry light- or medium-bodied white wine

2½ cups homemade chicken or vegetable stock or your favorite canned broth

¾ cup coarse polenta cornmeal

1 tablespoon chopped fresh basil leaves

½ cup freshly grated Parmesan or Pecorino cheese

Salt and freshly ground pepper

2 tablespoons olive oil

Oven-Dried Mediterranean Salad

Garnish if you like with shaved Parmesan or crème fraîche and baby arugula or mustard greens

LIGHTLY OIL A baking sheet or 8-inch cake pan and set it aside. Heat 1 tablespoon of the butter in a deep saucepan and add the shallots or onions. Sauté over medium heat until softened but not brown, about 3 minutes. Add the wine and stock and bring to a boil. Stir in the polenta meal until the mixture begins to thicken and then reduce the heat to low and stir regularly until the mixture is very thick, 10 to 12 minutes. Stir in the basil and cheese, and taste and season with salt and pepper. Pour the polenta onto the baking sheet or cake pan and, using a spatula or wet hands, smooth and even it out until it is about ½ inch thick. Chill in the refrigerator until firm. The polenta can be made ahead and stored covered in the refrigerator for a couple of days.

Cut the polenta into 4 pieces and heat the remaining butter and the olive oil in a large sauté pan. Brown the polenta over medium-high heat until crispy on both sides, about 5 minutes total. Place the polenta on serving plates and top with the salad and shavings of Parmesan or a dollop of crème fraîche and baby greens, if desired.

suggestion   The sautéed polenta slices are a great base for lots of different toppings. Any of the salsas or pasta sauces and the Wild Mushrooms *à la Grecque* (page 241) are good candidates. The pasta sauces can also top the polenta when it's still soft.

crispy risotto with oven-dried mediterranean salad

SERVES 4

This is a great way of using up leftover risotto, and I usually make extra just so that I can do this dish. If you don't have 3 whole cups of risotto left over, just make the cake in a smaller pan and don't expect to share it with so many people.

3 cups leftover risotto (see Note)
1 tablespoon chopped fresh basil leaves
1 tablespoon chopped fresh parsley leaves
1/2 cup freshly grated Parmesan or Asiago cheese
Sea salt and freshly ground pepper

4 tablespoons olive oil
Oven-Dried Mediterranean Salad (page 124)

Garnish if you like with shaved Parmesan or crème fraîche and baby arugula or mustard greens

MIX THE COOKED risotto with the herbs and cheese and season well with salt and pepper. Heat a heavy sauté pan over high heat and add 4 tablespoons of olive oil and then the rice mixture, packing it down well to form a cake about ¾ inch thick. (Note: You can also make smaller individual cakes.) Reduce the heat to medium and cook for about 5 minutes, until crisp and golden around the edges. Turn the cake over and cook for another 5 minutes, or until crisp and brown.

Turn the cake out onto a cutting board and cut into wedges. Place the wedges on warm plates and top with the Mediterranean Salad.

Garnish with shavings of Parmesan or a dollop of crème fraîche and baby greens, if desired.

NOTE: If risotto is not already in your repertoire, you can learn to make a basic version by following the directions for Oven-Dried Cauliflower, Corn, and Red Pepper Risotto on page 123. Just leave out the oven-dried vegetables and olives; the herbs are optional.

couscous risotto with oven-dried mushrooms and tomatoes and pecorino cheese

SERVES 4 TO 6 AS A MAIN COURSE

Here's a variation on the risotto theme above. This recipe uses a kind of couscous known as moughrabiye or Israeli couscous. It is made from the same toasted semolina as the regular granular couscous with which we are most familiar, but it is formed into larger round balls about the size of whole peppercorns. There is an even larger variety known as Lebanese couscous that can also be used in this dish; they are about the size of petite peas and take longer to cook. This also makes a nice side dish for simply cooked meats, fish, and poultry.

½ cup chopped shallots or green onions (white parts only)
1 tablespoon slivered garlic
2 tablespoons olive oil or butter
2 cups Israeli couscous (called *moughrabiye*)
½ cup dry white wine
4 cups homemade chicken or vegetable stock or your favorite canned broth

1 tablespoon grated lemon zest
1 cup diced oven-dried tomatoes
1 cup oven-dried portabella mushrooms
¼ cup chopped chives
½ cup (or more) freshly grated Pecorino cheese

IN A SAUCEPAN over medium heat, sauté the shallots and garlic in olive oil until lightly colored. Add the couscous and sauté for a minute or two longer. Add the wine and ½ cup of the stock and cook, stirring occasionally, until the liquid is nearly absorbed. Add the remaining stock ½ cup at a time and continue to cook and stir each time until the stock is nearly absorbed. Continue in this manner until the couscous is tender but still has some texture (about 10 minutes total). Stir in the lemon zest, tomatoes, mushrooms, chives, and cheese, and serve.

oven-dried pineapple and plums with rosemary syrup and cardamom ice cream

SERVES 4 TO 6

This recipe has three terrific building blocks in it, and you can combine all of them, as I do here, or make any one of them alone. I've raved enough about the oven-dried fruit: here's a great way to show it off. The quantity of each dried fruit per serving is up to you. The Rosemary Syrup is a great example of a simple technique for a sophisticated taste: it's easier to prepare than a package of Jell-O, but the flavor is subtle and outrageous. Serve it and everyone will think you're a culinary genius. I've paired it with exotically spiced homemade ice cream, but to simplify the whole recipe, or if you don't have an ice cream maker, you can use store-bought vanilla ice cream (with or without the cardamom blended in). Or you can simply top the dried fruits with some sweetened crème fraîche or sour cream or even use softened fresh goat cheese, then drizzle with the syrup.

Oven-dried pineapple
Oven-dried plums
Rosemary Syrup
Cardamom Ice Cream

Garnish if you like with fresh mint sprigs and edible flower petals (borage and calendula are two of my favorites with this)

ARRANGE THE PINEAPPLE and plums in shallow serving bowls, and spoon 2 to 3 tablespoons of Rosemary Syrup over the fruits. Place a small scoop of the ice cream on top and garnish with a mint sprig and edible flowers, if using. Serve immediately.

rosemary syrup

¾ cup sugar
¾ cup dry white wine
¼ cup fresh rosemary leaves
1 tablespoon peeled and chopped fresh
   ginger

½ teaspoon whole peppercorns
2 tablespoons fine balsamic vinegar, or
   to taste

IN A MEDIUM saucepan, combine all the ingredients, with ½ cup water, bring to a boil, then reduce the heat and simmer, partially covered, for 10 minutes. Cool, strain, and store covered in the refrigerator indefinitely. MAKES 1½ CUPS

cardamom ice cream

6 egg yolks
⅓ cup sugar
3 cups light cream or half-and-half
1 tablespoon ground cardamom

1 teaspoon very finely chopped lemon
   zest
¼ teaspoon ground white pepper
Drops of fresh lemon juice

IN A BOWL, whisk the egg yolks and sugar together until light and fluffy. In a saucepan over moderate heat, heat the cream, cardamom, zest, and pepper to a simmer. Remove from the heat and slowly whisk the hot cream mixture into the eggs mixture.

Return the mixture to the saucepan and cook over medium heat, stirring constantly, until the mixture begins to thicken. Do not allow it to boil or you will curdle the eggs. When the mixture thickens, remove the pan from the heat and immediately pour the mixture through a fine mesh strainer into a clean bowl. Add a few drops of lemon juice to cool the mixture slightly. Cover the bowl loosely and quickly chill in an ice water bath or in the freezer for 10 minutes. Place the cooled mixture in an ice cream maker and proceed according to the manufacturer's instructions. MAKES ABOUT 1 QUART

8 pot-roasting

A Traditional Method with Contemporary Appeal

Pot-roasting is most certainly an ancient technique, one that works equally well whether you're using a heavy iron pot over an open fire, the hot coals at its base, or a modern oven. Pot-roasting is also the perfect way to cook tough pieces of meat—pretty much the only kind available in days gone by.

The French, who are very precise in how they describe cooking methods, would call pot-roasting a *braise*. Braising is cooking (generally meats) in a tightly covered pot with a small amount of liquid. The technique is ideal for tougher cuts of meat, which contain more collagen, or connective tissues. Long, gentle cooking in a closed pot slowly converts the collagen to gelatin without burning the outside of the meat. This is not a technique you'd use for more expensive, tender cuts of meat, since they have much less connective tissue and they'll just end up dried out. The other advantage for the health-conscious cook is that pot-roasting renders (melts) much of the fat from the meat so it can be skimmed from the sauce. If the pot roast is made a day ahead, not only does its flavor improve, but the chilled fat can be removed more easily.

Braising is without question one of the least demanding classical techniques. If it's a pot roast with a lot of vegetables and flavoring ingredients, a certain amount of prep time is required. But once everything is in the pot, you're free. The results are not only delicious but also economical and allow for and encourage all kinds of flavor experimentation. If that weren't enough, the cooking aromas make your whole house smell heavenly!

keys to successful pot-roasting

~ **Buy a good, heavy ovenproof pot with a tight-fitting lid.** This is key. I think the best are heavy cast iron, and I prefer those that are enameled, like those from Le Creuset or Copco. Go for the Dutch oven shape; it's deep enough to allow you to cook in quantity and part of the joy of pot roasts is having leftovers to weave into other dishes.

~ **Brown the meats well before adding the liquid.** The purpose of browning is not to "seal in juices," as we're often told, but to caramelize the sugars in the meat, which deepens the flavor of the final dish. In order for the meat's exterior to caramelize, it needs to be browned over high heat. Take the trouble to brown all the sides, whether you're cooking one large piece of meat, which we call a roast, or small cubes, which we call a stew.

Following are recipes that should make you an expert pot roaster. Feel free to adjust the flavor ingredients. For instance, I use fennel seeds in my basic pot roast; if you don't like it, you should leave it out, or replace it with another spice. The only essentials are the meat, a little fat for browning, and the liquid for braising.

basic beef pot roast

SERVES 6 TO 8

The ingredients list calls for thickly sliced carrots, celery, and onions; when I'm teaching this dish and homey ones like it, I tell students to take the vegetables and "just whack them up"—the rougher the better.

**3 pounds beef tri-tip or boneless chuck
  roast**
Salt and freshly ground black pepper
4 tablespoons olive oil
4 cups thickly sliced onions
1 ½ cups thick celery slices
1 ½ cups thick carrot slices
¼ cup slivered garlic
¼ teaspoon hot red pepper flakes
3 cups hearty red wine
**4 cups homemade beef or chicken stock
  or your favorite canned broth**

**3 cups canned diced tomatoes with
  their juice**
2 large bay leaves
2 teaspoons fennel seeds
**3 tablespoons chopped mixed fresh
  herbs, such as basil, parsley, and
  chives**
**2 teaspoons cornstarch mixed with
  2 tablespoons cold water or wine
  (optional)**

PREHEAT THE OVEN to 375°F.

Trim all visible fat from the beef and season it with salt and pepper. Heat the olive oil in a heavy-bottomed Dutch oven or casserole, and over high heat, brown the meat well on all sides. Remove the meat from the pot and set it aside. Place the onions, celery, carrots, and garlic in the pot and cook over medium heat, stirring occasionally, until the vegetables just begin to color and the onions are translucent.

Add the pepper flakes, wine, stock, tomatoes, bay leaves, fennel, and herbs and bring it all to a simmer. Return the meat to the pot, cover it, and place it in the oven for 2 to 2½ hours, or until the meat is very tender and almost falling apart. (How can you tell how tender it is? Poke at it with a fork.)

Remove the meat from the pot and set it on a cutting board. Strain the liquid from the vegetables. (I suggest setting a colander in a big bowl or pot and scooping the vegetables into it first. Then you can probably lift the cooking pot and safely pour the liquid through the colander.) Let the liquid sit for a few minutes while the fat rises to the surface. Using a shallow spoon, skim off and discard as much of the fat as you can. Return the liquid to the original pot and boil it over high

BEST CUTS FOR POT-ROASTING AND STEWING

You can substitute all kinds of meats other than those called for in a recipe. The approach is basically the same if you are using pork shoulder or butt in place of the beef chuck or lamb shoulder. This chart lists the cuts that I think are best for pot-roasting, but be sure to ask your butcher too. Butchers, like hardware store owners, can be a little intimidating to the insecure shopper, but a relationship with one is well worth cultivating.

BEEF	VEAL	LAMB	PORK
Chuck	**Chuck**	Shanks	**Loin**
7-bone pot roast	Chuck roast*	Shoulder*	Pork loin*
Chuck roast	Blade roast	Breast	Blade end pork loin
Blade roast	**Brisket or breast**	Boneless leg of lamb	roast
Chuck-eye roast	Boneless breast	Short leg	Sirloin roast
Cross-rib roast*	**Sirloin**	Lamb neck‡	**Shoulder**
Brisket	Sirloin roast*		Shoulder*
Whole brisket	Top round		Boston butt
Brisket first cut	**Other**		**Leg (fresh ham)**
Brisket front cut	Rump roast		Whole or half leg*
Sirloin†	Shoulder roast		Shanks
Tri-tip	Shanks		
Sirloin roast			
Short ribs			
English-style			
Flanken-style			
Other			
Oxtail			
Flank steak			
Shanks			
Bottom round			

*Available bone-in or boneless.
†Can be used, but today's beef is leaner so cuts from the chuck are preferred.
‡Very flavorful, but not much meat compared to bone.

heat until it is reduced by approximately a third (just use your eyes) to concentrate the flavors. If you like a thicker, more gravy-like sauce, you can thicken the liquid by stirring in the cornstarch mixture. Taste the sauce, and season with salt and pepper if you think it needs it.

Slice the meat and return it and the braising vegetables to the pot. At this point, you can refrigerate or freeze the pot roast. As it chills, more fat will rise to the surface and congeal, making it easier to remove. Warm it through on the stovetop and serve: meat, vegetables, sauce, and all.

slow-cooked beef stew or pot roast

SERVES 6

This is a variation of an ancient Italian recipe called Peposo, so named because it uses a lot of pepper. It's a no-brainer as far as preparation goes, and it stays in the oven all day. Something happens in the long slow cooking that gives the meat great flavor and texture and mellows the pepper. If you still have a Crock-Pot or other slow cooker, now is the time to drag it out. Traditionally, this was served over slightly stale, crusty bread topped with the braising liquid, but you can also serve it with potatoes (mashed or roasted), polenta, or pasta. Cut the meat into stew-sized chunks before cooking, if you prefer.

Classic Italian gremolata is one of my favorite seasoning blends: a light, loose mixture that adds a spike of flavor to innumerable dishes. You can make it quickly by hand or super-quickly with a mini food processor.

3 tablespoons olive oil
2½ pounds lean stewing beef
16 whole garlic cloves, peeled
2 tablespoons or so cracked black pepper (*not* ground: put several tablespoons of black peppercorns in an envelope or a fold of waxed paper and smack it with something heavy)

4 cups canned diced tomatoes with their juice
2 cups red wine, preferably a full-bodied hearty one
1 cup chopped fresh basil leaves
Salt

Gremolata

PREHEAT THE OVEN to 275°F.

Heat the olive oil in a heavy-bottomed Dutch oven or casserole, and over high heat, brown the meat well on all sides, working in batches if you have cubed the meat. Pour off the fat and add the garlic, pepper, tomatoes, wine, and basil to the pot. Cover tightly, set it in the oven, and cook for 8 to 10 hours (yes, that's right). The idea is to bring the mixture to a very gentle simmer. Check occasionally, and if the liquid begins to cook away, add a little boiling water and turn down the oven temperature slightly. When the meat is very tender, lift it out of the pot and let the liquid sit for a few minutes while the fat rises to the top. Skim as much fat as possible from the liquid, then return the meat to the pot. At this point, you can refrigerate or freeze the stew if you want to. As it chills, more fat will rise to the surface and congeal, making it easier to remove. Warm the meat through, if necessary, taste and season with salt, and serve it topped with a sprinkling of Gremolata, if desired.

gremolata

3 large garlic cloves
1 cup packed fresh parsley leaves

2 to 3 tablespoons grated lemon zest
1/2 teaspoon or so salt

IN A MINI food processor, pulse the garlic to coarsely chop. Add the parsley and lemon zest and pulse a few more times to finely chop it all. Be careful not to turn it into a paste; it should be loose and airy. Alternatively, you can chop it all together by hand, which is ultimately more fulfilling. Add salt to taste. MAKES ABOUT 1/2 CUP

asian-flavored short ribs

SERVES 4 TO 6

It's hard to screw up short ribs. You just need to cook them slowly and gently for the meat to become softened and luscious. Once cooked, they can be served as is or pulled from the bone and turned into a great topper for rice or noodles, or used for a fantastic hash. Since short ribs contain a fair amount of fat, I like to braise them ahead and then refrigerate so that I can lift off and discard the congealed fat. This is my variation of the Chinese "red cooking" technique, which refers to slow cooking in a broth with soy sauce and sugar, among other things. It can be used with many different meats, such as pork or lamb shoulder.

4 pounds beef short ribs with bones, trimmed of excess fat and cross-cut in 2-inch pieces
Salt and freshly ground pepper
5 tablespoons olive oil
1 ½ cups chopped green onions (white and green parts)
2 tablespoons peeled and finely chopped fresh ginger
1 cup chopped carrots
1 ½ cups light- or medium-bodied red wine

4 cups homemade beef or chicken stock or your favorite canned broth
¼ cup rice vinegar
1 cup soy sauce
3 tablespoons packed light brown or palm sugar
2 tablespoons Asian chili-garlic sauce
3 pieces dried tangerine peel or 3 tablespoons finely grated orange zest
1 tablespoon Chinese five-spice powder (see Glossary and Pantry)
2 teaspoons cornstarch mixed with 2 tablespoons cold water (optional)

PREHEAT THE OVEN to 375°F.

Season the ribs lightly with salt and pepper. In a heavy-bottomed Dutch oven or casserole, heat 3 tablespoons of the olive oil, and brown the ribs over high heat. Remove the ribs from the pot, set them aside, and pour off any fat from the pot. Add the remaining 2 tablespoons olive oil, the onions, ginger, and carrots to the pot and sauté until they are lightly browned, 3 to 4 minutes. Add the wine, stock, vinegar, soy sauce, sugar, chili-garlic sauce, tangerine peel or orange zest, and five-spice powder. When everything is simmering, return the ribs to the pot, cover tightly, and place in the oven for 2 ½ to 3 hours, or until the meat is very tender and almost falling off the bone.

TO SERVE IMMEDIATELY: Transfer the ribs from the pot to a serving bowl or individual plates, keeping a bone with each piece if desired, and cover with foil to keep warm.

Strain the cooking liquid into a clean pot, discarding the solids. Let the liquid sit for a few minutes while the fat rises to the top. Skim off as much of the fat as possible. Boil the liquid uncovered until it is reduced by about a third, about 5 minutes. If you like a thicker, more gravy-like sauce, lower the heat, stir in the cornstarch mixture, and simmer for another 3 to 4 minutes. Taste the sauce, season it with salt and pepper if you think it needs it, and pour it over the ribs.

TO MAKE AHEAD: Transfer just the ribs from the pot to a storage container. Strain the liquid into a separate storage container, and refrigerate both for up to 3 days. At serving time, you can easily remove the congealed fat from the surface of the chilled liquid. Then proceed with the boiling, reducing, and thickening described above. Reheat the ribs in the finished sauce, and enjoy.

adobo pork roast

SERVES 6 TO 8

This recipe came from the Mexican kitchen crew at my restaurant in Santa Rosa, California, and was a favorite at staff meals. The process is a little different from the previous recipes, because the meat is cooked on the stovetop and the sauce is prepared separately. (For more information on the chile varieties, see the Glossary and Pantry.) The long list of suggested accompaniments is traditional; you can make as few or as many of them as you like.

FOR THE PORK

2 tablespoons olive oil

3 1/2- to 4-pound boneless pork shoulder
   or butt

2 cups homemade chicken stock or
   your favorite canned broth

2 large bay leaves

3 whole cloves

12 peppercorns

FOR THE SAUCE

4 large dried ancho or mulato chiles

2 or 3 dried guajillo or New Mexico
   chiles

1 dried chipotle chile

2 cups chopped white onions

1/2 teaspoon fennel seeds

1 tablespoon dried oregano (preferably
   Mexican)

1 teaspoon cumin seeds

3 tablespoons chopped garlic

1 cup diced tomatoes, fresh or canned

2 tablespoons olive oil

Salt and freshly ground pepper to taste

Accompaniments: Finely shredded
   green cabbage, sliced radishes,
   cilantro, chopped fresh tomatoes and
   chiles, fresh raw sweet corn, lime
   wedges, sliced avocado, tortilla chips

TO PREPARE THE PORK: In a large heavy-bottomed pot, heat the olive oil and brown the pork on both sides over high heat. Add the stock, bay leaves, cloves, peppercorns, and enough water to cover by half an inch or so. Bring the liquid to a boil over medium heat, skimming off and discarding any scum that rises to the surface (it sounds awful and doesn't look much better, but it's nothing to worry about). Reduce the heat, cover the pot, and simmer for 2 to 2 1/2 hours, or until the pork is very tender. Remove the pork from the pot and set aside. Pour the liquid through a strainer into a bowl, discarding the solids. Let the liquid sit for a few minutes while the fat rises to the surface, and then skim off as much of the fat as possible (it's the oily liquid floating on top). (If you are making this ahead, refrigerate the strained stock separately from the pork. The congealed fat can then easily be removed from the surface.)

TO MAKE THE SAUCE: Remove the stems and seeds from the chiles and place them in a bowl. Cover them with boiling water and set aside to soften for 30 minutes (do your best to keep them submerged while they soak). Saving the soaking liquid, transfer the chiles to a blender along with the onions, fennel, oregano, cumin, garlic, and tomatoes, and puree until very smooth. In a large saucepan, heat the olive oil and add the chile puree. Cook over medium heat for 4 to 5 minutes, stirring constantly. Add 2 to 3 cups of the strained and defatted pork stock, along with a cup or so of the reserved chile soaking liquid, and simmer uncovered over moderate heat for 15 minutes. If the sauce seems too thick, you can add additional stock. Season with salt and pepper to taste.

Slice the pork and add it to the sauce. Simmer for 5 minutes or so to allow the meat to warm through and absorb the flavor of the sauce. Serve the stew in bowls, passing the accompaniments as desired.

oxtails braised in red wine

SERVES 8 TO 10

This is one of those warming, old-time winter dishes made with an inexpensive cut of meat that many cooks have forgotten about. "Oxtails" don't actually come from oxen (which are castrated bulls used mainly as draft animals). They are the tails of ordinary beef cattle. Oxtails are very high in collagen, which when cooked breaks down into a mouth-filling, unctuous texture. Dried porcini add a wonderful flavor note to this and almost any recipe in this lesson, but if you can't find them or if they're too expensive, you can leave them out. I love this hearty concoction served with good homemade or other fresh egg noodles.

5 pounds oxtails cut at least 1 inch thick
Salt and freshly ground black pepper
1 cup flour, for dredging
3 tablespoons olive oil
4 cups pearl onions or cipollini, peeled
2 cups carrots, sliced on the diagonal (for looks)
1 cup sliced celery
2 cups quartered crimini mushrooms
6 garlic cloves, peeled and quartered
2 medium fennel bulbs, cored and cut in wedges

6 cups hearty, full-bodied red wine preferred
3 cups homemade chicken or beef stock or your favorite canned broth
1 teaspoon juniper berries, slightly crushed (see Note)
2 large bay leaves
3 cups canned diced tomatoes with their juice
1/2 ounce dried porcini mushrooms (optional)

PREHEAT THE OVEN to 375°F.

Trim the oxtails of any excess fat and season well with salt and pepper. Dredge them in flour (dip them in and roll them around) and shake off the excess. In a deep Dutch oven or casserole, heat the olive oil and over high heat, brown the oxtails in batches on all sides. Remove the oxtails from the pot, set them aside, and pour off all but about 3 table-spoons of the fat from the pot. Add the onions, carrots, celery, crimini mushrooms, garlic, and fennel, and sauté over high heat until they are lightly browned, about 5 minutes—they don't need to be cooked through. Transfer the vegetables to a bowl and set them aside. Return the oxtails to the pan along with the wine, stock, juniper berries, bay leaves, tomatoes, and dried mushrooms, if using. Cover and bake for 2 1/2 hours.

(If you left the vegetables in for this whole cooking time, they would be mush by the end. In this dish, I like them to retain some texture.)

Take the pot out of the oven and skim off as much of the fat as possible (it's the clear liquid floating on top). Add the reserved vegetables to the pot, cover, and return the pot to the oven. Cook an additional 40 to 50 minutes, or until the vegetables are tender. Check on it a couple of times to make sure that the oxtails are nearly covered with liquid. Add more stock or wine as needed.

TO SERVE IMMEDIATELY: Remove the pot from the oven, and skim off as much of the fat as possible. Taste the sauce and season with salt and pepper if you think it needs it. Serve the stew with some or all of the bones, depending on your preference.

TO MAKE AHEAD: Transfer the stew to a storage container (or let the pot cool down) and refrigerate for up to 3 days. At serving time, you can easily remove the congealed fat from the surface of the chilled stew. Reheat the stew on the stovetop, and serve.

NOTE: Juniper berries are available in jars in the spice aisle of bigger supermarkets.

brisket braised in coffee

SERVES 6 TO 8

My grandmother never threw anything away—including old coffee too bitter to drink, which she'd incorporate into various dishes, including her famous pears poached in coffee. As a child, I thought this was a little weird. But in fact, as coffee sits, its bitterness increases as its acids and tannins are developed. In other words, old coffee has some of the same qualities as dry wine, and so can enhance a dish in the same way. You don't, by the way, need to use old coffee for this recipe, but it should be good and strong. Brisket is certainly one of the most versatile and universally appreciated cuts of meat, whether it's part of a Kansas City or Texas barbecue, sliced for a Vietnamese pho, simmered for an Italian bollito misto, corned for St. Patrick's Day, or pot roasted for Rosh Hashanah. This is one of my favorite ways to prepare this humble cut. Like most stews or braises, it's even better reheated the next day.

4 pounds beef brisket, trimmed of
    excess fat
Salt and freshly ground black pepper
4 tablespoons olive oil
3 large yellow onions (about 1 1/2 to 2
    pounds total), sliced
1/4 cup sliced fresh garlic
2 tablespoons (or more) pure chile
    powder, such as ancho or Chimayo
    (see Glossary and Pantry)
2 teaspoons whole fennel seeds

2 teaspoons cumin seeds
2/3 cup packed light or dark brown
    sugar
2/3 cup apple cider vinegar
4 cups strong brewed coffee
1 cup homemade chicken, meat, or
    vegetable stock or your favorite
    canned broth
1 14 1/2-ounce can diced tomatoes with
    their juice

PREHEAT THE OVEN to 300°F.

Season the meat liberally with salt and pepper. In a deep Dutch oven or casserole, heat 2 tablespoons of the olive oil and brown the brisket on both sides over high heat. Remove the meat from the pot, discard the fat, and wipe the pot out.

Add the remaining 2 tablespoons of olive oil to the pot and sauté the onions and garlic over high heat until they just begin to color. Add the chile powder and sauté, stirring for a minute more, until fragrant. Add the fennel, cumin, sugar, vinegar, coffee, stock, and tomatoes, and bring to a simmer. Return the brisket to the pot (fat side up, if you want to be very correct), cover, and place in the oven for 3 to 3 1/2 hours or until the meat is very tender.

Leaving the oven on, transfer just the meat from the pot to a cutting board. Puree the braising liquids and vegetables until smooth any way you can (an immersion blender is the easiest way, or you can transfer everything carefully to a food processor or blender, in batches if necessary). Taste the sauce and season with salt and pepper if you think it needs it. Return the pureed sauce to the pot, place the meat fat side up in the pot, and bake *uncovered* for 30 to 45 minutes more, or until the brisket is nicely glazed. Transfer the meat to a cutting board (last time, I promise) and slice thinly across the grain. Serve the meat with the warm sauce spooned over it, or refrigerate the sliced brisket in the sauce for up to 3 days, and reheat on the stovetop.

herb and pistachio–stuffed veal pot roast

SERVES 4 TO 6

We just don't see much veal anymore. Unfortunately, it got a bad rap because of the inhumane way some ranchers raised the young animals. There is, however, "ethically and humanely grown" veal in the marketplace—ask for it! Here, I use the boneless shoulder roast, but the boneless breast is also delicious. These cuts are high in collagen, which makes for greater richness than we usually associate with veal. The herb and pistachio stuffing is actually a pesto, and any of the pestos (page 38) will "work"; if something else appeals to you more than the pistachio, give it a try instead.

3 pounds or so well-trimmed boneless
    veal shoulder roast (ask the butcher
    to do this for you)
Pistachio Pesto (page 45)
Salt and freshly ground pepper
3 tablespoons olive oil
¼ pound pancetta or bacon cut into
    large dice
2 cups chopped white or yellow onions
2 cups chopped white mushrooms
2 teaspoons chopped garlic

1½ cups chopped fresh fennel or
    2 teaspoons fennel seeds
2 cups homemade chicken stock or
    your favorite canned broth
1½ cups white wine, preferably
    medium-bodied
¾ cup heavy cream
2 tablespoons finely chopped fresh
    parsley leaves
1 tablespoon finely grated lemon zest

PREHEAT THE OVEN to 350°F.

Unroll the meat, carefully removing any netting or string that may be wrapping it, and spread the pesto mixture liberally on the inside. Roll the roast back up tightly and rewrap with the netting or tie with string. Season the roast liberally with salt and pepper. In a Dutch oven or heavy pot large enough to hold the roast, heat the olive oil and brown the roast well on all sides over high heat. Remove the meat from the pot and set aside.

Pour off all but 2 tablespoons of the fat from the pan, and add the pancetta, onions, mushrooms, garlic, and fennel. Sauté over medium heat until the vegetables are softened and just beginning to color. Add the stock and wine and bring to a boil. Add the veal, cover the pot, and roast in the oven for about 1½ hours, until the veal registers an internal temperature of 155°F. on an instant-read thermometer.

Transfer the meat to a cutting board and cover loosely with foil.

Carefully strain the liquid into a bowl, pressing down on the solids. Wipe out the pot and return the liquid to it. (Of course, you can just strain the liquid directly into a clean pot if you don't mind having two pots to wash when you're done.) Add the cream, bring the liquid to a boil, and cook over high heat for about 5 minutes, or until the liquid is reduced and is as thick as a light sauce. Turn off the heat, stir in the parsley and lemon zest, taste the sauce, and season with salt and pepper if you think it needs it. Remove the net or string from the veal, slice it thickly, and serve with the hot sauce spooned over it.

pot-roasted chicken with vegetables

SERVES 4 TO 6

In France, roast chicken is taken as seriously in the professional kitchen as it is in the home. Their basic approach is to select a young, free-range chicken, season it, brown it deeply in a heavy, deep casserole, then cover and roast in a medium-hot oven until it's done. What could be easier? I've watched the process many times, and I've noticed that it is the small things that make the difference: a good fresh chicken, duck, or goose; fat or real lard for browning; good sea salt and freshly ground pepper; sometimes some other seasoning, like a little lemon or ginger, but just as often not. The chicken roasts with the cover askew so that the skin crisps (completely covered, the chicken will tend to steam). The chicken always rests for 5 minutes or so before carving so that all the juices can redistribute in the meat.

One of the great classic roast chicken recipes uses the pot roasting method and adds 40 cloves of unpeeled garlic (yes, 40) along with a little wine and whatever other vegetables you might like. As the garlic roasts, its pungent flavor is tamed and it becomes almost subtle, infusing everything with its sweet flavor. The chicken is brought to the table in its pot, which was traditionally sealed with a flour and water paste under the rim of the lid. When the seal was broken and the lid lifted, the room was filled with a fantastic bouquet. Though I lose that effect, I like to remove the lid for the last 15 minutes of roasting, to crisp and brown the skin.

1 4- to 5-pound roasting chicken	2 cups celery cut into thick slices
4 tablespoons butter	Salt and freshly ground pepper
2 tablespoons olive oil	40 unpeeled garlic cloves
¼ pound thick-sliced pancetta or bacon cut into large dice	2 whole bay leaves
2 cups carrots cut thickly on the bias	2 cups homemade chicken stock or your favorite canned broth
2 small onions, peeled and cut into 8 wedges each	2 cups dry white wine

PREHEAT THE OVEN to 450°F. Remove the giblets from the chicken and save for another use or discard. (I toss them all except the liver into a container in my freezer. When I have enough, I use them to make stock.) Rinse the chicken well, remove any excess fat, and pat dry. Tuck the wings behind the body and tie the legs and tail together so that the chicken will hold its shape. Heat 2 tablespoons of the butter and the olive oil in a deep, heavy casserole and brown the chicken on all sides, about 8 minutes. Remove the chicken, set aside, and pour out all but a tablespoon of the fat. Return the casserole to the heat, add the pancetta, and sauté until browned and crisp. Remove the pancetta and add the remaining 2 tablespoons of butter, along with the carrots, onions, and celery, and sauté over medium heat until the vegetables are just beginning to color, about 5 minutes. Season liberally with salt and pepper.

Return the chicken to the casserole and add the pancetta, garlic cloves, bay leaves, stock, and wine. Cover tightly and roast in the oven for 45 minutes. Uncover and continue to cook for another 15 minutes or until the juices run clear when the thickest part of the leg is pierced and the chicken is nicely browned.

Remove the chicken and vegetables from the pot, arrange them on a platter, and keep warm (covering it all with foil works fine). Discard the bay leaves and skim as much fat as possible from the juices left in the pot (it's the clear liquid floating on top). Taste the sauce and season with salt and pepper. Carve the chicken and serve with the vegetables and the sauce on the side.

9 grilling

The Ancient Cookfire

Cooking
foods
outside
on a grill is one of my earliest food memories. As a little kid, I

lived with my grandparents, and we often went on fishing trips to remote

lakes and streams in the Colorado Rockies. We caught a lot of trout, especially

rainbows and cutthroats, and my grandmother would salt and pepper them

inside and out, wrap them in bacon, and grill them over hot coals along with

fresh corn or whatever else we had at the moment. It couldn't have been sim-

pler but, man, was it delicious! Grilling is certainly a primeval technique. Pre-

historic folk no doubt rigged all kinds of ways to cook over coals and fire.

For purposes of this lesson, I'm defining "grilling" as *quick cooking of

tender meats and vegetables outside over hot coals*. It also includes the alternative

method of using a ridged grill pan to cook quickly in the kitchen, on

the stovetop over high heat.

The term "barbecue," which is often used interchangeably with "grill," actually refers to a different technique. Despite the fact that everyone applies the word to a typical backyard cookout, any Southerner will tell you that to barbecue means to cook a relatively tough cut of meat slowly over low heat with lots of smoke to both flavor and tenderize it. The word comes from the Spanish *barbacoa*, which originally described the apparatus for slowly cooking or drying meats over an open flame. I don't want to get too hung up on the differences, but it's useful to understand them.

Like all techniques, grilling requires a little skill and experience to do it well. Way back in 1941, James Beard noted, "Grilling, broiling, barbequing—whatever you want to call it—is an art, not just a matter of building a pyre and throwing on a piece of meat as a sacrifice to the gods of the stomach! For while barbequing is a very old and primitive way of cooking, it is also one of the most appetizing methods of dealing with meat known to man, and it deserves to be done with some semblance of technique, accuracy, and care." Beard's secret was to make sure you had an even distribution of heat from coals that were "veiled in a lovely white ash" before you started cooking. He went on to advise, "A good fire, good coals, and patience, rather than speed, should be your watchword."

Grilling is a dry-cooking method very much like sautéing or oven-roasting, but with the added benefit of the smoky flavor that comes from cooking over coals or a live fire (by the way, gas grills are perfectly acceptable). What makes all of these dry-cooking techniques so enticing is that each helps foods develop a flavorful crust, the result of caramelization. When high heat is applied to foods, the natural sugars present in all living things begin to brown. Also, a process known as the Maillard reaction begins: sugars and proteins interact to produce new chemical structures, and as heat continues to be applied, these structures break apart and form more new structures, each of which has a distinctive taste or aroma. Hundreds of new compounds are produced. The result of all this is that browned food meshes all these flavors together, and just tastes better! Since grilling uses the highest heat of all cooking methods, it's the best technique for maximizing caramelization or browning.

To review (and this will be on the exam): when grilling, we want food to cook quickly over high heat. That means grilling works best for foods that are tender and cook quickly. We're looking to brown or sear the outside for maximum flavor and still have interiors that are moist and juicy. The risk is that we can quickly overcook and dry out the food in our desire to maximize flavor. In grilling, as in life, there is no great gain without some small gamble.

So where do we start?

first . . . the grill

There is an almost endless variety of grills on the market. The primary question facing most of us is: do I get one with a cover or not? My vote is to get one with a cover. The purpose of the cover is to hold heat in so that you can cook larger cuts of meat or whole birds and the like, which take longer to cook. The cover is *not* there to help you control flame or flare-ups (even though we sometimes resort to that). You do that by using the two level heat combination that I'll describe in just a minute. I also suggest you get one that has as large a grill surface as you can comfortably house and handle. This will give you the best chance to actually use the direct or indirect heat methods described below. Make sure that the cover is tight-fitting and look for one that uses thick, stainless steel rods (at least ¼ inch in diameter) for the grill surface. Thick rods hold the heat better when you place food on them and are less likely to stick. Stainless is also easier to clean.

One of the joys of grilling is that you don't need pots, pans, and skillets. Cleanup is pretty easy. All you need is a stiff wire brush, available at any hardware store, to do the job. Be sure to brush the grill clean right when you finish cooking, while the coals are still hot. Cooked-on food comes off easily then and is consumed by the coals. A little additional tip: cover the grill with a layer of heavy-duty aluminum foil immediately after you've removed the food and while the fire is still hot. This traps the heat and burns off the fat, grease, and other stuff, leaving a white dust that is easily brushed off. If you're using a gas-fired grill, you can accomplish the same thing by leaving the grill on for 10 minutes or so after covering.

next . . . what fuel and how do I light it?

For most Americans, composite briquettes are the fuel of choice. They're convenient and widely available. My advice: *don't* use them. They often include petroleum products and other chemicals, and who needs that on their food? Instead, use untreated hardwood charcoal (also known as charwood) such as mesquite. Hardwood charcoal is produced by burning wood slowly in a low-oxygen atmosphere until nearly all of the wood's solids have been converted to carbon. Hardware charcoal contains no additives of any kind. It burns cleaner and hotter than composite briquettes and can be regulated more easily because it is almost pure carbon. I find that it pays to purchase hardwood charcoal in 40-pound bags from a hardware store, feed store, or big-box retailer. The cost can be at least 60 percent less.

To light your fire, the only choices are a chimney starter or an electric coil starter. Lighter fluid, a petroleum product, may be just a smidge faster but is clearly unacceptable in terms of what it does to the atmosphere. You can make your own chimney starter by removing both ends from a 2-pound or larger coffee can and, with a church key or can opener, punching a few holes around the bottom to provide oxygen. To use, set it in the bottom of your grill on top of the fire grate. Crumple up some newspaper to fill it halfway, fill it the rest of the way with charcoal, and light the newspaper. This will start the charcoal burning; when it's red hot, dump it out and add as much charcoal as you are going to need on top. In another 15 minutes or so, all the charcoal will be going. Spread it out so that you have two levels of heat as described below.

cooking strategies

There are basically two:

1. Direct and Indirect Heat: Direct heat is what we're used to: cooking the food directly over the fire or hot coals. Direct heat is best for smaller, tender foods, such as chicken breasts, burgers, vegetables, fish, and the like—foods that can be cooked through in less than 15 minutes. Indirect heat involves cooking the food away from the heat, that is, coals on one side of the grill and food on the other. With a gas grill you only turn on one side of the grill and leave the other side, where the food goes, off. In this case, we would cover the grill so that it functions more like a convection oven. Indirect heat grilling is best for larger pieces of meat, such as roasts, legs of lamb, or turkeys, that will take more than 30 minutes to cook through. You can use a combination of the methods by first searing the food directly over the coals to give color and caramelization, and then moving the food away from the coals to finish cooking slowly.

2. One and Two Level Fires: When using the direct heat method, you have two options. If you're cooking something like shrimp, which cooks in just a couple of minutes over a hot fire, a straightforward, one level fire is fine. For foods that take a little longer to cook, I recommend building a two level fire, where half the cooking area is at high heat (a couple of layers of hot charcoal) and the other half is lower (a single layer or less). You can move the food between the two as needed, either to sear and caramelize or to finish cooking slowly. If you're using a gas grill, turn one half on high and the other on medium-low. For all my grilling, no matter what the food, I always use the two level method, because it gives me the most flexibility.

some final tips

~ Be sure to have everything organized and next to the grill before you start cooking. More good food has been ruined by someone forgetting something and having to run into the house to find it.

~ Keep a spray bottle full of water next to the grill to dampen flare-ups and to cool things down (including the cook!) if you need to.

~ Always start with a clean grilling surface. Oil it lightly after it's hot and before you place any food on it.

~ Only cover the grill when you are cooking items that will take longer than 30 minutes. For items that take a short time to cook, covering will give off-flavors to the food. If you've got something like bone-in chicken breasts or thick-cut chops, which are "in between," an alternative is to move them to the cooler part of the grill and cover them with a metal roasting pan or pie pan so that they can finish cooking without the outside becoming charred.

~ Wood chips to create smoke are a waste with the direct heat method since we don't cover the grill—so don't use them! Save them for those times when you use the indirect heat method and cover the grill.

~ To test to see if a grill is ready to cook on, many cooks use the "open hand test": hold your hand about 6 inches above the grill. If you can hold it there for about four seconds before it becomes too hot to stand, the fire is ready. If you have to move your hand sooner, the fire is still too hot. If you can hold it there longer, the fire is too cool, and you'll need to either turn up the gas or add more coals.

There are lots of ways to add flavor to the foods that we grill. Marinades soak the food with flavor before it hits the heat. Rubs can be as simple as rubbing good salt and freshly ground pepper on the food before grilling. Sauces are either put on just as the food finishes cooking or served at the table. Examples of all of these are included in the recipes below.

Okay . . . let's cook something!

grilled fresh lobster

SERVES 2

I was turned on to grilled lobster through Jasper White's book Jasper White's Cooking from New England, and now it's my favorite way to cook lobster. The shells char as the meat cooks, giving the lobster a delicious flavor. Buy lobsters alive. Before you split it, the lobster can be killed humanely by inserting a knife decisively at the spot where the head joins the body. This severs the spinal cord, dispatching it instantly. Alternatively, it can be killed by plunging it into boiling water for 2 to 3 minutes.

2 whole lobsters (about 1¾ pounds each)
Olive oil
Salt and freshly ground pepper

Simple Herb Butter Sauce
Fresh lemon wedges

PREPARE A CHARCOAL fire or preheat a gas grill using the two level method (page 152). Split the lobsters in half lengthwise and gently crack the claws. Remove and discard the long thin intestinal tract that runs the length of the lobster and also the lumpy head sac that is located near the eyes. Brush the shell and tail meat with olive oil and season with salt and pepper. Place the lobsters, shell side down, directly over medium coals. Liberally brush on the Simple Herb Butter Sauce, working some of it into the cracked claws. Repeat this again in a couple of minutes.

When the shell begins to char a bit, move the lobsters to a cooler spot on the grill and cover them with a metal roasting pan. Cook for 4 to 5 minutes more or until the meat is just cooked through. (It should be slightly translucent in the center.)

simple herb butter sauce

4 tablespoons butter
2 tablespoons olive oil
1 tablespoon minced shallots or roasted garlic (see Glossary and Pantry)

2 tablespoons mixed chopped fresh herbs of your choice
2 teaspoons fresh lemon juice
Salt and freshly ground pepper

IN A SMALL pan, heat the butter and oil over medium heat. Add the shallots and cook, stirring, until they have softened but not browned, about 3 minutes. Remove the pan from the heat, stir in the herbs, lemon juice, salt, and pepper, and keep warm. MAKES ABOUT ½ CUP

grilled oysters with hog wash

SERVES 4 TO 6

Some of my favorite oyster producers are the folks at Hog Island Oyster Company, who farm oysters on Tomales Bay, north of San Francisco. They have a rustic picnic ground there, where you can buy oysters to eat either raw on the half shell or grilled until they just pop open. It usually only takes a couple of minutes for the steam to build up inside the closed oyster. I love to top these with a vinaigrette I've named "Hog Wash," which goes well on either grilled or raw oysters.

2 dozen (or more) oysters in the shell   **Hog Wash**

PREPARE A CHARCOAL fire or preheat a gas grill. Place the oysters, with rounded or cup side down, directly over a hot fire. Within 2 to 3 minutes, the oysters will pop open. You may have to "help" some of them open with an oyster knife. Don't cook longer or the oyster will dry out. Discard the top shell, spoon on a teaspoon or two of Hog Wash, and eat!

hog wash

¾ cup seasoned rice vinegar
2 tablespoons finely chopped shallots
¼ cup fresh lime juice, strained
¼ cup finely chopped fresh cilantro leaves

I teaspoon seeded and finely chopped jalapeño chile, or to taste
Salt and freshly ground pepper to taste

COMBINE ALL THE INGREDIENTS and refrigerate for at least 30 minutes to let the flavors marry and develop. Can be made a day ahead and stored covered in the refrigerator. MAKES ABOUT I CUP

grilled tortillas with fresh chiles and pickled red onions

SERVES 4

Tierra Vegetables, a farm near Healdsburg, California, grows all kinds of fresh chiles and also makes dried chiles and marvelous smoked chipotle chiles, all of which you can mail-order. They once served me this incredibly potent sandwich; it remains one of the most memorable things I have ever eaten—a paragon of simplicity and an explosion of flavor. It is not for the faint of heart.

2 to 3 pounds mixed fresh sweet peppers and hot chiles of your choice
8 large (10- to 12-inch) flour tortillas

8 ounces sliced asadero, Jack, or other melting cheese
Pickled Red Onions

PREPARE A CHARCOAL fire or preheat a gas or stovetop grill. Slowly grill the peppers over medium-low heat so that they char just slightly and cook through in about 10 minutes. Split the peppers in half and cut out the stems and seeds. Scrape off and discard any charred skin and set the peppers aside.

Place the tortillas on the grill over low heat and place about 1 ounce of cheese over half of each tortilla. Top the cheese with an assortment of peppers and cook until the cheese just melts. Fold the tortilla over and eat along with some of the Pickled Red Onions. Yum!

pickled red onions

2 small red onions (about 8 ounces total)
½ teaspoon cumin seeds, toasted, if possible, and ground
½ teaspoon dried oregano
2 garlic cloves, peeled and sliced

½ cup white wine vinegar or cider vinegar
2 teaspoons sugar
Salt and freshly ground pepper to your taste

PEEL THE ONIONS and slice them into ⅛-inch-thick rings. Blanch them in a small saucepan of lightly salted boiling water for just a few seconds, then immediately drain and run under cold water.

Return the onions to the (empty) pan and add the cumin, oregano,

garlic, vinegar, and sugar. If the onions are not completely covered, add some water to the pan. Bring to a boil, then immediately remove the pan from the heat and pour everything into a bowl to cool. These should be made at least a couple of hours ahead of time and set aside for the flavors to develop. Taste and season with salt and pepper. Store covered in the refrigerator for up to 2 weeks. MAKES ABOUT 1 1/2 CUPS

grilled eggplant, red pepper, and arugula sandwich with basil-mint pesto

SERVES 4

This vegetarian sandwich is dressed with one of my favorite pestos, but you can use any pesto that you like. You did make some extra and store it in the freezer, didn't you?

1 large (about 1 1/4 pounds) eggplant, stem end removed
Olive oil
Salt and freshly ground pepper
2 medium red bell peppers, halved, seeds and stem removed
4 thick, 3-inch-square pieces of focaccia, split in half

Basil-Mint Pesto (page 45)
1 cup lightly packed young arugula leaves, tough stems removed
1 small cucumber, peeled and thinly sliced on the bias
Reduced Balsamic Vinegar (page 161)

PREPARE A CHARCOAL fire or preheat a gas or stovetop grill or broiler. Slice the eggplant into eight 1/4-inch-thick rounds, brush both sides of each slice with olive oil, and season lightly with salt and pepper. Lightly brush the peppers with olive oil. Grill or broil the eggplant and peppers on both sides until the eggplant is browned and cooked through and the peppers are softened and lightly charred. With the point of a knife, lightly scrape the peppers to remove any loose charred skin.

Spread focaccia halves liberally with pesto. Top the bottom slice of focaccia with grilled eggplant slices, peppers, arugula, cucumbers, a sprinkling of salt and pepper, and drops of balsamic vinegar. Top with the remaining focaccia and serve.

all-purpose grilling rub

MAKES ABOUT I CUP

This is my basic rub for meat, poultry, and fish. A dry rub (as opposed to a wet rub, which is liquidy from the inclusion of oil or something else) is traditionally used with slow-cooked barbecue. Dry rubs are also a useful flavoring technique for high-heat grilling. Just be careful not to burn them or they'll get bitter.

If you try this rub and you like it (or, indeed, if you don't like it), maybe you'll be emboldened to invent your own. Any combination of your favorite spices or dried herbs is a good jumping-off point.

⅓ cup sweet paprika
⅓ cup ground dried, medium-hot
   chiles, such as ancho or guajillo,
   or a combination

2 tablespoons kosher or sea salt
I tablespoon ground cumin
2 teaspoons ground allspice
I ½ tablespoons sugar

MIX ALL THE ingredients together. Store any unused portion tightly sealed in the refrigerator for up to 3 months.

grilled pork tenderloin with cranberry ketchup

SERVES 4

Here's a quick dinner from the grill that gets it flavor from a dry rub. For a less assertive flavor, you can just rub the meat with a kosher salt and freshly ground pepper. The Cranberry Ketchup may even wean you away from the supermarket stuff.

2 I-pound pork tenderloins
2 tablespoons olive oil

All-Purpose Grilling Rub
Cranberry Ketchup

PREPARE A CHARCOAL fire or preheat a gas grill using the two-level method (page 152). Rub the tenderloins with the olive oil, and then rub 2 tablespoons or so (or to your taste) of the All-Purpose Grilling Rub gently onto the meat. Grill directly over a hot fire, turning a couple of times, until the meat develops a nice browned crust, about 5 minutes.

Once the tenderloins are well browned and seared, move the meat to a portion of the grill where the heat is lower and continue to cook until the center of the thickest part is just slightly pink, about 12 minutes. Remove the meat from the grill and allow it to rest for 3 or 4 minutes. Slice on the bias and serve with a generous spoonful of Cranberry Ketchup on each portion.

cranberry ketchup

12 ounces fresh or frozen whole cranberries (that's the size of the package sold all across the country)
1 medium yellow or white onion, peeled and finely chopped (about 1 1/2 cups)
3 tablespoons finely chopped garlic
1/2 cup red wine
1/2 cup wine vinegar or apple cider vinegar
3/4 cup sugar
1/2 teaspoon five-spice powder
1/4 teaspoon red chile flakes
2 tablespoons soy sauce

COMBINE ALL THE ingredients in a deep nonreactive saucepan (the acid in the cranberries and vinegar will react with aluminum and uncoated cast iron, causing off-flavors). Bring to a simmer over medium heat, partially cover, reduce the heat, and simmer gently for about 30 minutes, stirring occasionally, until the mixture is as thick as . . . ketchup (watch the pot, not the clock). In a regular blender or food processor, or using an immersion blender, puree the mixture, then strain it through a medium strainer, pressing down hard on the solids. Store covered in the refrigerator for up to 6 weeks. If you are familiar with home canning techniques, you can process it in a water bath to store at room temperature for up to a year. MAKES ABOUT 2 CUPS

NOTE: If cranberries aren't available, you can use other berries or stone fruits like apricots or peaches. If using these other fruits, which are sweeter than cranberries, you'll want to reduce the sugar a bit.

grilled beef *tagliata* with rosemary, capers, and lemons

SERVES 4 TO 6

This dish epitomizes the best of Italian cooking. Just a few great ingredients treated simply, but the result is unforgettable. I still remember the first time I had this at a roadside trattoria. Like all Italian recipes, this has infinite variations, so here's my version. Tagliata, from the Italian tagliare, means "carved" or "cut." The meat is cut into thin slices, which produces a lot more surface area on which to drizzle seasoned oils or condiments.

²/₃ cup plus 2 tablespoons fragrant extra virgin olive oil

6 large garlic cloves, thinly sliced

2 tablespoons chopped fresh rosemary leaves

2 teaspoons cracked black pepper (see Note)

1½ pounds New York strip steak or sirloin, about 2 inches thick, excess fat removed

Salt and freshly ground black pepper

6 cups lightly packed tender young arugula

Reduced Balsamic Vinegar

3 tablespoons Fried Capers

Lemon wedges

PREPARE A CHARCOAL fire or preheat a gas or stovetop grill. In a small saucepan over low heat, cook ²/₃ cup of the olive oil and the garlic until the garlic is lightly browned and beginning to crisp. Take the pan off the heat, stir in the rosemary and cracked pepper, set aside, and keep warm.

Rub the steak liberally with 2 tablespoons of the olive oil and season liberally with salt and pepper. Grill the steak over high heat until rare to medium rare. (If you do this on the stovetop with a ridged grill pan, you'll need plenty of ventilation!) Transfer the steak to a cutting board and let it rest for 5 minutes or so. This allows the juices to "retreat" back into the meat and redistribute themselves.

Spread the arugula on a serving platter. Slice the steak thinly across the grain. Arrange the meat on top of the arugula and pour the warm seasoned oil over the meat. Drizzle with Reduced Balsamic Vinegar and scatter Fried Capers over all. Serve with lemon wedges.

NOTE: To get the right consistency, put the peppercorns in a clean envelope or fold of waxed paper and smack it with something heavy.

reduced balsamic vinegar

Here it is, the moment you've all been waiting for and a useful restaurant trick well worth knowing. Boil some balsamic vinegar, uncovered, over high heat, until it is reduced by a little more than half—say 60 percent. As it cools, it will thicken into a syrup that can be drizzled over all manner of things. Its advantage over straight-out-of-the-bottle balsamic is that in this state, it "stays put." It can be stored at room temperature almost indefinitely.

fried capers

When capers are fried, they take on a different flavor and texture that I really like. Drain the capers well, pat dry with paper towels, and then fry them in small batches in about ¼ inch of hot olive oil until the buds begin to open and are lightly browned and crisp. Drain on paper towels. Can be done a few hours in advance.

achiote-grilled sea bass

SERVES 6

Here, I've marinated the fish in a paste made with annatto seeds, or achiote, before grilling. Annatto seeds are used extensively in Mexican and Caribbean cuisines. They contribute not only a bright orange-red color, but also a subtle flavor. You can buy prepared achiote pastes that are perfectly fine to use, though I've included a recipe. If you cannot find annato seeds, substitute paprika, either sweet or hot. Citrus Salad is a fantastic accompaniment if you feel like doing a little something extra.

Achiote Paste

1 1/2 pounds fresh sea bass fillets or other firm-fleshed white fish or large scallops

2 cups mixed young savory salad greens, such as arugula, watercress, and spinach

1 large avocado, peeled, pitted, and sliced

Garnish if you like with fresh cilantro sprigs

Accompaniment: Citrus Salad (page 53)

PREPARE A CHARCOAL fire or preheat a gas or stovetop grill. Smear the Achiote Paste on both sides of the fish and marinate for 15 to 30 minutes. Quickly grill the fish over high heat until just done. Be careful not to overcook it. Arrange the greens on a serving platter or plates, top with the fish and avocado, and garnish with cilantro sprigs, if desired.

achiote paste

2 tablespoons finely ground annatto seeds (sometimes labeled achiote)

1 tablespoon olive oil

1 tablespoon pure chile powder, such as ancho

2 tablespoons chopped fresh garlic

1 teaspoon whole allspice (about 5), toasted and ground

1/2 teaspoon ground cinnamon

2 teaspoons honey, or to taste

2 teaspoons dried oregano (preferably Mexican)

1 teaspoon salt

1/3 cup or so fresh orange or tangerine juice, or enough to make a smooth paste

COMBINE THE ANNATTO seeds, olive oil, chile powder, garlic, allspice, cinnamon, honey, oregano, and salt in a blender. Blend, adding the juice a bit at a time until the mixture is a smooth paste. Store covered in the refrigerator for up to a week. Can also be frozen. MAKES ABOUT 1/2 CUP

flatbread on the grill

MAKES 8 BREADS

If you've ever—or even never—thought about making bread, this is a great place to start. This flatbread is very versatile, and in addition to grilling it as I've done here, it can also be cooked in a heavy skillet on the stovetop, under the broiler, or in a preheated 500°F. oven on a pizza stone. Whatever the method, flatbreads only take a couple of minutes to cook. Also note that the dough can be refrigerated after the first rise and baked the next day. The seasoning may be varied according to your tastes and menu. Try adding minced fresh herbs to the dough while kneading. Some cracked black pepper would also be great for a little added zip. Following are some other ideas for these flatbreads.

1 package active dry yeast
1¼ cups warm water (not over 110°F.)
2¾ cups unbleached all-purpose flour, plus additional for rolling
¼ cup whole wheat flour or coarse rye flour

2 teaspoons kosher salt
2 teaspoons crushed fennel seeds (optional)
Olive oil for brushing breads

COMBINE THE YEAST and water in the bowl of an electric mixer. Let it rest until frothy, about 15 minutes. Using the paddle attachment, incorporate the flours into the yeast mixture. Beat in the salt and fennel. Switch to the dough hook and knead for 5 to 7 minutes. Remove the dough and place it in a lightly oiled bowl, turning the dough over to coat it completely with oil. Cover the bowl with plastic wrap and allow the dough to rise until it has doubled in size, about 1 hour. Punch the dough down (deflate it by pushing it down with your fists), cover the bowl again, and let it rise a second time until doubled, about 45 minutes.

Prepare a hot charcoal fire or preheat a gas or stovetop grill. Turn the risen dough out onto a work surface and divide it into 8 pieces. Roll each piece into a ball. Place the balls on a floured cookie sheet, cover with a damp towel, and let them rest for 20 minutes (if you try to roll out the dough right away, it will be too rubbery, springing back into shape and refusing to stay rolled out). On a lightly floured work surface, roll the balls out until they are about 7 inches across. Dust with flour if needed as you roll to keep them from sticking. Lightly brush the disks with olive oil. Place the disks, oiled side down, on the grill. The breads will begin to rise almost immediately. When golden brown on the underside, brush the top with oil, flip the breads over, and cook until brown. Remove from the grill and serve warm.

variations   KULCHAS
~ After turning, top with 2 to 3 tablespoons of mixed sautéed onions and chopped fresh mint leaves and fold over into a half-moon.
~ After turning, top with 2 to 3 tablespoons of a mixture of drained feta cheese, lemon zest, and chopped fresh mint leaves and fold over.

CALZONES
~ Top the dough rounds with 2 to 3 tablespoons of a mixture of freshly grated Parmesan and coarsely ground black pepper and fold over to enclose. Grill the half-moons on both sides until puffed and brown.
~ Top the dough rounds with 2 to 3 tablespoons of a mixture of grated fontina cheese, grilled red peppers, and grilled zucchini and fold over to enclose. Grill the half-moons on both sides until puffed and brown.

PIZZAS
~ After turning, top with a simple tomato sauce made with fresh basil and roasted garlic. Grill until the underside is done.
~ In the summer, I love a topping of grilled figs, creamy blue cheese, and crisp, cooked pancetta or prosciutto.

grilled indian-spiced chicken kebabs

SERVES 4 TO 6

While grilling is great for chicken, it's risky with boneless, skinless breasts, which are easily rendered dry and tasteless by high heat. The key is a marinade and short cooking. Tikka paste is a great time-saver and can be bought in stores that carry Indian ingredients, or even sometimes in the "ethnic foods" section of large supermarkets. The chicken benefits from the long marinating time, because yogurt is not as acidic as other marinades.

2 to 3 tablespoons bottled tikka paste

6 to 8 tablespoons plain yogurt

1 tablespoon olive oil

1 1/2 teaspoons minced garlic

1 1/2 teaspoons peeled and minced fresh ginger

1/4 to 1/2 teaspoon cayenne pepper

1 1/2 pounds boneless, skinless chicken breasts, cut into 1-inch pieces

Accompaniments: lettuce leaves, cucumber slices, lime wedges, and Fresh Mint-Cilantro Chutney

COMBINE THE TIKKA paste, 6 tablespoons of the yogurt, the olive oil, garlic, ginger, and red pepper powder in a bowl. The mixture should be a thick paste. If not, add more yogurt. Mix well. Add the chicken pieces to the yogurt mixture, and mix thoroughly to coat. Cover and marinate in the refrigerator for 3 to 4 hours or overnight.

Prepare a charcoal fire or preheat a gas or stovetop grill.

Prepare 12 6- or 8-inch bamboo skewers by soaking them in warm water for at least 30 minutes. Thread the chicken on the skewers, leaving about 1/2 inch between the pieces. Grill the skewered chicken over medium-high heat for about 8 minutes, or until the meat is no longer pink in the center, turning once or twice. Serve on lettuce leaves and top with cucumbers, a squeeze or two of lime, and the chutney.

fresh mint-cilantro chutney

1 1/2 cups lightly packed fresh mint leaves

1/2 cup lightly packed fresh cilantro leaves

1/2 teaspoon ground cumin, lightly toasted

1/2 teaspoon sugar

1 teaspoon finely chopped jalapeño or serrano chile, or to taste

1/4 cup fresh lime juice

1/3 cup plain yogurt

Homemade vegetable or chicken stock or your favorite canned broth

Salt and freshly ground pepper

COMBINE THE MINT, cilantro, cumin, sugar, chile, lime juice, and yogurt in a blender or food processor and process until smooth, adding a bit of stock or water to help, if needed. Taste and season with salt and pepper. Can be made up to 2 hours ahead and refrigerated.
MAKES 1¼ CUPS OR SO

grilled spiced lamb chops

SERVES 4

In America, we are finally beginning to use and appreciate the world of spices. This rub combines the savory and the sweet to flavor the lamb; it's equally delicious on chicken or rich fish, like tuna. I've specified "frenched" chops, which means that you remove the fat and sinew along the rib bone, which makes for a more attractive presentation (ask your butcher to do it). I like to serve these chops with quickly sautéed greens.

I 3-inch cinnamon stick
I tablespoon whole coriander seeds
I tablespoon cumin seeds
2 whole allspice
2 tablespoons sweet paprika
½ teaspoon cayenne pepper, or to taste
2 teaspoons packed light or dark brown sugar
⅓ cup olive oil

2 tablespoons finely chopped garlic
I cup finely chopped fresh parsley leaves (tender stems are okay)
3 tablespoons finely chopped fresh mint leaves (tender stems are okay)
2 8-bone lamb racks, frenched and cut into 8 2-bone chops (about 2½ pounds total)
Sea or kosher salt

BREAK THE CINNAMON stick into small pieces and grind with the coriander, cumin, allspice, paprika, cayenne, and brown sugar in a coffee or spice grinder, until very fine. In a separate bowl, mix together the olive oil and the garlic, and then stir in the spice mixture along with the parsley and mint. Coat the lamb well with the mixture, massaging it in a bit to help it stick. Cover and marinate for at least 2 and up to 8 hours in the refrigerator.

Prepare a charcoal fire or preheat a gas or stovetop grill. Remove the chops from the refrigerator and bring them to room temperature before grilling. Season the lamb liberally with salt and grill directly over medium-high heat until rare to medium rare, 6 to 8 minutes.

10 soufflés

For some
reason,
soufflés seem
to intimidate many cooks. They really shouldn't. In many respects,

soufflés are farm foods, made from very basic ingredients generally avail-

able on every farm: eggs, butter, milk, flour, and a little cheese, to which

you can add whatever else may be on hand. I can remember my grand-

mother, who was no French chef, making them often, usually for the

lighter, quicker evening meal we called supper. Soufflé-making has a

method, and once you understand how it works, you'll see how open to

improvisation it is. For our exploration here, I am focusing on warm,

oven-baked soufflés, those that are eaten straight out of the oven. The term

soufflé nowadays is also applied to cold, usually sweet preparations whose

airy texture is supported by gelatin or whipped cream or both. To purists,

these are more accurately described as mousses.

The name *soufflé* comes from the French verb *souffler*, which means "to breathe," "to whisper," or "to blow up," in the sense of inflate. This aptly describes a soufflé's delicate, ethereal texture that seems to disappear in your mouth as you eat it. Behind this apparent magic is a straightforward technique that anyone can achieve by following the instructions, and despite all the sitcom jokes about nervous housewives and slammed doors, soufflés are actually pretty simple. They are made up of two components: a *base*, which is usually a thick, milk-based white sauce (what the French call *béchamel*) but can be anything from creamy cooked cereals to thick vegetable purees, and *whipped egg whites*, folded in just before the soufflé is baked. The base is the flavor carrier, the whites provide the puff. In the oven, the air trapped in the egg whites expands as it heats, causing the whole mixture to rise. A high oven temperature of 375 to 400°F. will produce a soufflé with a creamy texture. That same mixture baked longer at 325 degrees will yield a soufflé that is firmer and more uniformly cooked. You can make the choice depending on what you like.

As we examine how soufflés come together, you'll learn to make a white sauce, which has many applications beyond soufflés; you'll get some tips about beating egg whites; and we'll look at "folding," a manual procedure worth knowing how to do right. We'll explore a few of my favorite recipes for both savory and sweet soufflés. I'll bet that once you've made a couple of these, they'll become a regular part of your repertoire. A couple of other notes before we start.

~ Most soufflés can be prepared ahead, frozen in their uncooked state for up to 2 weeks, and then baked straight from the freezer. All you have to do is double the baking time listed and they rise almost as much as those freshly made. You can also prepare a soufflé mixture a few hours ahead and hold it in the refrigerator until baking time.

~ Soufflés can be cooked ahead and reheated! Known as twice-cooked soufflés, these are usually baked in individual serving sizes, cooled, taken out of their dish, and then reheated at serving time with a splash of cream. More pudding-like, they do puff again and are a delicious variation. See, for example, my Twice-Baked Goat Cheese Soufflés (page 178).

~ Soufflés can be baked flat and rolled with fillings and also baked "free-form." (See page 174 for one variation.)

Many recipes call for attaching a parchment or foil collar around the outside of the baking dish before adding the batter, which makes the soufflé rise even higher in the dish for a dramatic presentation at serving time. I've never liked this because the collar can slip during baking and sometimes be a bit of a pain to remove before serving. Who needs it?

If soufflés are so simple, how come all the jokes?

Does it take a little practice to make a *perfect* soufflé? Yes, it does. Do you need to make a *perfect* soufflé? No, you don't. If you pay attention in class (i.e., follow my directions), you will make a *delicious* soufflé—and that's a perfect supper.

improving the stability of whipped egg whites

traditionally, the French called for beating egg whites in a copper bowl to improve the stability (staying power) and texture of the beaten whites. Although there are competing theories about what's at work here (some think the acidity of the copper, some think it's ions), it really does work. Unfortunately copper bowls are expensive (and also a pain to keep bright and clean), so the next best alternative is either to use a pinch of cream of tartar (tartaric acid) in the whites or to pour a couple of teaspoons of vinegar into the mixing bowl and then wipe it out with a paper towel. The trace of vinegar (acetic acid) that remains also seems to help stabilize the whites. Also, it's imperative that the whites are absolutely free of any fat. Even a tiny speck of the yolk will cause the whites to be less stable and they won't whip up nearly as much. A final note—eggs are easier to separate when cold. However, for maximum puff and volume, the whites should be allowed to come to room temperature before whipping.

basic cheese soufflé

SERVES 4 TO 6

This is the one to get started with because it incorporates all of the individual techniques for putting a soufflé together. Traditionally, the soufflé is baked in a straight-sided dish that the French call a charlotte. They are nifty looking, usually white with fluted sides, and are widely available in cookware stores (and there's a good chance you already own one even if you've never thought of making a soufflé). You can, however, use any round oven-proof dish that is straight-sided, at least 4 inches deep, with a capacity of 6 cups or so.

6 eggs
4 tablespoons butter
2 tablespoons finely and freshly grated
   Parmesan or Asiago cheese
3 tablespoons flour
1 cup milk or light cream, warmed
   (a perfect use for the microwave)

1/2 teaspoon freshly grated nutmeg
1 teaspoon salt
1/2 teaspoon freshly grated pepper,
   preferably white
2 tablespoons finely chopped chives
1 cup finely grated Gruyère, cheddar, or
   other melting cheese of your choice

PREHEAT THE OVEN to 375°F.

SEPARATING THE EGGS: Put all the egg whites in a perfectly clean, grease-free large bowl. Put 4 of the egg yolks into a smaller bowl. You will have 2 egg yolks left over. (If you are new to separating eggs, the easiest way is to crack the shell firmly, then pull the halves apart over the egg whites bowl, catching the yolk in one half and letting the white run out. Rock the yolk back and forth between the two shell halves, letting as much of the white run out as possible. Drop the yolk into the yolk bowl. It is very important not to get any yolk into the egg whites—they won't beat up if you do. But it doesn't matter if there's white in with the yolks—there always is.) Set the 2 bowls of beautifully separated eggs aside.

PREPARING THE BAKING DISH: With your fingers, lightly rub a tablespoon or so of the butter all around the inside of the dish. Sprinkle the Parmesan inside the dish and roll the dish around in your hands to lightly coat the entire inside—the bottom and all the way up the sides. Set the dish aside in the refrigerator to chill a bit. A chilled dish seems to keep the butter in suspension better as the soufflé bakes.

PREPARING THE SAUCE BASE: Melt the remaining butter in a saucepan over medium heat. Add the flour and cook, stirring, for 2 to 3 minutes without letting it brown (this step cooks the flour so that it doesn't have a raw "floury" taste). Slowly whisk in the warm milk, a little at a time. Bring the mixture to a boil, stirring constantly, and cook for 3 to 4 minutes. The sauce will be very thick. Stir in the nutmeg, salt, and pepper and remove the pan from the heat. What you've made here is a white sauce, or béchamel. Beat a little of this warm base slowly into the egg yolks. This "tempers" or gradually warms them so that they are less likely to scramble. Whisk this mixture back into the rest of the base and set aside.

BEATING THE EGG WHITES: In a clean bowl, with a hand or stand mixer beat the egg whites just until stiff but still shiny and moist-looking as they are in the photograph at lower left. This means that the fluffy egg whites should stay in standing peaks when you lift out the beaters. (If the whites are no longer shiny and start to "clump," they have been overbeaten, as in the photograph at right.) See Improving the Stability of Whipped Egg Whites (page 170).

FOLDING THE EGG WHITES AND FINISHING THE SOUFFLÉ: Sprinkle the chives over the sauce base and with a rubber or silicone spatula, stir a quarter of the whipped egg whites into the base. Do this quickly. This lightens the mixture so that you can fold in the remaining whites. Here's a little lesson in folding: Scoop the rest of the whites onto the top of the sauce base. With the edge of the spatula, cut down into the whites, drag the spatula along the bottom of the bowl toward you, and bring the sauce mixture over the top of the whites. Turn the bowl a quarter of a turn, and sprinkle on some of the grated Gruyère. Cut down through the whites, drag the spatula along the bottom, and bring the sauce mixture over the top. Repeat until the whites, cheese, and sauce are just combined (see photograph opposite). This is one of those techniques that's harder to describe than to demonstrate, but it's worth trying to do it right. What should be going through your mind is that you are doing every-thing you can to thoroughly and evenly mix the egg whites, sauce base, and cheese without deflating the egg whites. Stirring will deflate them.

Spoon the mixture into the prepared dish, gently smoothing the top and bake for 25 to 30 minutes or until the soufflé is puffed and golden brown (see Note). *Keep the door closed for at least the first 20 minutes so that the soufflé can set. If your oven doesn't have a glass window and you're tempted to peek,* **don't!** When done, serve immediately. To maintain as much of the puff as possible when serving, plunge an upright serving spoon and fork straight down into the center of the soufflé and then pull the crust apart and scoop out a serving.

Congratulations.

NOTE: For a firmer soufflé, bake in a 325°F. oven for 35 to 40 minutes.

variations

SPINACH OR BROCCOLI SOUFFLÉ Stir ½ cup cooked and finely chopped spinach or broccoli into the warm sauce base after the addition of the egg yolks. Reduce the grated Gruyère quantity to ½ cup.

MUSHROOM SOUFFLÉ Stir ¾ cup very finely minced oven-dried portabella mushroom (page 117) into the base before the egg whites are added. Reduce the Gruyère quantity to ½ cup.

SEAFOOD SOUFFLÉ Sauté 3 tablespoons finely chopped shallots or green onions in a little butter or olive oil until soft. Add 3 tablespoons white wine and continue to cook until the wine is evaporated. Remove from the heat, and add ½ to 1 cup finely chopped or diced shrimp, crab, or salmon (smoked or otherwise), and stir into the warm sauce base after the addition of the egg yolks. Reduce the grated Gruyère quantity to ⅓ cup.

SOUFFLÉ ON A PLATTER You don't have to bake a soufflé in a dish. You can bake any soufflé flat on an ovenproof platter. It's still a soufflé. One of my favorite dishes for company is to take the Basic Cheese Soufflé mixture above and mound it over fresh asparagus that has been cooked briefly but is still crisp. Sprinkle the egg mixture with a little additional cheese and bake for 15 to 18 minutes in a preheated 425°F. oven or until the soufflé is puffed and brown. Serve it immediately. You can do the same thing with other vegetables like endive or cooked artichoke hearts. Also, experiment with fish fillets, like salmon or any other that will cook in the same time as the soufflé.

INDIVIDUAL SOUFFLÉS All soufflés can also be baked in individual ramekins prepared as you would a larger dish. Cooking time will be 18 to 20 minutes or so depending on the mixture.

cheese grits soufflé

SERVES 6 TO 8

One of the hallmarks of Southern cookin' is grits—ground dent corn simmered with water, milk, or stock, whose most famous accompaniment is red-eye gravy made from ham fat and coffee. (I worked with a chef from the South who swore by the addition of a little Coca-Cola.) Here, grits are woven into a soufflé. Use old-fashioned stone-ground grits if at all possible. They take longer to cook, but the flavor is infinitely better than the so-called instant or quick-cooking varieties. I love the grits from Hoppin' John's in Charleston, South Carolina. Any cooked cereal—farina, cream of rice, cream of wheat— can be the base for a soufflé. Use these proportions to guide your experiments.

2 tablespoons butter

2 tablespoons freshly grated Parmesan
   cheese

2 cups homemade chicken or vegetable
   stock or your favorite canned broth

1 cup light cream or half-and-half

1 cup grits, preferably stone-ground

6 large eggs

1 1/2 cups grated cheddar, fontina, or
   Gruyère cheese

3 tablespoons finely minced or mashed
   poached or roasted garlic

3 tablespoons chopped chives

Salt and freshly ground pepper

Drops of hot sauce to taste

BUTTER A 2-QUART soufflé or straight-sided baking dish and lightly coat with the Parmesan, turning the dish to coat the whole interior. Chill in the refrigerator.

In a deep saucepan over high heat, bring 1 cup of water, the stock, and the cream to a boil. Stir in the grits, reduce the heat, and stir regularly until the mixture is smooth, creamy, and thick, about 15 minutes.

Separate the eggs, leaving the whites in a large bowl and the yolks in a medium bowl.

Beat the egg yolks and then slowly beat in a little of the grits mixture to warm and temper the yolks. Stir in the rest of the grits, along with the cheese, garlic, and chives, and slightly overseason (yes, that's right) with salt, pepper, and drops of hot sauce. You can set this mixture aside covered and at room temperature for up to 2 hours before proceeding.

Preheat the oven to 375°F. In a separate bowl, beat the egg whites until stiff. Stir a quarter of the whites into the grits mixture to lighten it and then fold in the remaining whites and spoon the mixture into the chilled soufflé dish. Bake for 35 to 40 minutes or until the mixture is set, puffed, and golden brown. Serve immediately.

chocolate soufflé

The procedure for making a chocolate soufflé is exactly the same as for making a cheese soufflé. For more detailed descriptions of techniques, see Basic Cheese Soufflé (page 171). This chocolate soufflé is a little denser than traditional versions; its great attribute, however, is that it can be prepped ahead and held in the refrigerator for up to a day before baking. Allow a little longer baking time if you are taking it straight from the refrigerator.

Unsalted butter and granulated sugar for the dishes
4 large eggs
8 ounces finely chopped, good quality bittersweet chocolate
1 tablespoon unsalted butter
1 tablespoon flour
1/2 cup milk, warmed
1 teaspoon vanilla extract

2 teaspoons finely grated orange zest
1/8 teaspoon cream of tartar
1/4 cup sugar
Garnish if you like with powdered sugar or lightly sweetened raspberry puree (just throw some fresh or frozen raspberries into the food processor with a little sugar; strain if you don't like the little seeds), or both

PREHEAT THE OVEN to 375°F.

PREPARING THE BAKING DISHES: Lightly butter eight 1/2-cup soufflé dishes or a 1 1/2-quart soufflé dish. Sprinkle with granulated sugar, shaking and rotating the dishes to coat every surface, then pour out any extra sugar. Refrigerate the dishes until ready to use.

SEPARATING THE EGGS: Separate the eggs, leaving the whites in a large bowl and the yolks in a small one. Lightly beat the yolks. Set it all aside.

PREPARING THE SAUCE BASE: Melt the chocolate in a double boiler over barely simmering water, stirring occasionally, and set aside. In a saucepan, melt the butter, add the flour, and cook over medium heat for 2 to 3 minutes. Add the milk and whisk until the mixture is smooth, then bring to a boil. Reduce the heat and continue to cook for 3 to 4 minutes or until the sauce base is very thick. Remove from the heat, and whisk a little of the warm base mixture into the egg yolks to temper them. Then whisk this mixture into the remaining base. Stir in the melted chocolate, vanilla, and zest, and set aside.

BEATING THE EGG WHITES: In a separate bowl, beat the egg whites with the cream of tartar until soft peaks form (they should still be drooping over, not standing up stiffly, when you lift up the beaters). Sprinkle in the ¼ cup sugar gradually and continue to beat until the whites are stiff but not dry.

FOLDING THE EGG WHITES AND FINISHING THE SOUFFLÉ: Stir a quarter of the whites into the chocolate mixture to lighten it, and then carefully fold in the remaining whites. Pour the mixture into the prepared soufflé dishes and place on a baking sheet. (You don't need the baking sheet for a single large soufflé dish.)

Bake for 15 to 17 minutes, until a wooden skewer inserted into the center of the soufflé comes out moist but not gooey. Soufflés will puff and crack before they are done, so don't worry. One large soufflé will take 35 to 40 minutes.

Remove from the oven, dust with powdered sugar, and garnish each serving with a spoonful or two of fresh raspberry puree, if desired.

twice-baked goat cheese soufflés with watercress and oven-dried tomatoes

SERVES 6

The preparation of this soufflé mixture is the same as for the cheese and chocolate soufflés above. I've condensed the instructions here, but you can refer to those recipes if you need a little more support. The technique of twice-baking is a little different in that you first bake the soufflés in a water bath. The resulting texture is more pudding-like than the Basic Cheese Soufflé above.

5 tablespoons butter

4 eggs

4 tablespoons flour

1 ½ cups warm milk

4 ounces fresh soft goat cheese

1 tablespoon freshly grated Parmesan cheese

2 tablespoons mixed chopped fresh herbs, such as parsley, chives, and tarragon

Salt and freshly ground black pepper to taste

2 cups light cream or half-and-half

2 large bunches watercress, woody stems discarded

6 ripe Roma or other tomatoes, oven-dried (see page 117) and cut into large dice

1 teaspoon finely grated lemon zest

PREHEAT THE OVEN to 360°F.

Using 1 tablespoon of the butter, lightly coat the insides of six ½-cup soufflé dishes and refrigerate. Separate the eggs. You will need 4 egg whites and 3 egg yolks. (You can throw out or save the extra—see page 181.) Melt the remaining butter in a saucepan, stir in the flour, and cook over medium heat for 2 to 3 minutes. Gradually stir in the milk and bring just to a boil. Reduce the heat and simmer for 3 to 4 minutes, stirring regularly.

Mash the goat cheese and add it to the milk mixture, along with the Parmesan and herbs. Stir until smooth and remove from the heat. Cool for a few minutes and then stir in the egg yolks. Season to taste with salt and pepper.

Separately beat the egg whites to stiff peaks and fold quickly into the cheese mixture. Divide the mixture among the buttered dishes and smooth the surfaces. Place the dishes in a baking pan with raised sides, and pour boiling water into the pan to come two-thirds up the sides of the soufflé dishes. Transfer to the preheated oven and bake for 20 minutes or until the soufflés are firm to the touch and well puffed. Remove the soufflé dishes from the oven and the pan and cool slightly.

With your fingers, gently ease the soufflés out of the dishes and place them in a lightly buttered, ovenproof dish just large enough to hold them so that they are not touching. Cover loosely with plastic until ready to serve.

To serve, preheat the oven to 375°F. Remove the plastic and pour the cream over the soufflés to moisten them well. Bake in the preheated oven for 15 minutes or until the soufflés have swelled and are golden brown. Reserve the warmed cream from the baking dish.

Arrange the watercress on plates. Place a warm soufflé in the middle of each plate. Pour the warm cream over the soufflés and sprinkle the tomatoes and lemon zest over them. Serve immediately.

sweet semolina soufflé

SERVES 6

Semolina is the hard durum wheat used to make the best dried pastas. It is widely available at Italian markets and also by mail-order through many baking suppliers, such as The Baker's Catalog. In countries around the Mediterranean, semolina also serves as the base for various sweet desserts. This soufflé is relatively dense and pudding-like.

Unsalted butter and granulated sugar
   for the dishes
2 cups half-and-half
1/2 teaspoon cardamom seeds, lightly
   crushed
1-inch piece of vanilla bean
1 small cinnamon stick, broken
1 3-inch strip of orange peel
1/3 cup sugar
Pinch of salt
1/2 cup coarse semolina flour
3 large eggs, separated

1 tablespoon finely grated lemon zest
1/4 cup coarsely chopped golden raisins,
   tossed with 1 teaspoon flour to
   lightly coat

Garnish if you like with powdered sugar
   or a lightly sweetened berry puree
   (just throw some fresh or frozen
   berries into the food processor with a
   little sugar; strain if you don't like the
   little seeds or bits of skin), or both

PREHEAT THE OVEN to 350°F.

Lightly butter six 1/2-cup ramekins, sprinkle lightly with sugar, and turn to evenly coat. Set aside in the refrigerator.

Combine the half-and-half, cardamom, vanilla bean, cinnamon, and orange peel in a saucepan and bring to a simmer. Remove the pan from the heat and set aside to steep for 20 minutes. Strain the liquid into a clean saucepan. Split the vanilla bean and scrape the seeds into the cream. Add the sugar and salt and return the liquid to a simmer over medium heat. Whisk the semolina into the liquid in a steady stream, reduce the heat, and continue to stir until the mixture thickens, about 2 minutes. Remove from the heat.

In a small bowl, lightly beat the egg yolks, then beat in a little of the semolina mixture to warm and temper them. Stir the yolk mixture into the rest of the semolina. In a separate bowl, beat the egg whites to stiff peaks. Stir a quarter of the egg whites into the semolina base to lighten the mixture and then fold in the remaining whites along with the zest and raisins. Spoon into the prepared ramekins and arrange in a baking pan just large enough to hold the ramekins without them touching. Pour enough boiling water into the pan to reach three-quarters up the sides of the dishes and bake for 30 to 35 minutes or until the tops are puffed and golden brown. Remove from the pan and let them cool for a few minutes.

Unmold each soufflé by turning it out into your hand, and then place it right side up on a serving plate. Spoon on some berry puree and dust with powdered sugar, if desired. Serve immediately.

what do I do with the egg yolks if I haven't used them all in the soufflé?

Well, you can freeze egg yolks, but yolks frozen alone become very gelatinous and are almost impossible to use. So beat either ⅛ teaspoon salt or 1 teaspoon sugar or corn syrup into the yolks before they're frozen. Obviously, whether you add salt or sugar will depend on how you think you'll use them later on (be sure to label the container). You can keep them covered in the freezer for up to 4 months. Extra egg whites are much easier. Just pour them into a container, seal them well, and they last in the freezer up to 6 months.

11

two approaches to pasta, west and east

Pasta is a staple for most of us. It has existed in Asia for many centuries and, despite the legend of Marco Polo, it has been part of Mediterranean cuisine since the Roman Empire and probably before. Noodles and filled pastas are eaten all over the world, but I'm most drawn to preparations with Italian and Asian points of view, so that's what we're working with here.

You already know what's great about pasta: you can cook it quickly and easily, it offers limitless possibilities for saucing and flavoring, and it's a great value. The downside of this ease is that it's made us lazy, or perhaps disrespectful. We seem to think that since the pasta is so easy to prepare, we might as well throw any old thing from a jar or refrigerator case on top of it. I say: resist! Take advantage of pasta's ease not by belittling it, but by showing it off. With the tiniest bit of effort, you can make a fresh and interesting sauce—and pasta will become a treat instead of a fallback.

Is fresh pasta better than dried?

No. They are two different foods with different properties. Fresh pasta is one of the world's great foods, and it's surprisingly easy to make from scratch, but our interest here is in sauces to pair with the long-lasting, commercially prepared dried pasta already filling your cupboard. Don't apologize for using dried pasta. It too is a great food.

Are all dried pastas the same?

The quality of dried pasta depends especially on the flour from which it's made. Good Italian pasta is made from hard durum wheat, also called semolina, because it is very tough and will not turn starchy or gluey when cooked—unless, of course, you overcook it! It keeps its texture even when softened, what the Italian call *al dente* or "to the tooth." This chewiness is highly prized. Look for the words "100 percent hard durum wheat" or "semolina" when you buy dried pasta. And if you ever see imported Italian artisanal pasta (labelled *artigianale* in Italian) for sale, buy it. Because of the old machinery used to extrude and shape the pasta (bronze instead of teflon or stainless steel), the lower temperature at which it's dried, and the superior flour used, this pasta has a much rougher surface texture and higher residual humidity. This makes it cook more evenly, and absorb and hold the sauce better—it is a revelation. Italian artisanal brands may be pricey for pasta, but even at boutique prices, they're cheap for dinner—and worth every cent.

Asian pastas are made from a number of flours, including wheat, rice, buckwheat, yam, and mung bean. They have different flavors, textures, and traditional uses, and there are encyclopedic books devoted to Asian noodles if you're interested in learning more.

The key thing to remember is that the flavor of the pasta is an important component. Many people have the mistaken idea that pasta is only there to carry the sauce. Some of the greatest pasta dishes, Mediterranean or Asian, focus on the pasta, with the sauce playing a secondary role.

Why so many different shapes? And must clam sauce always be eaten with linguini?

I've suggested shapes with each sauce in this lesson but, as you've no doubt experienced, there are more shapes and sizes out there every day. Familiar combinations are part tradition, part whimsy. Classically, long pasta goes with thinner-bodied, smoother sauces like tomato. Chunkier, thicker sauces tend to go better with shorter pasta. The idea is to find a match that maximizes contact between pasta and sauce and is easy to manage on the fork.

What about adding oil to the pasta cooking water and rinsing cooked pasta?

You'll often see these instructions in pasta recipes. Don't add oil to pasta water! It doesn't do anything other than float on top and then, when you drain the cooked pasta, coat it so your sauce tends to slip off. Rinsing also creates slippery pasta. When cooked pasta is just drained, its surface is a little starchy and sticky, so sauce clings better. This is the preferred approach for Italian pasta dishes. Interestingly, however, most Asian pastas *are* rinsed after cooking because the slippery texture is prized. Also, Asian pastas are often added later in the preparation of a dish or are used cold, so rinsing is a way to keep them from sticking and also stop them from cooking further.

For Italian-inspired pastas, the hot, cooked pasta is combined with the sauce just before serving, which is the best way to maximize contact between noodle and sauce and to give the pasta a chance to absorb a little of the sauce before it gets to your mouth. In the Italian method, if the cooked pasta is tossed together with the sauce as soon as it is drained, you don't have to worry about sticking and clumping. Make sure the sauce is ready to go by the time the pasta is ready to drain, have a big enough serving bowl at the ready, toss, and serve immediately.

THE RECIPES in this lesson are divided by the cuisines that inspired them, and I hope that will open up your pasta horizons rather than restricting them.

ITALIAN-INSPIRED PASTA There is a world of possibility beyond tomato sauce and pesto. The best sauces tend to be highly flavored, with the goal of complementing the taste and texture of the pasta without overwhelming it.

lemon sauce with spaghettini

SERVES 4 TO 6

1 pound dried spaghettini (thin spaghetti)
1/2 cup (1 stick) butter
2 tablespoons olive oil
2 tablespoons finely chopped shallots or green onions (white parts only)
1 tablespoon finely chopped garlic
2 tablespoons finely grated lemon zest

3 tablespoons fresh lemon juice
Salt and freshly ground pepper
3 tablespoons chopped fresh basil leaves
3 tablespoons chopped fresh parsley leaves
3/4 cup freshly grated Pecorino, Parmesan, or Crottin cheese, plus extra for garnish

BRING AT LEAST 4 quarts of lightly salted water to a boil in a large pot. Stir in the spaghettini and cook until al dente. Drain, reserving a cup of the pasta cooking water.

While the pasta is cooking, melt the butter and olive oil over medium heat in a large sauté pan. Add the shallots and garlic, and sauté until the vegetables are softened but not brown, 1 to 2 minutes. Stir in the lemon zest and juice and season lightly with salt and pepper. Stir in the hot spaghettini, and remove from the heat.

Add the herbs and cheese and toss quickly, adding enough of the reserved pasta water to keep everything moist. Serve in warm bowls with additional cheese on top, if desired.

artichoke and olive sauce with conchiglioni

SERVES 4

This recipe is an excellent demonstration of chopping as both technique and flavor-maker. The sauce isn't even cooked, but by chopping all these tasty things up small, you end up with a dish that is vibrant and complex in the mouth, full of flavor and texture.

Conchiglioni are shell-shaped pasta, a nice shape for a sauce like this, because the little bits of olive, artichoke, and pepper get trapped inside the shell, making each bite different. This is great for a weeknight supper, because you can toss the sauce ingredients together one night (or weekend afternoon) and have an instant great meal the next.

I 6½-ounce jar marinated artichoke hearts, drained and coarsely chopped
I cup diced red bell peppers, raw or roasted (see Glossary and Pantry)
⅓ cup chopped, pitted green or black olives, or a combination
⅓ cup chopped lightly toasted walnuts
¾ cup loosely packed fresh basil leaves, chopped (you should have about ⅓ cup)

I tablespoon minced garlic
¾ cup extra virgin olive oil
⅓ cup freshly grated Pecorino or Parmesan cheese, plus extra for garnish
I teaspoon finely grated lemon zest
Drops of fresh lemon juice to taste
Freshly ground pepper to taste
12 ounces dried conchiglioni

COMBINE THE ARTICHOKE hearts, peppers, olives, walnuts, basil, garlic, olive oil, cheese, zest, juice, and pepper in a serving bowl (or a storage container if you're making it ahead) and stir it all together. Store covered in the refrigerator for up to 3 days. Bring it up to room temperature before using.

Cook the pasta in lightly salted boiling water until al dente. Drain and toss with the sauce. Serve immediately with a sprinkling of additional cheese, if desired.

laurie's broccoli sauce for pasta

SERVES 4 TO 6

This is a recipe of sorts from the late Laurie Colwin, a novelist and editor who also wrote for Gourmet magazine. I was always deeply touched and amused by her writing. She talked about recipes in the larger context of how the preparation of food was an essential ritual of life and love. Here's a quote to illustrate: "The table is a meeting place, a gathering ground, the source of sustenance and nourishment, festivity, safety, and satisfaction. A person cooking is a person giving: even the simplest food is a gift. . . . I know that young children will wander away from the table, and that family life is never smooth, and that life itself is full, not only of charm and warmth and comfort but of sorrow and tears. But whether we are happy or sad, we must be fed. Both happy and sad people can be cheered up by a nice meal!"

Many of her essays and columns are collected in two books: Home Cooking and More Home Cooking. They were published in the early 1990s, so you may have to search for them, but they're worth the effort! I wish that I could have known her personally but in many ways, I feel that I do.

And if you need a little more guidance than Laurie's casual description below, here are some suggested quantities for the ingredients:

I pound broccoli crowns (no stems)
3 tablespoons olive oil
2 large garlic cloves
Salt and freshly ground pepper
Juice of ½ lemon

⅓ cup homemade chicken stock or
 your favorite canned broth, to thin
 sauce, if necessary
I pound dried ziti or fusilli
½ cup freshly grated Parmesan or
 Pecorino cheese

"NOW TO broccoli. How some people hate it! However, it turns into a sleek, rich pasta sauce. First you steam it. Then you sauté it in dark green olive oil with two cloves of garlic until the garlic is soft. Then you toss it all in the blender with pepper, a pinch of salt, the juice of a half lemon, more olive oil and serve it on ziti or fusilli with lots of grated cheese, and no one will suspect what is being served."

fresh mussel sauce with linguini

SERVES 6

Fresh mussels are quick and easy to cook and practically make their own sauce. Those that we buy in the market today are generally farm-raised and, as a result, are much cleaner and don't need to be "purged" of grit and sand before cooking. Substitute clams if you like them better. The traditional recipe calls for a long pasta but you can use anything you want. You can also remove the mussels from the shell before combining with the pasta. I don't serve this with cheese, but you can if you want.

6 tablespoons butter or olive oil
I cup finely chopped onions
2 tablespoons finely chopped garlic
2 cups crisp, light-bodied white wine
⅓ cup chopped fresh parsley leaves
I tablespoon finely grated lemon zest
I teaspoon fennel seeds, crushed (fold in waxed paper or a clean envelope and smack with the bottom of a skillet if you don't have a mortar and pestle)

Big pinch of red pepper flakes (optional)
4 pounds mussels in the shell, well washed and "beards" removed
Freshly ground pepper
I pound dried linguini

HEAT THE BUTTER in a pot large enough to hold the mussels. Add the onions and garlic and sauté over medium heat until softened but not brown, 2 minutes or so. Add the wine, parsley, zest, fennel, red pepper, if desired, mussels, and a grinding or two of black pepper. Cover tightly and bring to a boil over high heat. Reduce the heat to medium and simmer for 3 to 4 minutes, still covered, until the mussels open. Discard any that don't open.

While the mussels are cooking, cook the linguini in lightly salted boiling water until al dente. Drain, place in warm bowls, and ladle the mussels and their cooking liquid over the pasta. Serve immediately.

tuna sauce for pasta

MAKES ABOUT 2 CUPS

In Italy, this sauce is a traditional component of vitello tonnato, a classic dish of cold braised veal sliced and garnished with this sauce along with oil-cured olives, lemon slices, and braised young vegetables. It's also great with pasta, either hot or cool. I especially like it cold on a warm summer day. This recipe makes enough to sauce up to 1 1/2 pounds dried pasta. If you are concerned about eating or serving a raw egg yolk, you can substitute one that has been coddled or even hard cooked. If you can find Italian tuna in olive oil, buy it for this sauce. This is the best tuna noodle casserole you'll ever eat.

3/4 cup extra virgin olive oil
1 teaspoon minced garlic
1 6 1/2-ounce can tuna packed in oil
1 egg yolk
4 to 6 anchovy fillets, rinsed
3 tablespoons fresh lemon juice
1/3 cup heavy cream

1/4 cup or so homemade chicken stock
   or your favorite canned broth
3 tablespoons drained and chopped
   capers
1/3 cup minced fresh flat-leaf parsley
Salt and freshly ground pepper,
   preferably white

IN A BLENDER or food processor, combine the olive oil, garlic, tuna, egg yolk, anchovies, and lemon juice and process briefly to puree. Transfer the mixture to a small mixing bowl and stir in the cream and stock gradually until the sauce is thick enough to coat the back of a spoon. Stir in the capers and parsley, taste, and season with salt and pepper, if you think it needs it.

a "sauce" of roasted peppers, fried eggs, and bread crumbs

SERVES 4

The sauce here happens as the ingredients are mixed. The toasted bread crumb topping is often used in Italy to dress up simple pasta dishes. These are also delicious sprinkled on simply cooked vegetables and fish.

3 tablespoons butter

I cup coarse dry bread crumbs (I like Japanese-style panko)

I tablespoon finely chopped garlic, either fresh or poached

1/2 cup freshly grated Parmesan or Pecorino cheese, plus extra for serving

1/4 cup finely chopped fresh parsley leaves

2 large red bell peppers

2 tablespoons capers, drained and rinsed

6 tablespoons extra virgin olive oil

Salt and freshly ground black pepper

I pound dried pasta (shape of your choice, such as bow-ties or radiatore)

4 large eggs

MELT THE BUTTER in a large skillet over medium heat. As soon as the foam begins to disappear, stir in the bread crumbs. Lower the heat slightly and cook, stirring constantly, until the bread crumbs begin to brown. Add the garlic and sauté for a minute more or until the crumbs are golden brown. Remove from the heat, cool, and stir in the Parmesan and parsley. Set aside. (The crumbs can be made a day or two ahead; store tightly covered in the refrigerator. Wait to add the parsley until serving time.)

Char or roast the peppers, then peel, seed, and chop into 1/4-inch dice (see Glossary and Pantry). Be sure to catch all the juices and add to the chopped peppers in a bowl. Stir in the capers, 3 tablespoons of the olive oil, and salt and pepper to taste and set aside.

Cook the pasta in at least 6 quarts of lightly salted boiling water until al dente. While the pasta is cooking, heat the remaining 3 tablespoons of olive oil in a sauté pan and gently fry the eggs until the whites are set but the yolks are still runny. Season well with salt and pepper.

Set aside 1 cup of the pasta cooking water, then drain the pasta. Divide the hot pasta among 4 warm pasta bowls and top with the red pepper mixture. Place a hot egg on top of each serving and then sprinkle with the bread crumb mixture. Serve immediately, instructing eaters to toss the mixture with 2 forks, gently breaking up the egg whites and letting the yolks act as a sauce. Add a little of the reserved hot pasta water if the mixture needs thinning. Enjoy immediately, passing and adding a little more cheese and pepper, if desired.

green herb sauce for pasta

MAKES ABOUT 2 CUPS

Tofu adds creaminess and body to this sauce without all the saturated fat that you'd get from cream. And of course, soy-based tofu also contributes healthful phytochemicals and quality protein. This is also good on either hot or cool pasta; the recipe makes enough sauce for 1 pound dried pasta.

I cup chopped fresh basil leaves
I cup chopped fresh spinach or romaine lettuce
$1/3$ cup chopped fresh chives or green onion tops
I tablespoon chopped fresh garlic or 3 tablespoons chopped poached garlic

$1/2$ block (about $3/4$ cup) silken tofu or soft regular tofu
$1/3$ cup freshly grated Parmesan or Pecorino cheese, plus extra for serving
2 teaspoons toasted sesame oil or hazelnut oil
Salt and freshly ground pepper to taste

COMBINE ALL THE ingredients in a food processor or blender and blend until smooth. The garlic flavor gets stronger and the greens start to lose their color the longer the sauce stands, so I think it's best used within an hour or so after pureeing.

NOTE: See Soy Foods lesson (page 286) for information on types of tofu.

ASIAN-INSPIRED PASTA Asian cuisines take a different approach to noodle dishes. For one thing, the sauce is not the main show, as it is in Italian and Italian-inspired dishes. Asian pasta dishes often include some other stuff—vegetables, cubes of tofu, bits of chicken, meat, or fish—that are not incorporated into the sauce. The sauces tend to be thinner and lighter and function as more of a foil for the noodles and other featured foodstuffs than as the star attraction. This next group of recipes of Asian-inspired pasta dishes is therefore set up differently. If you make the whole recipe, you'll generally have a complete, one-dish meal. The sauces and pasta alone together, while perhaps not substantial enough for a main meal, make wonderful side dishes, savory snacks, or midnight suppers—which happens to be a popular Italian use for a lightly sauced pasta dish too.

cold soba noodle salad
with orange soy sauce

In Japan, cold noodles dressed with a sweet and salty sauce using soy are served everywhere. This recipe transforms that dish into a delicious salad that I often use as a base for grilled vegetables, meat, and fish. Another kid-friendly taste sensation.

1 pound soba noodles or other thin noodles like angel hair
Drops of olive oil
3 cups lightly packed watercress leaves, woody stems removed

Orange Soy Sauce

Garnish if you like with fresh daikon sprouts or other radish sprouts

COOK THE SOBA noodles in boiling salted water until just done but still firm. Rinse in cold water and toss with drops of olive oil. Arrange the watercress on a serving platter or plates and top with the noodles. Drizzle with Orange Soy Sauce and top with daikon sprouts, if desired.

orange soy sauce

5 tablespoons soy sauce
1/2 cup fresh orange juice
2 tablespoons seasoned rice vinegar
2 teaspoons toasted sesame oil
1/4 teaspoon crushed red chile flakes

1 teaspoon peeled and very finely minced fresh ginger
1 teaspoon sugar, or to taste
3 tablespoons olive oil

COMBINE ALL THE ingredients and shake, whisk, or blend in bursts to emulsify and thicken. Adjust the seasoning to your taste. Store covered in the refrigerator for up to 3 days. MAKES ABOUT 1 1/4 CUPS

saigon shrimp with rice sticks and nuoc cham sauce

SERVES 4 TO 6

Many of the classic flavors and ingredients of Southeast Asia come together in this bowl. To be politically correct, I guess I should rename this Ho Chi Minh City Shrimp. The sauce is a favorite that I make up in larger batches and often toss with cooked thin noodles like Japanese somen for a quick small meal. Rice sticks, which are made from rice flour, come in a variety of widths and lengths. While the widest varieties need cooking like other dried noodles, the very fine ones are typically just soaked in warm water before being added to soups, stir-fries, or other preparations. You can also make this dish with bean thread noodles.

¼ pound thin rice stick noodles or vermicelli

1½ pounds medium shrimp, brined if desired, peeled, deveined, and patted dry (pages 271–72)

2 teaspoons Asian fish sauce

2 teaspoons peeled and finely minced fresh ginger

4 tablespoons vegetable oil

4 cups bean sprouts, rinsed and drained

½ cup garlic chives or 1 cup scallions (green parts only) cut into ¼-inch lengths

½ cup Nuoc Cham Sauce

⅓ cup coarsely chopped toasted peanuts

⅓ cup fresh cilantro leaves

Garnish if you like with fresh mint sprigs

COVER THE RICE stick noodles with warm water and soften for 20 minutes. Drain and arrange on a serving platter.

Toss the shrimp with the fish sauce and ginger and set aside. Heat a wok or heavy skillet over high heat and add 2 tablespoons of oil. When hot, quickly sauté the bean sprouts and chives for about 20 seconds. Spoon the cooked vegetables over the noodles.

Add the remaining 2 tablespoons of oil to the wok and sauté the shrimp over high heat until they just turn pink, about 2 minutes. Arrange over the rice sticks and vegetables and top with several spoonfuls of Nuoc Cham Sauce and a sprinkling of peanuts and cilantro. Garnish with mint sprigs, if using, and serve immediately.

nuoc cham sauce

²/₃ cup **Asian fish sauce (see Glossary and Pantry)**

²/₃ cup **rice vinegar**

Finely grated zest and juice from large limes

2 teaspoons **seeded and finely minced hot red chiles**

2 tablespoons **minced garlic**

5 tablespoons **sugar, or to taste**

COMBINE ALL THE ingredients and stir or shake to dissolve the sugar. Store covered in the refrigerator for up to 5 days. MAKES ABOUT 1¹/₂ CUPS

cold noodle salad with coconut peanut sauce

SERVES 4 GENEROUSLY

I make this at home all the time. If you can find them, fresh Chinese egg noodles are my favorites with this sauce; alternatively, use any fresh or dried long pasta, including good old spaghetti. I've used cooked chicken here (my favorite is the Ginger-Poached Chicken on page 214) but you can use shrimp or substitute sliced, oven-dried mushrooms (see page 117). In my experience, this dish has great kid appeal. (Omit the chili-garlic sauce if you need to.)

12 ounces fresh Chinese egg noodles or other fresh long noodles or 8 ounces dried long noodles of your choice
1 teaspoon toasted sesame oil
1 ½ cups finely julienned red bell peppers
1 ½ cups peeled, seeded cucumber sliced at an angle (for looks)

2 cups fresh bean sprouts or pea shoots, well washed
2 cups thinly sliced cooked chicken breast
Coconut Peanut Sauce
½ cup lightly packed fresh cilantro leaves

COOK THE NOODLES in a pot of lightly salted boiling water until just done but still firm. Drain, rinse with cold water, and drain again. Transfer to a mixing bowl, add the sesame oil, and toss to coat. Add the peppers, cucumber, and sprouts, and toss again. Arrange on a plate and top with the chicken. Cover with plastic and refrigerate for at least 30 minutes to chill. Drizzle the sauce over and sprinkle with cilantro.

coconut peanut sauce

3 tablespoons natural peanut butter
1 teaspoon Asian chili-garlic sauce
3 tablespoons homemade chicken or vegetable stock or your favorite canned broth, or water

⅓ cup stirred coconut milk
2 teaspoons packed light or dark brown sugar
2 tablespoons fresh lime juice
1 to 2 tablespoons soy sauce, or to taste

COMBINE ALL THE ingredients in a blender and blend until smooth. The sauce should have the consistency of heavy cream. Store covered in the refrigerator for up to 5 days. Return to room temperature before using.

MAKES ABOUT 1 CUP

seared scallops and noodles with salted black bean sauce

SERVES 4

This sauce uses the salted or "fermented" black beans that are a staple in Chinese cooking. They are sold in a variety of packages (see Glossary and Pantry). Finding good fresh scallops is sometimes difficult, so you can substitute whatever good fish or shellfish is available to you.

3 tablespoons olive oil

1 pound large fresh sea scallops, side muscle removed

3 tablespoons Chinese salted black beans, rinsed and chopped

2 tablespoons slivered garlic

2 tablespoons peeled and finely chopped fresh ginger

1 cup homemade chicken or fish stock or your favorite canned broth

2 tablespoons soy sauce

1 teaspoon or so sugar

1 pound fresh Chinese egg noodles or other long pasta of your choice

1/4 cup roughly chopped fresh cilantro leaves

1/2 cup thinly sliced green onions (white and green parts)

2 teaspoons lightly toasted sesame seeds

IN A WOK or nonstick skillet, heat 2 tablespoons of the olive oil and quickly sauté the scallops over high heat to brown them lightly on both sides, about 2 minutes total. Resist the temptation to move them around, which would interfere with the development of a beautiful golden crust. Be careful not to overcook them. The center of the scallop should remain translucent. Remove the scallops from the pan and set aside.

In the same pan, add the remaining tablespoon of oil, the black beans, garlic, and ginger, and sauté for 30 seconds over medium heat. Add the stock, soy sauce, and sugar, and bring to a boil. Boil for 2 minutes to reduce and thicken the sauce just slightly. Taste it and add more soy and sugar if you think it needs it. Remove the pan from the heat and keep the sauce warm.

Quickly cook the pasta in lightly salted boiling water until al dente. Drain and add to the black bean mixture. Toss, adding the scallops, cilantro, and green onions. Sprinkle with the sesame seeds and serve immediately.

part three

main
ingredient
lessons

12

chicken beyond the everyday

Why a lesson on chicken when there are none devoted to beef, pork, or lamb? There are a couple of reasons. The most obvious is that Americans eat a lot of it. It's relatively inexpensive, and there's nothing not to like about the taste. For the last twenty-five years or so, it's been the low-fat meat of choice, especially in the form of boneless, skinless breasts, which are even available on every fast-food menu in the country. Does this sound like faint praise? It is. I think chicken needs help. The other reasons for focusing on chicken are the issues around its production and labeling, which are windows onto commercial agricultural practices generally. We twenty-first century types are pretty much disconnected from the farm and any thought of how our food is grown. By understanding more, you can not only choose, buy, and eat better chicken but influence the decency and quality of this part of our food supply as well. The food called chicken has become so much a part of our daily menu that we don't even to think about the noble little birds that are its source.

I was lucky enough as a child to have spent a number of years on my grandparents' ranch in Colorado, where we had lots of chickens. They not only supplied us with eggs and meat, but as a bonus provided feathers for bedding and fertilizer for the garden. Additionally, the chickens were our best weather forecasters. We always knew that changes were in the air if the chickens "sang" at night more often than usual. If a hen or her chicks refused to leave their coops in the morning, we knew that especially heavy weather was due soon. My grandmother also used her chickens as a barometer for when to plant the garden. She believed that when the chickens molted, as they did every spring, it was a signal to begin planting. If the chickens molted from the head first, you should sow early; if from their posterior first, sow late.

Here are some chicken terms that need clarification and some issues of which we should all be aware:

"HORMONE FREE": Some of the biggest producers are now labeling their chickens "hormone free." Most consumers, I'm sure, assume that this is a good thing. Here's the scoop. Prior to 1960 or so, before being replaced by selective breeding and feed revisions, hormones were used to help make chickens more "uniform" and also to calm them down. If you've ever been around a chicken house, you know it can get pretty raucous. The truth, however, is that hormones have not been used in the poultry industry for nearly 40 years. Thus, any "hormone free" claims on poultry are irrelevant, since the entire poultry industry is "hormone free." The bigger issue is the next one.

USE OF ANTIBIOTICS: Unfortunately, it is a common practice on large factory farms to feed chickens a steady diet of antibiotics. Because they typically are grown in stressful crowded conditions, they are vulnerable to all kinds of diseases and afflictions. All it takes is for one chicken to get sick and the rest quickly follow. There is real concern among dieticians and the medical community about the consumption of "secondhand" antibiotics. (See also the discussion of farm-raised salmon, page 254).

"NATURAL" CHICKEN: This sounds great—but ever wonder what it means? In 1982, the USDA declared that any product could be labeled "natural" if it did not contain any artificial flavoring, coloring, chemical preservatives, or any other synthetic ingredient, and if the product is minimally processed. Minimal processing may include those traditional processes (smoking, roasting, freezing, drying, and fermenting) used to make food edible or preserve it or make it safe for human consumption. "Natural," as the USDA defines it, represents little more than a minimal standard. The label does not address the use of antibiotics or growth enhancers for poultry or any other growing methods. The word "natural" suggests that "natural" chickens are raised antibiotic-free—not so. Any conventionally grown chicken can qualify for a "natural" label claim.

"FREE RANGE": This joke of the '80s certainly sounds like a good and humane thing. In truth, there are no strict standards for using this term. "Free-range" generally means only that, in addition to an enclosed poultry house, the chickens have an outdoor pen, normally the same size as the house, in which to roam and forage. This does give them a little more exercise, fresh air, and sunlight, and a more varied diet than factory-raised chickens, who never go outdoors. But if you start talking to even some concerned and scrupulous chicken farmers, they'll tell you that chickens just aren't that interested in the great outdoors. The "free-range" label does not automatically guarantee humane treatment of these birds, but it delivers more for them and for us than poultry factory conditions. There are organizations that do inspect for humane treatment and certify such. Among those to contact are the Humane Society of the United States and the Humane Farming Association.

Here are my suggestions for what to look for when you buy a chicken:

1. It should be antibiotic free.

2. It should be humanely and wholesomely grown.

3. Ideally it should be organic and certified so by a reputable third party. This is now possible since the implementation of the new national organic standards, which took effect in October of 2002.

4. It should be fed a vegetarian diet, which is part of the new organic standard. Many commercially grown chickens are fed animal by-products, which we now know is a questionable practice at best. That old adage of "you are what you eat" applies equally to chickens, and as nature writer Michael Pollan says, "You are what what you eat eats too."

And now let's get into the kitchen.

How many breasts does a chicken have?

One? Two? It's one of the questions I get asked most in my cooking classes when we talk about using chicken breasts in a recipe. To be anatomically correct, chickens have one breast. (Picture a chicken walking around. . . . That front part, where you'd pin a medal or a corsage—that's the breast.) That breast is divided into two halves by the breastbone. (Picture a super-market package of "chicken breasts," bone-in, skin on, boneless, whatever. Each piece is *half* of a chicken's breast, though it is commonly called *a* breast.) Many recipe writers use some variation of the "two separate breast halves" or "one whole breast, unsplit." In real life (and that's what I'm opting for too), I think most of us define a chicken breast as half of a chicken's whole breast. . . . Okay? The French, who have always been more precise in matters of butchery and cuisine, define a chicken breast as having two *suprêmes*. This way there is no confusion.

Is the boneless, skinless breast the best the chicken has to offer?

I think if those folks who raise chickens had a choice, they'd figure out how to grow a chicken that was only breast and preferably without bones and skin! There's no question that the breast is a great cut of meat. It requires no preparation and lends itself to all kinds of saucing, flavoring, and manipulation because of its neutrality—qualities that are also the source of its limitations. The cheapest breast, and to my mind, the most flavorful, is the bone-in, skin-on breast. The next best alternative for flavor is the boneless skin-on breast, and the least desirable in terms of flavor is the boneless, skinless breast, which is also the most expensive. This last variation has become the most common because it's easy and quick to cook (a good thing) and because the Fat Police have deemed it the chicken of choice (not necessarily a good thing). If you've read about shrimp (page 268), then you know that the shells contribute a lot of flavor to a recipe. The same thing is true of the bones and skin of a chicken. Given a choice, I'd rather cook breasts, or any other part of the chicken, with the bone in and skin on. They'll not only be more flavorful (that's why we use them when we make stock) but juicier too. If fat is of concern, then remove the skin before serving and eating.

In this lesson, the recipes are organized by cooking technique: sautéing, roasting, poaching, and pan-roasting. This gives me a chance not just to talk about chicken but also to explore these basic cooking techniques and what they yield. Pot-roasting and grilling are two other ways to cook chicken to which I've devoted entire lessons (see pages 130 and 148).

GRADES AND STANDARDS FOR CHICKEN

BROILER-FRYER	A young, tender chicken about 7 weeks old that weighs 2½ to 4½ pounds when eviscerated. Cook by any method.
ROCK CORNISH GAME HEN	A small broiler-fryer weighing between 1 and 2 pounds. Usually stuffed and roasted whole.
ROASTER	An older chicken, 3 to 5 months old, which weighs 5 to 7 pounds. It yields more meat per pound than a broiler-fryer. Usually roasted whole.
CAPON	Male chickens 16 weeks to 8 months old that are surgically unsexed. They weigh 4 to 7 pounds and have generous quantities of tender, light meat. Usually roasted.
STEWING/ BAKING HEN	A mature laying hen 10 months to 1½ years old. Since the meat is less tender than that of young chickens, it's best used in moist cooking, such as stewing.
COCK or ROOSTER	A mature male chicken with coarse skin and tough, dark meat. Requires long, moist cooking.

SAUTÉING To sauté is to cook in a wide, shallow-sided pan over high heat using a small amount of butter or oil, or a combination of the two. Sautéeing chicken pieces gives you great flavor from the browning or caramelization of the skin with very little fat. That's why I recommend buying and preparing chicken skin on; if you can't buy it or you strongly prefer skinless chicken, sautéeing is still a fine approach. The outside of the meat will color a bit, but you just won't get the big flavor boost or the browned bits useful for making a pan sauce.

sauté of chicken breasts with vinegar

SERVES 4

You can find a version of this classic recipe in almost any French or "continental" cookbook from the past 75 or 100 years, and with good reason: the reduction of the pan juices, a little stock, and vinegar is piquant and easy—it just tastes elegant. If you don't like the herbs I've suggested, try others. And try different vinegars to see which you prefer. More pan sauces to accompany a sauté of chicken breasts are described in Simple Savory Sauces (page 70).

4 skin-on boneless chicken breasts, about 6 ounces each

Salt and freshly ground pepper

2 tablespoons olive oil

5 tablespoons butter

3 tablespoons finely chopped shallots or green onions (green and white parts)

I tablespoon finely chopped garlic

1/3 cup cider vinegar or red or white wine vinegar

1 1/4 cups homemade chicken stock or your favorite canned broth

I tablespoon tomato paste

2 teaspoons finely chopped fresh tarragon leaves

2 tablespoons finely chopped fresh parsley leaves

LIGHTLY SEASON THE chicken breasts with salt and pepper. In a sauté pan large enough to hold the breasts in one layer, heat the olive oil and 2 tablespoons of the butter over medium heat. Place the chicken in the pan skin side down and cook until golden brown. Turn over and cook until just done, about 8 minutes. (The best way to check is to stick a small thin knife into the thickest part. Any sign of pink, and the chicken's not ready. Try to get it out of the pan as soon as it reaches that point.) Transfer the chicken to a platter and keep it warm. (Covering the plate with foil works fine.)

Add the shallots and garlic to the pan and sauté until soft and just beginning to brown. Add the vinegar and stock, stirring to scrape up any browned bits from the bottom of the pan, and reduce the liquid over high heat until lightly thickened, about 3 minutes. Whisk in the tomato paste and any chicken juices from the platter, then take the pan off the heat and whisk in the remaining 3 tablespoons butter. Stir in the herbs and add salt and pepper to taste. Pour the pan sauce around the chicken and serve immediately.

ROASTING Roasting is a general term that refers to cooking in an oven at relatively high temperatures. Usually, the meat or other roasting food is cooked uncovered so that its exterior browns and caramelizes nicely. The conventional line between baking and roasting is the oven temperature: 350°F. or below for baking, above 400°F. for roasting. The truth of the matter is that it was probably restaurant menu writers who converted us all to universal use of the term *roast* for all uncovered oven cooking; at this particular moment, it just sounds better. Roasting works equally well with whole chickens and chicken parts.

simple soy-marinated and
roasted chicken breasts

SERVES 6

This is a favorite technique for preparing super-flavorful boneless chicken breasts. I generally roast several breasts at a time to have them on hand for salads, pasta, or other dishes that call for cooked chicken. It works equally well with chicken thighs and turkey breast. Also try this same marinade and approach with salmon steaks or fillets. Cooking times, of course, will need to be adjusted.

¾ cup soy sauce
¼ cup mirin (see Glossary and Pantry)
2 teaspoons toasted sesame oil

1 tablespoon Asian chili-garlic sauce
   (see Glossary and Pantry)
6 boneless, skinless chicken breasts

PREHEAT THE OVEN to 450°F. Combine the soy, mirin, sesame oil, and chili-garlic sauce in a dish or resealable plastic bag. Add the chicken breasts and marinate them for at least 15 minutes and up to 2 hours (remember to refrigerate them while they sit). Lightly oil a baking sheet, and arrange the breasts in a single layer. Roast for 15 minutes or until the meat is just cooked through and still juicy. If using bone-in breasts, you will need to increase the cooking time by 3 to 5 minutes.

suggestion
~ Serve on a bed of quickly sautéed spinach.
~ Slice and add either hot or cold to a salad.
~ These are delicious cold, which makes them great picnic fare.

basic roast chicken

SERVES 4 TO 6

I haven't talked much about kitchen equipment here, because I don't want people to think they can't make a recipe if they don't have the right pan. Still, having the best tool for the job can make life easier. A roasting pan is a heavyweight metal or Pyrex pan, 2 to 4 inches deep, that should accommodate a rack, which lifts the chicken above the fats and juices and allows the heat to circulate all around it. A V-shaped rack is ideal for roasting chicken (and other meats), because it holds it snugly, eliminating the need for trussing, a procedure called for in classical recipes. Collapsible-adjustable racks handle birds of varying sizes and are easier to store. If you don't have a good pan and a rack and you want to roast a chicken, do it anyway—to heck with the equipment.

I 4- to 5-pound roasting chicken
I medium lemon, quartered
4 whole unpeeled garlic cloves, smashed
2 to 3 whole sprigs of fresh herbs, such
    as thyme, rosemary, or sage
3 tablespoons extra virgin olive oil
Kosher salt and freshly ground pepper

1/2 cup white wine
1/2 cup homemade chicken or vegetable
    stock or your favorite canned broth
Fresh lemon juice
2 teaspoons chopped mixed fresh herbs,
    such as parsley, chives, chervil, and
    basil

PREHEAT THE OVEN to 450°F. Remove the giblets and neck from the chicken and save for another use or discard. Rinse the chicken well under cold running water, pull off and discard any excess lumps of fat, and pat dry. Place the lemon, garlic, and herb sprigs in the cavity. Massage the olive oil into the skin and season generously with salt and pepper.

Set a V-shaped rack in the roasting pan, and place the chicken on it breast side up. Roast for 50 to 55 minutes, or until the thigh meat is no longer pink (165° to 170°F. on an instant-read thermometer). Using a bulb baster, pastry or barbecue brush, or—yes—a spoon, occasionally baste the chicken with its drippings as it roasts (every 10 minutes or so).

When the chicken is done, remove it from the rack, set it aside, and keep it warm. Add the wine and stock to the roasting pan and on the stovetop bring to a boil over high heat, stirring to scrape up any browned bits from the bottom of the pan. Boil until the liquid is lightly thickened and reduced by about a third. Taste and season with salt, pepper, and drops of lemon juice. Pour the sauce into a small warm pitcher and skim off the fat that rises to the top. Stir in the chopped herbs. Carve the chicken and serve with the sauce to spoon over it.

basic roast chicken
with lemon and chile glaze

1/2 cup fresh lemon juice

1/4 cup honey

1 1/2 tablespoons pure ancho or
California chile powder (see Glossary
and Pantry)

1/4 teaspoon cayenne pepper

1/2 teaspoon ground coriander

1/2 teaspoon ground cumin

1/2 teaspoon ground cinnamon

WHISK ALL THE ingredients together until well combined.

Follow the directions for Basic Roast Chicken, opposite. After the chicken has been in the oven for 20 minutes, begin basting with Lemon and Chile Glaze. The chicken will be so flavorful it won't even need the pan sauce. Just serve it with the pan juices, if you'd like, skimmed of excess fat (the clear liquid floating on top).

basic roast chicken
with sweet tamarind glaze

3 tablespoons tamarind pulp (see
Glossary and Pantry)

1/2 cup boiling water

1 tablespoon garlic crushed through a
press

1 tablespoon ginger juice (use the garlic
press to extract from fresh ginger)

1 teaspoon seeded and finely minced
hot chile, such as serrano or Thai

1/4 cup rice vinegar

2 tablespoons honey, or to taste

1 tablespoon soy sauce

STIR AND MASH the tamarind into the boiling water and steep for 10 minutes. Strain, pressing solids with a spoon to extract all juices. In a small saucepan, combine tamarind liquid with remaining ingredients and heat over medium heat, stirring, until the honey dissolves.

Follow the directions for Basic Roast Chicken, opposite. After the chicken has been in the oven for 20 minutes, begin basting generously with Sweet Tamarind Glaze. The chicken will be so flavorful it won't even need the pan sauce. Just serve it with the juices, if you'd like, skimmed of excess fat (the clear liquid floating on top).

POACHING One of the easiest ways to cook chicken is to cook it in liquid. You need nothing more than a big saucepan and decent stock— your favorite canned broth is just fine. You can vary the flavors by lacing the poaching liquid with anything that appeals: lemon juice, wine, fresh herbs, dried spices—whatever. Weirdly, the risk with poaching is that the chicken can become dry and tough if it's cooked too long or too hard. The key is—yes—not to cook it too long or too hard.

poached chicken breasts

MAKES 4 BREASTS

This basic recipe for poaching chicken breasts yields not only a moist, tender breast but also a delicious broth that can be used for soups and sauces—or to poach more chicken.

2 cups crisp, light-bodied white wine

3 cups homemade chicken stock or
   your favorite canned broth

3 whole cloves, or 6 juniper berries, or
   1 whole star anise, or 12 Sichuan
   peppercorns . . . (you can see where
   I'm going with this)

1 large bay leaf

1/2 cup coarsely chopped green onions
   (green and white parts) or 1/4 cup
   coarsely chopped fresh parsley
   (leaves and stems are fine)

4 large bone-in chicken breasts

IN A DEEP skillet or saucepan that will allow the breasts to sit in a snug single layer, combine the white wine, stock, cloves, bay leaf, and green onions. Bring the mixture to a boil and then reduce the heat and simmer for 3 to 4 minutes to extract some flavor from the seasonings. Place the chicken breasts into the simmering stock, which should cover the chicken completely; if it doesn't, add some additional wine or stock. Cover the pan and simmer slowly for 6 minutes (check periodically to be sure the liquid is not boiling hard and adjust the heat if necessary). Turn off the heat and allow the breasts to sit covered for 15 minutes. They should just be cooked through at this point. Remove and proceed with the salad that follows or other uses.

Carefully strain the poaching liquid through a fine mesh strainer and store covered in the refrigerator for up to 5 days or in the freezer for up to 6 months. This provides a delicious stock for soups, stews, and sauces.

poached chicken breast salad
with curry buttermilk, apples, and pecans

SERVES 6 TO 8

I love to prepare this salad—old-fashioned but never boring—for picnics. My favorite way to eat it is to roll it up in tender lettuce leaves. To toast the curry powder, add it dry to a small saucepan and stir it over medium heat for a minute or two or until you can smell its fragrance.

4 Poached Chicken Breasts
2 cups peeled, cored, and diced tart-sweet apples, such as Fuji
2 cups red seedless grapes, halved
1 1/2 cups diced fresh fennel or celery
1 cup lightly toasted pecans or cashews

FOR THE CURRY-BUTTERMILK DRESSING
2 teaspoons grated orange zest
2/3 cup mayonnaise
1/2 cup sour cream
1/4 cup buttermilk
2 teaspoons honey, or to taste
2 teaspoons fresh lemon or lime juice
2 to 3 teaspoons curry powder, lightly toasted
Salt and freshly ground pepper

PULL THE CHICKEN breast meat from the bones and discard the bones and the skin. Cut the meat into bite-size pieces and add it to a bowl along with the apples, grapes, fennel, and nuts.

In a separate bowl, whisk together all the dressing ingredients except the salt and pepper. Stir the dressing into the chicken mixture, taste, and season with salt and pepper. Store in the refrigerator. This is best eaten the same day it's made.

ginger-poached chicken and stock

MAKES 3 QUARTS FLAVORFUL STOCK AND 1 OR 2 POUNDS
DELICIOUS CHICKEN

This yields two flavorful products: a whole tender poached chicken and a savory stock that can be used for soups and sauces. The Chinese refer to this method as "white-cooked," which means it's cooked very slowly without soy sauce. It produces a delicate, juicy chicken that is great for Cold Noodle Salad with Coconut Peanut Sauce (page 198), to name just one of its many uses. The slow cooking also helps ensure that you have a nice clear stock, which is aesthetically pleasing at the very least. I've reduced the stock to concentrate its flavors, but you don't have to. Taste and make up your own mind.

1 4- to 5-pound fresh chicken
5 quarts water
2 large bunches of green onions, chopped

¼ pound fresh ginger, washed and coarsely chopped (no need to peel)
1 star anise (optional) (see Glossary and Pantry)

IN A LARGE stockpot, combine all the ingredients. Slowly bring the water to a simmer and skim off any scum that appears. (It sounds awful and doesn't look much better, but it's nothing to worry about.) Reduce the heat, cover, and cook for 25 minutes. Check occasionally to make sure that the water is just barely moving, and adjust the heat as necessary. Turn off the heat and let it stand covered until cool, about 2 hours. Remove the chicken from the pot to a large cutting board or platter (to catch the juices), and pull off the meat, discarding the skin and bones. The only way to do this is with your fingers.

Strain the stock, discarding the solids. Refrigerate it to chill it. Remove and discard the congealed fat, which will have risen to the top. If you want to concentrate the flavor, transfer the stock to a clean pot, bring it to a boil, and reduce over high heat to about 3 quarts (this will take 15 to 20 minutes). Strain again. Store covered in the refrigerator for up to 5 days or in the freezer for up to 6 months.

suggestion A simple way to serve the chicken is to slice it and sprinkle with a top-quality sea salt, such as Maldon or fleur-de-sel, or with a homemade fla-vored salt, such as sour salt (2 parts salt to 1 part ascorbic acid crystals) or chile salt (2 parts salt to 1 part pure ground chile powder, such as ancho or New Mexico).

a favorite chicken sandwich

If you slice thin little pieces of chicken and arrange them with Caramelized Onion Jam and watercress on small croûtes (either crackers or toasted slices of baguette), you will have an elegant hors d'oeuvre with the same ingredients.

Ginger-Poached Chicken
Whole-grain peasant-style bread, such as Swiss health bread

Caramelized Onion Jam
Bunch of watercress, woody stems removed

PULL MEAT FROM the bone or slice it, as you prefer. Layer it on the bread with some jam and the watercress and top with another slice of bread. Eat.

caramelized onion jam

This concoction, which I sometimes call a jam and sometimes a cooked chutney, is one of my favorite sweet-tart savory flavor-makers, a condiment with a lot of potential. Try it with grilled lamb or on a toasted blue cheese sandwich.

2 tablespoons olive oil or butter
2 large white onions, peeled and thinly sliced (about 4 cups)
2 tablespoons (or more) roasted garlic
Big pinch sugar

2 tablespoons balsamic vinegar, white if possible
1½ tablespoons chopped golden raisins
Salt and freshly ground pepper

IN A LARGE heavy-bottomed sauté pan, heat the olive oil and sauté the onions, stirring until they are just beginning to color, about 8 minutes. Add the garlic and sugar and continue to cook until the onions are rich golden-brown and very soft. This will take another 15 to 20 minutes or so. If the onions are browning too fast, add a tablespoon or so of water and reduce the heat. Stir in the vinegar and raisins and season with salt and pepper. Serve warm or at room temperature. Store covered and refrigerated for up to 5 days. Like all jams, this one can be canned using the water bath method. MAKES ABOUT 1½ CUPS

soy-poached chicken salad with sweet chilli-ginger sauce

SERVES 6

This recipe combines some interesting components that you'll find in any Asian grocery store. Poaching chicken in a soy-flavored broth is an old Chinese technique; once made, the broth can be reused by straining, boiling for a couple of minutes, and then storing in the refrigerator for up to 2 weeks or in the freezer. By the way, I'm using the spelling of chilli as it appears on the bottle!

2 pounds bone-in chicken breasts or thighs
Soy Poaching Liquid
3 cups mixed young savory greens, such as spinach, arugula, mustard, and cress

½ pound jicama, parsnips, or kohlrabi, peeled and finely julienned
Sweet Chilli-Ginger Sauce

Garnish if you like with savory sprouts, such as onion or radish

REMOVE ALL VISIBLE fat and skin from the chicken and discard. Add the poaching liquid to a deep saucepan and bring to a simmer. Add the chicken and simmer gently for 6 to 8 minutes or until the chicken is just cooked through. Turn off the heat and let the chicken stand in the liquid for at least 30 minutes to absorb flavor.

To serve, remove the bones from the chicken and shred or thinly slice the meat. Arrange on plates, along with the greens and jicama. Drizzle with Sweet Chilli-Ginger Sauce and garnish with savory sprouts, if desired.

NOTE: The longer the chicken stays in the poaching liquid, the more flavor and color it will absorb. The chicken can be prepared a day ahead if desired. Be sure to remove it from the poaching liquid before storing in the refrigerator—otherwise you'd have too much flavor and color, I think.

soy poaching liquid

3 cups water
3/4 cup dark soy sauce
1/3 cup sugar
1/3 cup **Chinese black vinegar (see Note)**
  or balsamic vinegar
4 tablespoons peeled and chopped fresh
  ginger

4 large garlic cloves, bruised
Juice and half the peel of I medium
  orange
3/4 teaspoon fennel seeds
I large star anise
I 3-inch piece cinnamon stick
1/4 teaspoon crushed hot chile flakes

COMBINE ALL THE ingredients in a deep saucepan and simmer for 5 minutes.

NOTE: Koon Chun brand black vinegar is widely available in Asian markets.

sweet chilli-ginger sauce

2 teaspoons finely minced fresh ginger
2 teaspoons peeled and finely minced
  fresh garlic
2 tablespoons soy sauce
1/2 cup **Thai sweet chilli sauce, or to**
  taste (I like Mae Play brand)

2 tablespoons fresh lime or lemon juice,
  or to taste
2 to 4 tablespoons homemade chicken
  stock or your favorite canned broth,
  or water

COMBINE THE GINGER, garlic, and soy sauce in a blender and pulse briefly. Add half the chilli sauce, the fresh lime juice, and enough stock to achieve the desired consistency, and pulse a couple of times more. Taste and add additional chilli sauce to your own taste. Store covered in the refrigerator for up to 1 week. MAKES ABOUT I CUP

PAN-ROASTING Pan-roasting is a hybrid technique used commonly in restaurants and perfectly suited to the home. Food is quickly sautéed on one side to brown it, then the pan is set in the oven, where the more gentle surrounding heat preserves the food's juiciness as it finishes cooking. This also allows you to ignore it for a few minutes—always a boon. Note that you will need an *ovenproof* sauté pan (i.e., one without a plastic handle).

pan-roasted chicken breasts with asian butter sauce

SERVES 6

This marinade calls for kaffir lime leaves, a marvelously aromatic ingredient that can be found fresh or frozen at Southeast Asian grocers. If you live in an area where citrus grows, you can also grow your own in pots or in the ground. Substitute lime zest if you can't find them. This recipe makes a generous amount of sauce; use as much as you like.

2 tablespoons Asian chili-garlic sauce
   (see Glossary and Pantry)
1 tablespoon Asian fish sauce
   (see Glossary and Pantry) or
   2 tablespoons soy sauce
1 tablespoon fresh lime juice
2 kaffir lime leaves, very thinly sliced, or
   1 tablespoon finely grated lime zest
6 large bone-in chicken breasts
4 tablespoons olive oil

BUTTER SAUCE
1¼ cups homemade chicken stock or
   your favorite canned broth
1 teaspoon Asian fish sauce
½ teaspoon very thinly sliced hot red
   chile, or to taste
2 tablespoons unsalted butter, softened
2 tablespoons chopped fresh cilantro
   leaves
2 teaspoons fresh lime juice, or to taste

Garnish if you like with fresh cilantro
   leaves and lime wedges

COMBINE THE CHILI-GARLIC sauce, fish sauce, lime juice, and kaffir lime leaves, and rub the breasts with this mixture. Cover and refrigerate for at least 1 and up to 6 hours.

Preheat the oven to 400°F. Heat the olive oil in an ovenproof skillet over medium heat. Add the breasts skin side down and cook until browned, about 4 minutes. Turn the chicken skin side up and transfer the pan to the oven for 15 to 18 minutes, or until the chicken is just cooked through. While the chicken is cooking, prepare the Butter Sauce.

FOR THE BUTTER SAUCE: In a saucepan, combine the stock and fish sauce, and boil over high heat until the liquid is reduced to about $1/3$ cup. (You can learn to eyeball this. When the pan is empty, put $1/3$ cup of water in it to visualize what it looks like.) Add the red chile. Take the pan off the heat, and whisk in the butter a bit at a time to thicken and enrich the sauce. Stir in the cilantro and lime juice and keep warm, if necessary (a small thermos works well).

Serve the chicken with the sauce spooned over the top. Scatter with cilantro leaves and serve immediately with lime wedges.

variation   I often make this dish with an elaborate lemon grass and bok choy risotto. Sautéed bok choy and aromatic white rice, either steamed or cooked in chicken stock, make excellent accompaniments with a lot less effort.

13   dried beans

Jewels of the Plant Kingdom

With the revision of the Food Guide Pyramid by the USDA in 1996, and its emphasis on eating a more plant-based diet, Americans have begun to "rediscover" beans. Most people are familiar with the grocery store varieties such as pinto, navy, garbanzo (chickpeas), black, and kidney, all of which are delicious and should be a part of every pantry. They are highly nutritious and provide the basis for all kinds of inexpensive yet satisfying recipes. Beyond these familiar varieties is an intriguing realm of beans that many of us are completely unaware of. Today, thanks to the efforts of organizations like Seed Savers Exchange, which is dedicated to preserving biological diversity, we are also being "reintroduced" to heirloom varieties such as Scarlet Runner, Christmas Lima, Tongues of Fire, Appaloosa, Esther's Swedish, and other colorful and colorfully named beans.

One of humankind's oldest cultivated crops, beans have been around for at least 10,000 years. Beans were found in Egyptian tombs and are referred to frequently in the Bible. Beyond their worldwide use as food, beans (and legumes in general) have tremendous agricultural value. They are natural nitrogen producers and are critical in crop rotation, the goal of which is to renew the vigor of the soil. Bean cultivation is one of the key tools in sustainable agriculture programs.

Botanically, beans are mature seeds from the enclosed pods of the large plant family known as Leguminosae (lentils, peas, and even carob also belong to this family, though from a cook's point of view, they are not beans). For our purposes, there are two bean types (excluding string beans): *fresh shelling beans*, which are consumed fresh from their pods, and *dried beans*, which are dried to be consumed later. Fresh shelling beans are generally only available for a few weeks each summer. In addition to peas, the ones I usually look for fresh are favas, which come to market in late spring; limas, cranberry beans, and black-eyed peas, which appear mid-to-late summer; and soybeans, which come to market in summer and fall. In their fresh form, they offer a unique textural and flavor alternative to their dried counterparts, and their great advantage is that they cook very quickly straight from the pod. Farm markets are usually the best places to find fresh shelling beans. Our focus in this lesson, however, will be on dried beans, which are available all year round.

Beans take a long time to cook, or soak, or something, right? Plus, there's that side effect . . .

In my cooking classes, the two reasons students give most often for not cooking and eating more dried beans are the long, overnight soaking time usually recommended and "gas"! A few years ago, the USDA came up with a technique that helps deal with both of these issues and it's called the quick soak method. It makes dried beans ready to cook in an hour, and it helps eliminate the insoluble sugars that cause gas.

TO SOAK BEANS

It's very simple: First wash the dried beans thoroughly and pick through them to remove any pebbles or other inedible matter. (Remember, dried beans are a natural agricultural product that comes to us right from the field, just like any fruit or vegetable.) Place the washed beans in a deep saucepan and add enough cold water to cover by at least 4 inches. Place the pan on the stove over high heat and bring it to a boil. As soon as the water boils, remove the pan from the heat and let it sit for 1 hour. What we're looking for here are beans that are plump with no wrinkled skins. Drain the beans in a colander and rinse them well. They are now ready to cook and less likely to cause gastric distress.

Why does this work? The initial quick blanching releases into the water a lot of the sugars, known as oligosaccharides, that are the main cause of gas. When you drain and rinse the beans, many of those sugars go right down the drain.

many cooks believe that you can further "de-gas" beans by adding the herb epazote (either fresh or dried) to the *cooking* water (not the "quick soak" water) as they do in Mexico, or a piece of the dried seaweed kombu (available in Asian and natural foods stores) as the Japanese do. Both of these will purportedly further reduce those evil little gas-producing insoluble sugars. Some food scientists debunk this, but I have to tell you that I'm a believer.

TO COOK BEANS

The beans have been drained and rinsed, right? Now return them to the pot, again covering with 4 inches or so of cold water. Bring the beans to a boil and then reduce the heat so that they simmer gently. Partially cover the pot, and cook until the beans are tender. This can take anywhere from 15 minutes to 2 hours or more depending on the variety and other factors discussed below. Check to make sure the water stays at a gentle simmer and that the beans are always covered by at least 1 inch of water.

BEANS: Cooking Times and Uses

BEANS (SOAKED)	COOK TIME	PRESSURE COOKER	USES
ADZUKI OR AZUKI	45 to 60 minutes	5 to 8 minutes	Rice dishes, salads
BLACK	1 to 1½ hours	8 minutes	Rice dishes, soups, salads; used in Mexican, Caribbean, and Latin American dishes
CANNELLINI or WHITE KIDNEY	45 to 60 minutes	5 to 8 minutes	Soups, salads, pureed
CHRISTMAS LIMA	60 minutes	5 to 8 minutes	Soups, salads, stews
CRANBERRY	45 to 60 minutes	6 to 8 minutes	Italian bean dishes and soups
ESTHER'S SWEDISH	45 to 60 minutes	6 to 8 minutes	Soups, salads, baked casseroles, pureed
FAVA (DRIED)	35 to 40 minutes	4 to 7 minutes	Soups, salads, side dishes
FLAGEOLET	1 to 1½ hours	5 to 9 minutes	Soups, stews, salads, side dishes, often served with lamb
GARBANZO (chickpeas)	1 hour	5 to 8 minutes	Salads, soups, hummus
GREAT NORTHERN	1 to 1½ hours	5 to 8 minutes	Soups or cassoulets
LIMA BEANS, large	45 to 60 minutes	Not recommended	Vegetable side dish, add to soups, salads
LIMA BEANS, baby	1 hour	Not recommended	Vegetable side dish, add to soups, salads
NAVY or SMALL WHITE	45 to 60 minutes	5 to 8 minutes	Pork and beans, baked beans, soups and stews, pureed
PINK	1 to 1½ hours	6 to 8 minutes	Soups, chili
PINTO	45 to 60 minutes	5 to 7 minutes	Soups, chili, refried beans, Mexican dishes
RED	1½ to 2 hours	6 to 9 minutes	Soups, salads, rice dishes
RED KIDNEY	1 to 1½ hours	5 to 8 minutes	Soups, salads, rice dishes
SOYBEANS*	45 to 60 minutes	5 to 7 minutes	Soups and mashes

* In America, dried soybeans have not yet become "mainstream" but they should. I love them fresh or fresh frozen (also known by their Japanese name, *edamame*) but cooked from their dried form, they can be pretty bland. Pan-roasting brings out their nutty, toasty flavor, and it's very simple to do. Cooked soybeans can substitute in almost any bean recipe.

Rinse the soybeans well and then place them in a large, nonstick skillet over high heat. When the beans start to sizzle, stir until their surfaces are dry. Continue to stir. The skins will first shrivel and then smooth out and begin to split to reveal the creamy interior of the bean. This will take 3 to 4 minutes. When the beans begin to brown in spots (be careful not to burn them!) remove the pan from the heat and continue stirring for another minute or so to cool them down.

Transfer the beans to a deep saucepan, cover with at least 4 inches of cold water, and bring to a boil. Reduce the heat to a simmer, partially cover, and cook them until tender, 45 minutes to 1 hour. Skins will tend to come off as they cook. You can remove and discard the skins if you like.

My simple rules for cooking dried beans are these:

~ Don't add salt or acidic ingredients, such as tomatoes, citrus, or wine, to the cooking beans until the beans have begun to soften. Salt and acid can toughen the skins and result in uneven cooking. Although some bean varieties are unaffected by these additions, others are. To be on the safe side, I add these seasonings near the end of the cooking time, when the beans are almost done.

~ If you are going to combine different beans in the same finished dish, cook each separately, since, as I've noted, each variety will have a different cooking time. I've never been a fan of those 18 or 36 or however many dried bean mixtures that are sold for soups.

~ Whenever you cook beans, make some extra and freeze them for later use. Beans freeze well and that way you can have recipe-ready beans in short order.

~ For bean salads, add vinaigrettes or other dressings while the beans are still warm; they will absorb the dressings better. If you're starting with frozen or cooled beans, warm them first in the microwave or on the stovetop.

~ Though bean varieties can generally be used interchangeably in any recipe, some are better for soups, some for salads, and some for purees, because of their texture, flavor, or appearance. Experiment and develop your own favorites. You really can't go wrong.

You can use your freshly cooked beans in the recipes below, or refrigerate them for up to 3 days, or freeze them. I store them in their cooking water either way.

COOKING TIME FOR BEANS WILL DEPEND ON SEVERAL FACTORS

~ **The variety:** Some varieties can cook in as little as 15 minutes; others can take 2 hours or more. The size of the bean does not determine how long it will take to cook.

- **How old the beans are:** Last year's crop will take longer than this year's. Unfortunately, the age of your beans is rarely something you can find out when you purchase them.
- **Quality of the cooking water:** Beans take longer to cook in hard water.
- **Altitude:** The higher you are, the longer it'll take.

Using a pressure cooker can reduce the cooking time by half or more. I know that some people think beans can cause a pressure cooker to explode, but they won't. It's an excellent tool for cooking beans. Just follow the manufacturer's instructions.

Is it okay to use canned beans?

You bet it is. Canned beans can be used in place of cooked dried beans in all of the following recipes and are perfectly acceptable. The only draw-backs I find with canned beans are that they are sometimes overcooked (i.e., mushy) and oversalted. Drain and rinse them well before using them in any recipe. If the recipe calls for the cooking liquid, use plain water or stock, if you have some on hand. Of course you will be far more limited in varieties, so do try cooking with dried beans sometime— you might like the difference.

Now . . . on to the recipes!

mashed white beans with roasted garlic

SERVES 4 TO 6 AS A SIDE DISH

This is an interesting alternative to mashed potatoes that is perfect with roasted meats, birds, and grilled vegetables. Use a white or cream-colored bean that has a soft creamy consistency, such as flageolet, gigande, cannellini, or navy.

2 medium heads of garlic
Extra virgin olive oil
Salt and freshly ground pepper
3 cups cooked white beans (save the liquid)

1 ½ tablespoons finely chopped fresh parsley, mint, or basil leaves, or a combination
½ cup or so freshly grated Parmesan or Pecorino cheese

PREHEAT THE OVEN to 375°F. Cut off the top quarter of two whole heads of garlic to expose each clove and drizzle with olive oil and a sprinkling of salt and pepper. Wrap the heads in foil and roast in the oven for 40 minutes or so, until the garlic is completely soft. Unwrap the garlic for the last 5 minutes to allow it to brown and caramelize a bit. (You can also do this in the toaster oven.) Set aside.

In a food processor, pulse-puree the beans, adding enough of their cooking liquid to make the consistency resemble mashed potatoes. They shouldn't be completely smooth. (Like potatoes, they become gluey and starchy if overprocessed.) Heat 2 tablespoons of olive oil in a pan large enough to hold the bean puree and squeeze the roasted garlic out of its skin into the pan. Sauté the garlic briefly, then add the bean puree and warm it through. Stir in the herbs. Taste and season with salt and pepper. Serve topped with freshly grated Parmesan cheese.

garbanzo and blue cheese hummus

MAKES ABOUT 1 CUP

This was one of those accidental recipes that happened when I was putting together an antipasto plate for a picnic. I had the cheese alongside the hummus and when I tasted them together, I loved the combination. It makes a wonderful spread for crusty bread or crostini topped with chopped ripe tomatoes, cucumber, and mint or basil.

1¾ cups or so cooked garbanzo beans
2 tablespoons roasted or poached garlic
1 teaspoon toasted sesame oil
1 tablespoon fresh lemon juice
⅓ cup or so buttermilk, homemade
   vegetable stock or your favorite
   canned broth, or bean-cooking liquid

2 ounces rich blue cheese, such as Great
   Hill, Maytag, or Bellwether Farms
Salt and freshly ground pepper

Garnish if you like with fragrant olive or
   nut oil and chopped chives or fresh
   parsley, or a combination

COMBINE THE BEANS, garlic, sesame oil, and lemon juice in a food processor, and process for a minute or two until the mixture is pureed. Add enough buttermilk to aid in the process. Add the cheese and process until smooth. Taste and season with salt and pepper if you think it needs it. For a really smooth texture, you can push the mixture through a medium strainer, but you can certainly leave it the way it is. Store covered in the refrigerator for up to 4 days.

To serve, scoop into a serving bowl or spread out on a plate and drizzle with fragrant oil and a sprinkling of chopped herbs, if desired.

cannellini bean and arugula salad

SERVES 8 TO 10 AS PART OF AN ANTIPASTO OFFERING

Cannellini beans are a traditional variety used often in the cooking of Northern Italy. They have a wonderful, creamy texture and are nearly white in color. They are also available canned. Look for fresh cannellinis at farmer's markets toward the end of summer. Once removed from their shells, fresh cannellini cook in just a few minutes.

4 cups cooked cannellini beans, drained
  and rinsed if using canned
2/3 cup coarsely chopped sun-dried
  tomatoes, dry- or oil-packed
3 tablespoons balsamic vinegar,
  preferably white
1/4 cup extra virgin olive oil
2 tablespoons chopped fresh mint leaves

1/4 cup chopped drained capers
3/4 cup chopped sweet red onions (soak
  in ice water for 30 minutes if strong)
1/2 cup or so fresh lemon juice
Salt and freshly ground pepper
3 cups lightly packed young tender
  arugula leaves

GENTLY COMBINE THE beans, tomatoes, vinegar, olive oil, mint, capers, and onions in a bowl along with 1/4 cup of the lemon juice. (If the beans are cold from the fridge, you can warm them slightly before combining.) Set aside for at least 1 hour to let the flavors develop and then taste and season with additional lemon juice, salt, and pepper. Stir the arugula into the salad just before serving.

black bean gazpacho salad

SERVES 8 TO 10

This is a variation—in form and content—on the popular Spanish cold soup. It is a terrific summer lunch salad or first course since, though it is very hearty, it is extremely refreshing. While some time is involved in chopping the vegetables, the salad comes together very easily. I often tell my students not to judge a recipe's degree of difficulty by the number of ingredients. This dish is a perfect example. It requires no skill to make. It's great for a crowd and stores well in the refrigerator for up to 3 days. And it's delicious. And it's healthy. What more could you ask for?

3 cups cooked black beans, just done (not mushy)

2 cups peeled and sliced red onions (soak in ice water for 30 minutes if strong)

1 tablespoon minced garlic

2 cups sliced cucumbers, from peeled, halved, and seeded cucumbers

2 cups seeded and diced tomatoes

1 cup diced red bell pepper

1 cup diced yellow bell pepper

2 teaspoons seeded and finely minced serrano chiles, or to taste

1 cup chopped fresh tomatillos (peel off those papery husks first)

1 cup fresh corn kernels, raw if tender or briefly blanched if not

1/2 cup roughly chopped fresh cilantro leaves

1/3 cup fresh lime juice

1 tablespoon Tabasco sauce, or to taste

1/4 cup olive oil

1 cup fresh or canned tomato juice

2 tablespoons chopped fresh oregano leaves or 2 teaspoons dried

Kosher salt and freshly ground pepper

Garnish if you like with lime wedges and avocado slices

IN A BIG bowl or directly in a storage container, combine the beans, onions, garlic, cucumbers, tomatoes, bell peppers, chiles, tomatillos, corn kernels, cilantro, lime juice, Tabasco, olive oil, tomato juice, and oregano. Chill at least 2 hours to allow the flavors to blend. At serving time, taste the salad and then season with salt and pepper, extra Tabasco, or lime juice—whatever you think it needs. Serve on well-chilled plates.

okra, peppers, and bean stew

SERVES 8

This rich stew is wonderfully aromatic thanks to its mix of spices and herbs, and it cooks in minutes. Different beans can really affect the look and "mouth feel"; try it with baby limas, with Tocomares Chocolate, and see. But the real reason for including it is to make a pitch for that under-appreciated vegetable, okra. For those who weren't raised with okra, it's a "joke" vegetable. Yes, it can be slimy if overcooked—so don't overcook it.

3 tablespoons olive oil

I pound white onions, thickly sliced

2 red bell peppers, stemmed, seeded, and cut in large triangles

I poblano or Anaheim chile, stemmed, seeded, and thinly sliced

$1/2$ teaspoon minced serrano or chipotle chile

3 tablespoons slivered garlic

2 cups ripe diced tomatoes (drained if using canned)

$1/2$ teaspoon lightly toasted fennel seeds, slightly crushed

$1/2$ teaspoon lightly toasted cumin seeds, slightly crushed

$1 1/2$ teaspoons dried oregano

$1/4$ teaspoon ground cinnamon

$1/2$ cup light- or medium-bodied white wine

$2 1/2$ cups homemade vegetable or chicken stock or your favorite canned broth

$1/2$ pound fresh okra, cut in half lengthwise

2 cups cooked beans, such as cannellini, baby lima, or specialty beans such as Tocomares Chocolate or Esther's Swedish

$1/3$ cup roughly chopped fresh cilantro leaves

Salt and freshly ground pepper to taste

Garnish if you like with additional chopped fresh cilantro or mint leaves

HEAT THE OLIVE oil in a skillet. Sauté the onions, peppers, poblano and serrano chiles, and garlic over medium heat, until they just begin to color and are crisp-tender, 7 to 8 minutes. Add the tomatoes, fennel, cumin, oregano, cinnamon, wine, and stock, and simmer for 3 to 4 minutes. Don't overcook—the vegetables should still have texture. Add the okra and continue cooking for 2 to 3 minutes or until the okra is barely tender (if you overcook, the okra becomes "slimy"). Stir in the beans and chopped cilantro and warm through. Taste and season with salt and pepper if needed.

To serve, ladle the stew into warm soup plates, garnish with chopped herbs, if using, and serve.

esther's swedish baked beans

One of the historic American dishes is Boston Baked Beans. The canned product is so ubiquitous, though, that people have forgotten what a worthwhile dish it is to make yourself. An authentic recipe would start with dried beans and salt pork for flavor and would cook all day in a low oven. It's easy to do, and I urge you to try it sometime. My version leaves out the salt pork and, if you start with cooked beans, it's easy and quick enough for a weeknight. For this recipe, I like a bean called Esther's Swedish, a variety that originated in Scandinavia. It is now grown in America and is a great bean to use in this dish because it holds its shape very well. You can certainly use a more common variety. To add a little crunch, top the beans with some coarse bread crumbs (Japanese-style panko being my favorite) that have been tossed with a little clarified butter or olive oil before baking. For a vegetarian "beans and weenies," add some marinated seitan or baked tofu to the mixture before baking. Both can be purchased already prepared in natural foods stores and many supermarkets. Of course, nonvegetarian beans and weenies is an option too.

I tablespoon olive oil

¾ cup sliced yellow or white onions

½ cup diced carrots

I tablespoon chopped garlic

⅓ cup white wine

3 cups cooked Esther's Swedish, navy,
    or great northern beans

⅓ cup dark molasses

2 tablespoons soy sauce

I tablespoon Dijon mustard

Salt and freshly ground pepper to taste

PREHEAT THE OVEN to 350°F. Heat the olive oil in a sauté pan, and cook the onions, carrots, and garlic over medium heat until lightly browned. In a large bowl (or in the sauté pan if it's large enough), combine the cooked vegetables with the wine, beans, molasses, soy sauce, mustard, salt, and pepper, and mix thoroughly. Transfer the mixture to a lightly buttered or oiled casserole. Bake uncovered for 35 to 40 minutes.

flageolet beans with mushrooms, tomatoes and gremolata

SERVES 4 TO 6

Combined with a salad of mixed greens, this dish makes a wonderful vegetarian meal. I like this recipe both warm and at room temperature. Again, any cooked bean that you like can be used.

3 tablespoons olive oil or butter, or a combination

8 ounces crimini mushrooms, cut in ¼-inch dice

Salt and freshly ground pepper

⅓ cup finely chopped shallots or green onions (green and white parts)

½ cup light- or medium-bodied white wine

3 cups seeded and diced fresh tomatoes (or substitute canned diced tomatoes, drained)

3 cups cooked flageolet, baby lima, or great northern beans

½ cup Gremolata (page 135)

IN A SAUTÉ pan, heat 2 tablespoons of the oil and add the mushrooms. Sauté quickly over high heat and toss to brown lightly on all sides. Season with salt and pepper, remove from the pan, and set aside.

Add the remaining tablespoon of oil to the pan along with the shallots and cook over medium heat until soft but not brown, 2 or 3 minutes. Add the white wine and tomatoes and cook until most of the liquid has evaporated, about 7 minutes. Add the reserved mushrooms, the beans, and half of the Gremolata mixture and toss gently to combine. Season with salt and pepper to taste. Serve, sprinkling the remaining Gremolata over the top.

14 mushrooms

The Meat of the Vegetable Kingdom

I'm willing to bet that most Americans were first introduced to mushrooms in the form of a bowl of Campbell's Cream of Mushroom soup. I was lucky to have grown up on a ranch in Colorado, and my first recollections of eating mushrooms were those that we gathered wild in late summer. I remember most the morels. They have a unique honeycombed and conical shape, and usually are black or dark gray in color but also occasionally white or yellow. Their hollow stem and core make larger morels ideal for stuffing, which is what my grandmother used to do with them.

Technically edible mushrooms are fungi, which is a vast kingdom of organisms—neither plant nor animal—in and of itself. As eaters and cooks, however, we mentally divide foodstuffs into either plant or animal, and since mushrooms are more like the former, we think of them as vegetables. I love mushrooms because of their ability to add deep, rich, earthy flavor to a dish almost in the same way that meat would; on their own, mushrooms' dense, chewy texture satisfies in a way that's different from "other" vegetables. For both of these reasons, I think of mushrooms as the meat of the vegetable kingdom, though to a true vegetarian, that may not seem like much of a compliment.

Before they were cultivated (which happened only in the last few hundred years) every mushroom eaten was taken from the wild. Who was the first person to eat a wild mushroom and what drove him to do it? The conventional wisdom is that their often exotic shape and color and especially aroma probably seduced that first eater.

The culinary history of mushrooms is long and rich; the culinary uses for mushrooms are almost endless. In this lesson, we explore mushrooms—fried, grilled, stewed, and sautéed, and in soups, sandwiches, elegant main courses, and a savory syrup—utilizing a dozen different varieties, including even the much maligned common button mushroom. A little mushroom will add interest and dimension to almost any dish. Many culinary mushrooms are available dried, and in that form they have often had a more concentrated flavor. Interestingly, like wine, many dried mushrooms will deepen with flavor as they age over a few years. The key is to store them properly in an airtight container and out of the light. Also try oven-drying mushrooms (see page 117) sometime. It's amazing how removing some of the water in any mushroom will power up its flavor.

For our purposes, most mushrooms fall into one of two categories: dried and fresh. Both cultivated and wild-gathered mushrooms are sold both ways.

Wild or cultivated, mushrooms should be moist and firm, neither dry and shriveled nor wet and slimy and should not have any soft or discolored spots. Cultivated mushrooms are certainly more uniform and usually in better condition than wild mushrooms, which can vary widely and are definitely more of an "adventure."

COMMON TYPES OF MUSHROOMS

The distinction between wild and cultivated mushrooms becomes a little fuzzy: once a mushroom has been cultivated it is classified as cultivated, but that doesn't mean it no longer grows wild.

FRESH CULTIVATED *Available year-round*	Button Crimini Portabella Hen of the Woods (Maitake) Enoki (Enokitake) Morel Oyster Pom Pom Blanc Cinnamon Cap Clam Shell Brown and White Trumpet Royale Nameko Shiitake
DRIED CULTIVATED *Available year-round*	Many of the above fresh cultivated mushrooms are available dried. With the exception of dried cultivated shiitake, the dried mushrooms usually called for in recipes are from wild sources.
FRESH WILD *Available seasonally*	Candy Cap (also called Maple Caps) Puff Ball Golden and White Chanterelle Matsutake Hedgehog Black Trumpet Porcini (Cepes or King Bolete) Morel Black and White Truffles
DRIED WILD *Available year-round*	Almost all of the wild mushrooms listed above are available dried, with the exception of Puff Ball. Other dried mushrooms commonly found in the market include Chinese Wood Ear (also called Tree Ears and Black Fungus).

We're often told to select only mushrooms with tightly closed caps with no gills exposed. This is a good way to judge the age of the mushroom, but I find that mushrooms that have opened up a bit are actually better for cooking. The resultant loss of moisture evidenced in "open" mushrooms concentrates and intensifies their flavor and makes them easier to sauté or otherwise cook. Mushrooms should have the odor of clean, damp earth. They should never smell ammoniated, which is a sign that they are rotting.

Don't store mushrooms in a sealed plastic package. Unfortunately many markets insist on selling them to us just this way. Sealed in plastic, they often become slimy, so get them out of that little "tomb" as quickly as possible and let them breathe. The best way to store mushrooms is in a paper bag or in a single layer in a paper-towel-lined dish or tray. The only exception to this is the cultivated enoki, which *should* stay sealed in plastic until used. Be sure to refrigerate all mushrooms until you use them.

If for some reason you have an overabundance of mushrooms, I find that sautéing them very briefly in butter or olive oil to barely cook them through and then immediately freezing them in a sealed container for up to 2 months is a good way to take care of them. In my experience, freezing raw mushrooms doesn't work well.

Never wash a mushroom, right?

How to clean mushrooms always seems to be a controversial question. One school of thought is that fresh mushrooms should be wiped with a damp cloth or brushed with one of those cool little mushroom brushes (you mean you don't have one?) and never rinsed. The rationale is that mushrooms are like little sponges that will soak up any water and become soggy and flavorless. The real deal is that mushrooms are about 90 percent water anyway, so what difference will a little more make? Since mushrooms live in or near the dirt, even if it's a sterile compost (as in the case of cultivated mushrooms), they often are dirty—with actual dirt—when we buy them. A quick wash in a colander is a much more efficient way to clean them than all that laborious brushing and wiping. In fact, cultivated button mushrooms, even when soaked in water for a minute or two, absorb very little water. My advice, then, for cultivated mushrooms is to wash them quickly under running water in a colander, drain, and give them a quick pat with paper towels to remove surface moisture.

Wild mushrooms are a little different. They do seem to absorb more water than their cultivated cousins, and often they are harder to get clean. Morels and chanterelles are notorious for hiding bits of dirt, pine needles, bugs, and the like. You often have to soak them for a few minutes in lightly salted water to flush out little critters. As a result, they can get a little soggy, and if you don't dry them, they can get slimy. I find that the best thing to do after washing them is to dry them as gently as you can and then spread them out in a single layer on a paper-towel-lined tray and put them *uncovered* in the refrigerator for a day or two before cooking. (If they are *really* soggy, you can try gently spinning them first in a salad spinner.) Refrigerators are a very drying environment. (That's why cheese, left uncovered, quickly dries out). With mushrooms, we can take advantage of that phenomenon.

Do dried mushrooms need washing?

Dried mushrooms do need to be cleaned, and they also need to be rehydrated. You can accomplish both things at once.

To rehydrate dried mushrooms: Rinse the mushrooms quickly, place them in a bowl, and cover with warm water. Let them sit for 15 minutes or until they've softened. Lift the mushrooms out of the water carefully, allowing any grit to settle to the bottom of the bowl, then strain the flavorful soaking liquid through a coffee filter and save it to add flavor to sauces and stocks. If you're using shiitake, wood ears, or other mushrooms that have tough stems, trim them away and discard.

basic sautéed mushrooms

Certainly the simplest, yet to my taste, the most delicious way to prepare mushrooms whether cultivated or wild is to sauté them quickly in a little butter and neutral vegetable oil. The goal here is to use high enough heat and cook a small enough quantity to allow their moisture to evaporate quickly, so the mushrooms will brown. Too often I see home cooks sauté too many mushrooms over too low a heat, and the mushrooms just sit there and steam and "burble," never developing their potential flavor. Even button mushrooms, which many cookbooks malign, can be pretty flavorful if you sauté them correctly and caramelize them a bit (or a lot). I like to sauté them to the point where they are deeply browned and beginning to crisp, almost like a chip. The flavor is fantastic!

A BASIC SAUTÉ OF MUSHROOMS: Slice cleaned mushrooms thickly (a little more than 1/8 inch). Add equal parts butter and oil to a large sauté pan —about 1 tablespoon of each for 3 cups of sliced mushrooms should be about right. The pan should be large enough to hold the mushrooms in a layer no more than 2 slices deep. If you are doing a lot of mushrooms, then do them in batches.

Heat the oil and butter over medium-high heat until the butter just begins to color. (The coloring of the butter gives a rich, nutty flavor but be careful not to burn it.) Add the mushrooms, turn the heat up to high, and sauté the mushrooms. At first they may appear a bit dry, but soon they will begin to release their moisture.

Add a few drops of oil if necessary. Stir and continue to sauté until the mushrooms are golden brown and very fragrant. Season with salt and pepper and stir in some chopped fresh herbs if you'd like: chives, parsley, and basil are all good.

suggestions ~ Use the mushrooms to fill an omelet.
~ Stir mushrooms into plain steamed rice or fresh pasta with butter.
~ Mound mushrooms atop grilled meat, fish, or vegetables.

fried curried shiitake mushrooms

MAKES 12 MUSHROOMS

Don't be scared off by the title; the mushrooms actually absorb very little oil as they cook. (I originally called this recipe Sautéed Curried Shiitake Mushrooms, but it wasn't technically correct.) I love these as little hors d'oeuvres or atop a freshly dressed crisp green salad. Rice flour is available in any health food store or Asian grocery if it's not in your supermarket. It produces a crisper coating than all-purpose flour.

Sea or kosher salt

12 large fresh shiitake mushrooms, all approximately the same size, stems removed, cleaned

¼ cup rice flour (see Note) or all-purpose flour

2 teaspoons curry powder, or to taste

Olive oil or other vegetable oil for frying

LIGHTLY SPRINKLE SALT on both sides of the mushrooms. Mix the flour and curry powder together and dust the mushrooms liberally with the mixture (tossing it all together in a paper bag is an easy way to go). Heat ⅛ inch of olive oil in a sauté pan over medium-high heat and cook the mushrooms on both sides until just done, about 2 minutes total. Serve hot.

NOTE: You can make your own rice flour by buzzing uncooked white rice in a coffee grinder until finely ground. Sift through a fine strainer before using. This is also a great way to clean a coffee grinder!

wild mushrooms à la grecque

Mushrooms "in the Greek manner" make a wonderful addition to a buffet table or an antipasti platter. I also use this recipe as a sauce or topper for grilled or broiled meats and fish. The approach works equally well for a wide variety of vegetables, including baby artichokes, cauliflower, baby carrots, etc. The key is to make sure not to overcook the mushrooms (or other vegetables) so that they still have some texture. If you don't have wild mushrooms, regular commercially grown mushrooms such as crimini or ordinary buttons will do fine. I usually make this using alba, clamshell, or trumpet royales from my friends at Gourmet Mushrooms, my neighbors here in Sonoma County.

1 medium white onion, peeled and cut into 8 wedges (leave some of the root end on to hold the wedges together)
Juice and slivered zest of 1 large lemon
2 bay leaves
2 tablespoons tomato paste
1/3 cup sugar
4 cups crisp, light-bodied white wine
1/4 teaspoon whole fennel seeds

1/4 teaspoon whole coriander seeds
1/2 teaspoon whole mustard seeds
1/4 teaspoon red chile flakes or Aleppo pepper, or to taste
6 large whole peeled garlic cloves
2 teaspoons kosher or sea salt
1 1/2 pounds wild or cultivated mushrooms, cleaned

IN A DEEP, nonaluminum saucepan, combine the onion, lemon juice and zest, bay leaves, tomato paste, sugar, wine, fennel, coriander, mustard, chile flakes, garlic, and salt, and bring it to a boil. Add the mushrooms, cover, and simmer for 8 to 10 minutes or until the mushrooms and onions are tender but not mushy.

Drain the mushroom mixture, reserving the broth, and set the mushrooms and onion aside. Return the broth to the pan, bring it to a boil over high heat, and cook uncovered to reduce by a third, about 6 minutes (you'll have approximately 4 cups of liquid that you want to reduce to about 2 1/2 cups). Combine the mushrooms and onion with the reduced liquid.

Store covered in the refrigerator for up to 1 week and serve warm or at room temperature.

wild mushroom paté

MAKES ENOUGH TO FILL A 3-CUP MOLD

The simplicity of this recipe belies its great taste. Serve with crisp little croûtes, toasts, or crackers of your choice. Though I call it Wild Mushroom Paté, a mixture of wild and cultivated mushrooms or cultivated mushrooms alone is equally tasty.

5 tablespoons butter

1/2 cup chopped shallots or green onions (white parts only)

1 1/4 pounds fresh wild and/or cultivated mushrooms, such as shiitake, oyster, and Cremini

2 teaspoons finely chopped garlic

2 teaspoons curry powder, or to taste

1/2 teaspoon ground cumin

1 cup toasted, preferably unsalted cashews

2 tablespoons toasted nut oil, such as walnut, or olive oil

Salt and freshly ground pepper

Garnish if you like with finely chopped mixed herbs, such as fresh parsley, chives, and basil leaves

HEAT THE BUTTER in a large sauté pan over moderately high heat. Add the shallots, mushrooms, garlic, curry, and cumin and sauté, stirring until the mixture is just beginning to brown and all the liquid exuded by the mushrooms has evaporated. Remove from the heat.

In a food processor, finely chop the cashews. Add the nut oil and continue to process to make a paste. Add the mushroom mixture and process till smooth. Taste and season with salt and pepper, then transfer to a terrine or other ceramic dish. The paté can be stored covered and refrigerated for up to 3 days. Allow it to return to room temperature and sprinkle with chopped herbs at serving time.

more about mushrooms

mushrooms and other fungi are no doubt the largest living group of organisms on earth. We are usually unaware of this, because all we see is the "fruit" of the mushroom. In actuality, the mushrooms we eat are like the fruit of an apple tree; the bigger part of the plant is the tree itself—the roots, trunk, leaves. The "rest" of the mushroom, called the mycelium, is usually underground, where it can occupy several acres. Reportedly one mushroom that occupied several square miles has been found in the Midwest!

wild mushroom hunter's soup

SERVES 6 TO 8

This is not a wild mushroom soup for hunters; it's a soup for wild mushroom hunters, one we threw together in camp after a day of wild mushroom hunting. The soup has few ingredients, and its flavor will vary depending on the type of mushrooms used. If you are lucky enough to have found some other wild edibles such as ramps (wild leeks) or a young cress, by all means, throw them in too!

1 1/2 pounds fresh wild mushrooms, cleaned

4 tablespoons olive oil

2 1/2 cups thinly sliced white or yellow onions

2 tablespoons slivered garlic

1 1/2 cups fresh or canned diced tomatoes in juice

6 cups homemade chicken or vegetable stock or your favorite canned broth

1/4 cup ruby port or amontillado sherry

2 tablespoons finely grated lemon zest

Salt and freshly ground pepper

Freshly grated Parmesan or Asiago cheese

Garnish if you like with chopped fresh herbs, such as parsley, chives, basil, or chervil, or a combination

SLICE THE WILD mushrooms thickly (at least 1/8 inch) and set aside. In a deep saucepan, heat 2 tablespoons of the olive oil and cook the onions and garlic over medium heat until they are lightly golden.

While the onion mixture is cooking, in a separate sauté pan over high heat, sauté the mushrooms in the remaining olive oil until they are cooked through and lightly browned. (If you're not comfortable having two pans going at once, finish the onions and garlic, remove the pan from the heat, then do the mushrooms.) Add the mushrooms to the saucepan with the onion mixture along with the tomatoes and stock. Bring to a boil and then reduce the heat and simmer for 3 or 4 minutes. Stir in the port and zest. Taste and season with salt and pepper just before serving. Serve in warm bowls or mugs garnished with a good sprinkling of cheese and chopped fresh herbs, if using.

mushroom-ginger soup with roasted garlic custards

SERVES 6

I love this soup. You can serve it without the custard, but with it, it becomes something very special (that means "impressive"), but still easy to do. If you have stock from Ginger-Poached Chicken (page 214), it would add great depth of flavor here; you might then want to cut the amount of additional ginger unless you're a ginger freak like me.

2 tablespoons olive oil

I pound fresh shiitake mushrooms, cleaned, stems discarded, thinly sliced

3 large garlic cloves, peeled and slivered

3 tablespoons peeled and finely slivered fresh ginger

8 cups homemade chicken or vegetable stock or your favorite canned broth

3 cups lightly packed watercress leaves, coarse stems discarded

2 teaspoons hot pepper sesame oil, or to taste

Salt and freshly ground pepper

Roasted Garlic Custards

3 green onions, sliced thinly diagonally on the bias (white and green parts)

I package (3 ounces) fresh enoki mushrooms, rinsed and ends trimmed

3 tablespoons finely slivered nori (dried seaweed) strips (optional)

IN A SOUP pot, heat the olive oil and sauté the shiitakes, garlic, and ginger over medium-high heat until the mushrooms just begin to color, about 5 minutes. Add the stock and bring to a boil. Immediately reduce the heat and stir in the watercress and hot pepper sesame oil. Taste and season with salt and pepper. Ladle the soup into wide bowls. Run a knife around the side of each custard to release it. Carefully place it in the center of each soup bowl. Garnish with green onions, enoki mushrooms, and nori strips, if desired, and serve immediately.

roasted garlic custards

3 large eggs
4 tablespoons roasted garlic
1 teaspoon salt
1/2 teaspoon freshly ground pepper

3/4 cup light cream or half-and-half
3/4 cup homemade chicken or vegetable
   stock or your favorite canned broth

PREHEAT THE OVEN to 350°F. Lightly butter or oil six 4-ounce ovenproof ramekins and arrange in a deep roasting pan. (Try to fit them in so that they are not touching each other or the sides of the pan.)

In a blender or food processor, combine the eggs, garlic, and salt and pepper. Process in short bursts until the garlic is fully incorporated and the mixture is smooth. Mix in the half-and-half and stock.

Divide the custard mixture among the prepared ramekins and fill the pan with enough boiling water to come three-fourths of the way up the sides of the ramekins.

Bake for 25 to 30 minutes or until the centers of the custards are just set. Remove the ramekins from the water bath and cool to room temperature before unmolding. (They can be made a day ahead and stored covered in the refrigerator, but don't unmold them until you're ready to serve them, and allow them to come to room temperature before serving.) MAKES 6 CUSTARDS

wild mushroom syrup

MAKES ABOUT ²/₃ CUP

This richly flavored condiment is the kind of thing you may never have considered making, but once you do, you'll find yourself using it on everything. I drizzle it on seared or grilled seafood such as scallops or halibut, on pasta and rice, and over warm salads. You can scale up the batch to make enough for special little gifts from your kitchen. It's also a great way to use fresh mushrooms that are a little over-the-hill and any shiitake stems— you know . . . the ones you've saved in your freezer for months.

1 ounce dried porcini or field mushrooms (about 1 cup)
1½ pounds mixed fresh mushrooms, such as crimini, oyster, and shiitake, cleaned
3 tablespoons unsalted butter or olive oil

2 tablespoons chopped shallots
1 tablespoon chopped garlic
¾ cup medium-bodied white or red wine
Salt and freshly ground pepper to taste

PLACE THE DRIED porcini in 1 cup of water and soak for 20 minutes to rehydrate. Carefully lift out the porcini, strain the soaking water through a coffee filter, and reserve the liquid. Chop the porcini. Coarsely chop the fresh mushrooms and set aside.

Heat the butter in a deep saucepan over medium-high heat, and add the shallots and garlic. Sauté for a minute or so, until the vegetables just begin to soften, then add the fresh and dried mushrooms. Turn the heat up to high and sauté until the mushrooms are lightly browned. Add the strained soaking water along with the wine and 3 cups of water. Bring to a boil and cook uncovered for 10 minutes to reduce by at least half. Skim off any scum that rises to the surface. Remove the pan from the heat.

Set a strainer over a clean saucepan, and pour the mushrooms and liquid into the strainer, pressing down heavily on the solids to extract all the liquid. Over high heat, continue to boil and reduce the liquid until it thickens slightly. Season with salt and pepper. Cover and store in the refrigerator for up to 4 weeks. Warm before using.

grilled portabella mushrooms

Grilled portabellas appear as the vegetarian option on practically every restaurant menu in the country these days. If they're a little bit of a cliché, they are also too delicious and versatile to ignore. I've suggested two of my favorite uses, but you'll think of more. The quantities, obviously, are infinitely flexible.

Large portabella mushrooms, cleaned
Olive oil, about 1 tablespoon per mushroom

Salt and freshly ground pepper

PREPARE A CHARCOAL fire or preheat a gas or stovetop grill. Wipe the tops of the mushrooms with a damp cloth and scrape out and discard the black gills with a teaspoon. Brush the mushrooms with olive oil and season lightly with salt and pepper. Grill the mushrooms over medium-high heat, turning once, until just cooked through but still firm, about 5 minutes total.

grilled portabella salad with citrus vinaigrette

Grilled Portabella Mushrooms
Grapefruit Vinaigrette (page 26)
   or Orange Nut Oil Vinaigrette
   (page 28)

Savory greens, such as arugula, mustard,
   cress, mizuna
Aged goat cheese, such as Crottin

WHILE THE MUSHROOMS are still warm, slice them ¼ inch thick (at an angle looks nice) and pour some vinaigrette over them. Toss gently and set aside at room temperature for at least an hour and up to a couple of days. (Store covered in the refrigerator. Bring to room temperature before serving.)

Serve the mushrooms on the greens, drizzled with a little more vinaigrette and topped with a slice or crumble of goat cheese.

grilled portabella sandwich
with artichoke aïoli

SERVES 4

Artichoke Aïoli

4 4-inch squares of focaccia, sliced in half

1½ cups lightly packed tender young arugula

2 medium red bell peppers, charred, peeled, and halved (see Glossary and Pantry)

4 Grilled Portabella Mushrooms (page 247)

Salt and freshly ground pepper

LIBERALLY SPREAD DRESSING on each half of the focaccia. Top the bottom halves with the arugula, bell peppers, and a mushroom. Season with salt and pepper, place the top halves of focaccia on top, and press gently together. Eat!

artichoke aïoli

6½-ounce jar of marinated artichoke hearts, drained and rinsed

3 tablespoons chopped poached garlic

⅓ cup freshly shredded or grated Parmesan cheese

3 tablespoons chopped fresh basil or parsley leaves or a combination

⅓ cup mayonnaise, homemade if possible

COMBINE THE ARTICHOKES, garlic, cheese, and herbs in a food processor and pulse several times to chop very finely. Add the mayonnaise and process to fully combine. Cover and store in the refrigerator for up to 3 days. MAKES ABOUT ¾ CUP

grilled portabella mushrooms with lentils and a spicy tomato broth

SERVES 8

This recipe brings together the "beef steak" of the vegetable world with some very flavorful components in a dish lusty enough to go with a rich red wine like Pinot Noir or Merlot. The lentils and tomato broth can be made a day or two ahead and reheated in a snap just before serving. When I'm really going all out, I deep-fry some thinly sliced parsnips for just one more flavor and texture note in the garnish.

8 large portabella mushrooms, all approximately the same size, cleaned
5 tablespoons olive oil
2 teaspoons roasted garlic, pureed
1 tablespoon balsamic vinegar

½ pound tender kale or chard leaves, tough center stem removed
Lentils
Spicy Tomato Broth

PREPARE A CHARCOAL fire or preheat a gas or stovetop grill. Remove the stems from the mushrooms and scrape out the black gills. Whisk together the olive oil, garlic, balsamic vinegar, and a light seasoning of salt and pepper, and lightly brush the mushrooms and kale with this mixture. Grill the kale leaves over medium-high heat until soft, lightly browned, and crispy around the edges. Set aside. Grill the mushrooms on both sides until just cooked through but still firm.

To serve, arrange the grilled kale leaves in a shallow, wide-rimmed bowl, along with a heaping spoonful or two of Lentils. Slice the mushrooms on the bias, and arrange them on top. Spoon the Spicy Tomato Broth in a ring around the Lentils and kale. Serve immediately.

lentils

1 tablespoon olive oil

¼ cup minced shallots or green onions
(white and green parts)

2 tablespoons minced garlic

⅓ cup diced carrots

⅓ cup diced celery

½ cup cleaned and chopped shiitake
mushrooms

3 tablespoons red wine vinegar, or to
taste

½ cup chopped canned tomatoes

1 teaspoon minced canned chipotle
chiles in adobo, or to taste

8 ounces green or brown lentils

2 cups clear homemade vegetable or
chicken stock or your favorite canned
broth, or water

Salt and freshly ground pepper

IN A SAUCEPAN over medium heat, warm the olive oil, and slowly sauté
the shallots, garlic, carrots, celery, and shiitakes until soft but not brown.
Add the vinegar, tomatoes, and chipotles. Raise the heat to high and stir
for 3 to 4 minutes or until the liquid is reduced by half. Add the lentils
and stock. Bring the liquid to a boil, reduce the heat to a simmer, and
cover. Cook for 20 minutes or until the lentils are tender but still hold
their shape and are not mushy. Add more stock if necessary. Taste and
season with salt and pepper. MAKES 1 QUART

spicy tomato broth

1 cup canned tomato juice (I like Muir
Glen organic)

1½ cups homemade vegetable, corn, or
chicken stock or your favorite canned
broth

1½ tablespoons prepared or freshly
grated horseradish

1 tablespoon fresh lemon juice

2 teaspoons sugar

Drops of hot sauce, such as Pickapeppa
or Tabasco (optional)

Sea salt to taste

WHISK ALL THE ingredients together at least an hour before serving to
allow the flavors to marry. If serving hot, it's best just to warm the broth
through—don't boil or even simmer—to release the fresh aromas of the
horseradish and lemon. MAKES ABOUT 2¼ CUPS

15   salmon

America's Favorite Fish

Americans love salmon. It's full of flavor, easy to cook, and the most available of all fresh fish to the home cook and restaurateurs alike. In truth, restaurant chefs often get a little frustrated because in many places around the country, the only fish that customers seem to want is salmon.

I love salmon, and living in Northern California gives me an occasional chance to go out and fish for some of those magnificent Chinook or king salmon. I'm sometimes asked, if I had to choose a last meal, what it would it be. For me, it would be a piece of roasted or grilled wild-caught king salmon with a glass of Russian River Pinot Noir. Heaven! (I hope. . . .)

What do you mean, "wild-caught"?

Whether you are aware of it or not, most of the salmon that we see in the market today are products of aquaculture—they've been raised on a fish farm. Like most other edible fish, salmon has suffered in recent decades from the twin problems of over-fishing and destruction of breeding habitat. As numbers declined, prices went up, and rather than backing off and giving the fish a chance to regenerate, it seems like it's human nature to want even more.

Enter aquaculture. In the 1970s, the Norwegians revolutionized the market for salmon by developing a method for farming them using large floating pens anchored in pristine sheltered fjords and bays. This technology spread around the world: to other northern European locations, to both coasts of Canada and the United States, and to New Zealand and Chile. I had a chance to visit Norway in the early 1980s to see salmon farming, and it really was quite amazing. Big floating pens contained hundreds of fish, originated in the farm's own nearby hatchery. Once released into the pens, they were fed several times a day on formulas containing fish meal and other nutrients, and as a result, grew quickly and efficiently. The net of this was that salmon, which had previously been limited by seasonal availability, now became available year-round in uniform and consistent quality and size. Prices dropped as efficiencies of farming increased, and this all helped to make salmon as universally popular as it is today.

There are a couple of dark clouds, however. The most successful species for farming is the Atlantic salmon. It adapts better to farm conditions than the Pacific species, which also grows a little more slowly. The Atlantic salmon, of course, is not native to the west coast of America and Canada or other places where salmon is farmed, but it is still the species of choice for farms in these locales. This poses a problem of ecological balance. Even though the fish are contained in pens, some do escape and colonize locally, and there is increasing concern about possible loss of native species.

Even in their native environment, there is concern that salmon bred for farming could interfere with their wild cousins, since the genetic differences of farm-raised salmon, which are bred to grow twice as fast, could wreak havoc with the gene pool of wild salmon.

As food, isn't farmed salmon the same as wild?

For me, farmed salmon have a different and less interesting flavor. They are fed formula food to accelerate their growth, they consume excess calories and don't get the same "exercise" as their wild counterparts, and their flesh is consequently softer. Also, they're significantly fattier, and even though it's "good" fat, high in omega-3, it may be too much of a good thing, at least gastronomically, if not nutritionally. Other issues cause greater concern. Since salmon are confined in much closer quarters than would occur in the wild, they are much more susceptible to disease. Aquafarmers routinely use antibiotics to prevent this, though admittedly less than they did in the industry's early years. Knowing now that overuse of antibiotics can actually foster the development of resistant microorganisms, this practice should be of concern to all of us. More disturbingly, farmed salmon are fed dyes derived from petrochemicals to color their flesh anywhere from pale pink to rosy red (farmer's choice) to mimic the color wild salmon achieve through their diet. And most troubling of all, two recent scientifically credible studies report unacceptably high levels of PCBs in farmed salmon.

So how do I buy good salmon?

One way to be sure that you're buying wild-caught salmon is to buy Alaskan. There are no fish farms in Alaska, where salmon farming was prohibited in 1990 to protect the wild stock from potential problems. The state's 40-year-old programs, which monitor every species to ensure that sufficient numbers escape capture to maintain the population, are a model for fishery management around the world.

Beyond ecological considerations, the most important tool to use in buying any seafood is your nose. There should never be a "fishy" smell, which is a prime indicator of old product. It's one of the reasons I've never particularly liked buying fresh fish from supermarkets where they shrink-wrap it in plastic trays—it's nearly impossible to smell.

If you're buying salmon with the head on, the eyes are a good clue to freshness. They should be firm and clear, not sunken and milky. The gills should be bright red and not brownish. Much of the salmon we buy has already been dressed (gutted, which should happen immediately after they're caught) and cut into steaks or fillets. Look on the inside of the belly. Any breaks in the creamy inner lining or any kind of discoloration (known as "belly burn") are an indication of careless or late cleaning.

Sometimes the skin is on, and if so, look to see if most of the scales are intact. If not, this could be a sign that the fish has been bruised. Pale patches on the red meat are a signal that the fish has been in prolonged direct contact with water or ice. This can result in flavorless, waterlogged meat. Finally, because salmon are a fattier fish, look at the fat layer near the skin, especially around the belly. It should be very light pink, not brown, which again is an indication of age.

Better than other fish, salmon lends itself to several cooking methods, each giving a different end result. In the recipes below, I'm using four: roasting, grilling, steaming, and curing.

ROASTING Salmon is a full-bodied, oily fish, which makes it an ideal candidate for roasting. Below are recipes utilizing two different approaches, low heat and high heat—which I suppose qualifies as baking, but to the contemporary ear, "roasting" just sounds better.

slow-roasted salmon

SERVES 6

This is the simplest recipe imaginable. What makes it work is that most of the natural fat in the salmon stays put and isn't cooked away by high heat. You end up with a beautifully buttery, moist piece of fish. The skin helps promote this by sealing in the juices and also contributes flavor of its own. You don't have to eat the skin if you don't want to, but do leave it on while the fish cooks. (Obviously, you can cook a single fillet or as many as you can fit in your oven; just use more or less herbs and lemon zest.)

Extra virgin olive oil
6 thick salmon fillets or steaks with skin on, about 5 ounces each
Salt and freshly ground pepper

½ cup chopped fresh herbs, such as tarragon, parsley, or chives
2 tablespoons finely grated lemon zest

PREHEAT THE OVEN to 250°F. Gently rub a little olive oil into the flesh side of the salmon and season it lightly with salt and pepper. (Rubbing the fish will also give you the chance to feel for any little bones, which you can pick out with your fingers or tweezers.) Lay the salmon skin side down on a nonstick or parchment-paper-lined baking sheet. Combine the herbs and zest and sprinkle over the top, gently pressing into the flesh. Roast in the oven for 22 to 25 minutes or until just cooked through but still slightly translucent in the very center (check with the tip of a knife). Serve warm or at room temperature.

variation   Instead of the chopped fresh herbs and zest, you could use one of the pestos (see page 38).

salmon fillet roasted in lemon butter

SERVES 6 TO 8

This is the flip side of the recipe above: a salmon fillet roasted fast in a super-hot oven. Try them both and see which you prefer. In this approach, the fish cooks in a fragrant bath of butter and herbs. I call for a whole fillet, or side of salmon, but you can also roast individual portions.

½ cup (1 stick) butter
4 tablespoons olive oil
⅓ cup crisp, light-bodied white wine
2 tablespoons fresh lemon juice
1 tablespoon finely grated lemon zest
1 teaspoon sugar

Salt and freshly ground pepper to taste
1 boned salmon fillet, 2 to 3 pounds, skin on or off
¼ cup mixed fresh chopped herbs, such as tarragon, chives, or parsley, or a combination

PREHEAT THE OVEN to 500°F. In a small saucepan, combine the butter, olive oil, wine, lemon juice and zest, sugar, salt, and pepper, and warm gently. Pour half of the mixture into a shallow roasting pan that will just fit the salmon fillet. Lay the fillet in skin side down, and then drizzle the remaining butter mixture over the top and sprinkle on the herbs. Cover the pan with foil and place in the oven. Roast for 8 minutes or so, then uncover and check for doneness in the thickest part of the fish with the tip of a knife. The flesh should be firm but still slightly translucent in the middle. (Most home oven thermostats are notoriously inaccurate, especially at very low and very high temperatures, so do check on the fish, and don't be surprised if it cooks even faster or needs a little more time.) If necessary, return the uncovered pan to the oven and roast 3 to 4 minutes more or until just done. Using two spatulas, remove the salmon to a warm platter and spoon the juices over the top. Serve warm.

GRILLING The weather in Northern California frequently just begs for outdoor cooking, so I use this method for preparing salmon. See the Grilling lesson (page 148) for lots of grilling tips and other recipe ideas.

grilled tequila-lime marinated salmon

SERVES 6

The marinade is also excellent with chicken or pork. As discussed in the Marinades lesson (page 54), the acidity in the marinade will change the texture of the fish if you leave it for too long. For chicken and pork, up to 4 hours is fine. One hour is the maximum for fish.

6 thick salmon fillets or steaks with skin on, about 5 ounces each

Tequila-Lime Marinade

PLACE THE SALMON in a nonreactive dish or resealable plastic bag, add the marinade, and refrigerate for up to 1 hour, turning once or twice.

Prepare a charcoal fire or preheat a gas or stovetop grill.

Remove the salmon from the marinade, and grill directly over medium-high heat on both sides until just cooked (it should still be slightly translucent in the middle), perhaps 5 minutes or so. Serve warm.

suggestion ~ If you're feeling ambitious, serve with a topping of Pineapple Melon Salsa (page 10).

tequila-lime marinade

¹/₂ cup tequila
¹/₂ cup fresh lime juice
¹/₃ cup fresh orange juice
I teaspoon Asian chili-garlic sauce, or to taste

I tablespoon olive oil
¹/₄ cup chopped fresh cilantro leaves
¹/₄ teaspoon salt

COMBINE ALL THE ingredients in a blender and blend until smooth.
MAKES ABOUT I ¹/₃ CUPS

grilled salmon with a lemon-balsamic glaze

SERVES 6

This one is going to knock your socks off. Once you've made the glaze (you can make it weeks ahead, and it's completely foolproof), you'll want to eat it on everything: salmon, grilled portabellas, tofu, pork tenderloin—you can't miss. I prefer to grill the salmon with the skin on because it contributes flavor and helps keep the fish in one piece when I turn it. If your preference is skin-off, then by all means, do it that way. A whole salmon fillet makes a really nice presentation too, as long as you can easily fit it and turn it on your grill. You can also pan-roast, broil, or steam the salmon, since the glaze goes on after it's cooked.

**6 thick salmon steaks or fillets with skin
   on, about 5 ounces each
Olive oil**

**Salt and freshly ground pepper
Lemon-Balsamic Glaze**

PREPARE A CHARCOAL fire or preheat a gas or stovetop grill.

   Rub both sides of the fillets with some olive oil and season lightly with salt and pepper. (Rubbing the fish will also give you the chance to feel for any little bones, which you can pick out with your fingers or tweezers.) Grill the salmon directly over medium-high heat on both sides until just cooked through, perhaps 5 minutes or so. Place on warm plates, drizzle with the glaze, and serve.

lemon-balsamic glaze

**1/2 cup balsamic vinegar
1/2 cup crisp, light-bodied white wine
2 tablespoons fresh lemon juice
2 tablespoons packed light or dark
   brown sugar**

**1/8 teaspoon freshly ground black
   pepper, or to taste**

COMBINE ALL THE ingredients in a small saucepan and bring to a boil. Cook uncovered over high heat until the mixture thickens, 3 to 4 minutes. Store covered in the refrigerator for up to 3 weeks. Warm slightly on the stove or in the microwave before using.

MAKES A LITTLE LESS THAN 1/2 CUP

grilled salmon with roasted red pepper sauce

SERVES 6

This is not a recipe so much as it is an example of how layering a simply made component, like the grilled salmon, with more elaborate make-ahead components can give you a dish of real sophistication with complex flavors and texture.

6 thick salmon fillets or steaks with skin on, about 5 ounces each
Extra virgin olive oil
Kosher salt and freshly ground pepper
Roasted Red Bell Pepper Sauce (page 79)

1 medium avocado, diced or sliced into fans, if you know how
Grilled Corn Salsa (page 9)
Crema (Mexican sour cream) or stirred sour cream (optional)

PREPARE A CHARCOAL fire or preheat a gas or stovetop grill.

Rub both sides of the fillets with some olive oil and season lightly with salt and pepper. (Rubbing the fish will also give you the chance to feel for any little bones, which you can pick out with your fingers or tweezers.) Grill the salmon directly over medium-high heat on both sides until cooked through, about 5 minutes. It should be slightly translucent in the center. Remove the skin if desired.

To serve, place about ¼ cup of the Roasted Red Bell Pepper Sauce on a warm plate. Lay a piece of salmon in the center and top with some avocado, a tablespoon or so of the Grilled Corn Salsa, and a drizzle of crema, if desired.

salmon and omega-3s

The fat in fish is rich in polyunsaturated fatty acids called omega-3s. Fattier fish, such as salmon, tuna, and mackerel, are especially good sources. These fatty acids reduce blood clotting and may lower the risk of coronary artery disease and fatal heart attacks. They may even be beneficial against rheumatoid arthritis and psoriasis, and there is some suggestion that they can reduce the risk of macular degeneration, a leading cause of blindness. There is no government recommendation for omega-3 intake, but we all should get as much as we can, and food is the best source. The American Heart Association suggests eating at least 2 servings of fish weekly, and especially salmon and tuna.

CURING This is an ancient technique, which the Scandinavians used before refrigeration. Salt draws the water out of the fish and unravels proteins in its flesh in a chemical process that parallels that of cooking with heat. Curing is a kind of alchemy that changes raw salmon to something silky and delicious.

gravlax or herb-cured salmon

SERVES 10 OR MORE AS AN APPETIZER

This is the classic preparation for gravlax. Dill is traditional, but I like to use a mixture of herbs. Once you've mastered this, you can flavor it in limitless ways. Here's the most important thing: gravlax is ridiculously easy to make, but because few people do it, it's incredibly impressive. You can serve hot dogs for Christmas dinner, but if you've started with a first course of homemade gravlax, your guests will think you're a brilliant cook.

1 boned salmon fillet, 3 to 4 pounds, skin on
½ cup kosher or sea salt
⅓ cup sugar
2 tablespoons finely grated lemon zest

2 teaspoons freshly ground black pepper
1 cup finely chopped mixed fresh herbs, such as dill, basil, tarragon, parsley, chives, mint, chervil, and cilantro
⅓ cup vodka, grappa, or aquavit

LINE A PAN just large enough to hold the salmon with a generous, overhanging layer of plastic wrap. Lay the salmon on top, skin side down. Feel the salmon carefully to find any little bones and remove them with your fingers or tweezers.

Mix the salt, sugar, zest, and pepper together and sprinkle over the salmon. Scatter the herbs over the fish, then sprinkle with the vodka. Wrap the salmon tightly with the plastic wrap and place a smaller pan directly on top of the wrapped salmon. Weight it with a brick, if you happen to have one, or some canned goods. Refrigerate for 1 to 2 days, turning the salmon over at least twice a day and pouring off the liquid.

To serve the gravlax, unwrap it and gently wipe off the curing ingredients. Slice it very thinly, at an angle, with long sawing strokes, leaving the skin behind. It's best if the slices are almost thin enough to see through. If you notice any dark meat against the rosy flesh, neatly cut it away because it can be a little strong and fishy-tasting. Serve with a squeeze of lemon. Cured salmon lasts in the refrigerator for 2 to 3 days.

- Serve in tea sandwiches or canapés with thinly sliced cucumber and watercress.
- Make Gravlax Tartare by tossing finely diced (not sliced) gravlax with extra virgin olive oil; serve it with a squeeze of lemon, chopped chives, salmon caviar, and toast or pumpernickel points.
- Layer it on warm flat bread or potato pancakes topped with thinly sliced sweet red onions, capers, and a dollop of sour cream.

gravlax and dill quesadillas with salmon caviar

MAKES 8 HORS D'OEUVRES

This is another festive use for the gravlax. You could substitute purchased smoked salmon or smoked trout or cooked shrimp and use any combination of melting cheeses that you like.

½ cup sour cream

4 tablespoons chopped fresh dill

2 teaspoons drained, rinsed, and chopped capers (optional)

Salt and freshly ground pepper to taste

3 8-inch flour tortillas

2 teaspoons Dijon mustard

1 cup grated Monterey Jack cheese

1 cup grated white cheddar cheese

3 tablespoons chopped red onion

2 teaspoons grated lemon zest

8 thin slices gravlax or smoked salmon

2 tablespoons salmon caviar, rinsed and drained

STIR THE SOUR CREAM, 2 tablespoons dill, and capers together. Season with salt and pepper and set aside for 30 minutes to let the flavors develop.

Preheat the oven to 450°F. Lightly brush the tops of the tortillas with mustard. Place 2 tortillas on an ungreased baking sheet. Sprinkle each with the Monterey Jack, cheddar, onion, remaining dill, and zest, and season with salt and pepper. Stack one tortilla on top of the other, and cover with the remaining tortilla. Bake in the oven until the tortillas are slightly crisp and the cheese has melted, 8 to 10 minutes. Alternatively, you can do this in a covered heavy skillet over medium heat.

Cut the quesadilla in eighths. Top each eighth with salmon, the dill sour cream, and salmon caviar. Serve immediately.

STEAMING Though poaching is one of the most popular techniques for cooking salmon, I prefer steaming. It seems to preserve more of the fish's flavor, and it's just as easy. Steaming, of course, is a very healthy way of cooking since no additional fats are added in cooking. (The sauce, of course, is a different matter!) In the recipes following, I use two different approaches: steaming on a rack in the oven and steaming on a plate in a bamboo (or other) steamer.

salmon steamed with black beans

SERVES 4

This is a full-flavored steamed dish. The Chinese are masters at this technique. Instead of salmon, you can use any meaty seafood, such as sea bass or even scallops or shrimp, adjusting cooking times accordingly. Oysters in the shell are also delicious. I usually use a Chinese bamboo steamer set over a pot of boiling water. The advantage of these steamers is that you can stack several on top of each other to easily double the recipe. If you don't have a bamboo steamer, you can jury-rig your own with any deep pot that has a tight-fitting cover and is wide enough to hold the steaming plate. Place an ovenproof ramekin on the bottom of the pot to elevate the plate above the boiling water.

2 tablespoons soy sauce or tamari

2 tablespoons dry sherry or Shaoxing (rice wine)

1 tablespoon packed light or dark brown sugar

2 tablespoons rice vinegar

1 tablespoon fresh lemon juice

1 tablespoon toasted sesame oil

Pinch of freshly ground white pepper

3 tablespoons homemade chicken or vegetable stock or your favorite canned broth

6 tablespoons olive oil

1 tablespoon finely sliced garlic

1¼ cups sliced shiitake mushrooms, stems removed and discarded

1 tablespoon peeled and very finely slivered fresh ginger

4 thick salmon fillets or steaks, about 5 ounces each

3 tablespoons Chinese dried (fermented) black beans (see Glossary and Pantry), rinsed well

IN A BLENDER, combine the soy sauce, sherry, brown sugar, vinegar, lemon juice, sesame oil, pepper, and stock and blend for a few seconds. With the motor running, slowly add 4 tablespoons of olive oil to form a lightly thickened sauce. Set aside.

In a sauté pan, heat the remaining 2 tablespoons of olive oil over medium-high heat and quickly sauté the garlic, mushrooms, and ginger until just cooked through. Place the fish on a heatproof plate (or plates) that will fit in your steamer. Top each fillet with some of the mushroom mixture and then spoon some of the blender sauce over that. Sprinkle the black beans around the fillets and carefully put the plate(s) in the steamer. Cover and steam over boiling water until the fish is just cooked through, about 10 minutes.

Serve with the mushrooms, black beans, and juices spooned over.

salmon steamed in the oven

SERVES 4 AS A MAIN COURSE

In this recipe, the salmon is cooked very slowly. Only a little steam is produced, but when captured in the oven, this gentle heat results in a succulent, buttery fish, since the fat in the fish is just melted, but not cooked away. Again, I suggest leaving the skin on to both keep the fish moist and add flavor, but you can do this skin off if you prefer. As with most of these recipes, you can steam a single fillet just as easily or do as many as will fit on your rack.

4 thick salmon fillets or steaks with skin on, about 5 ounces each
Extra virgin olive oil

Fresh lemon juice
Sea salt and freshly ground pepper

YOU'LL NEED A roasting pan at least 2 inches deep and a rack that will fit in it that's large enough to hold the salmon in a single layer.

Preheat the oven to 350°F. Place the pan in the oven and fill with an inch or so of boiling water (the actual amount depends on the height of the rack; just make sure the water doesn't touch the fish). Rub both sides of the fillets with olive oil and then rub in lemon juice. (Rubbing the fish will also give you the chance to feel for any little bones, which you can pick out with your fingers or tweezers.) Place the salmon skin side down on the rack and season with salt and pepper. Place the rack over the water in the pan and steam for 16 to 20 minutes or until the salmon is mostly cooked through but still slightly translucent in the center (check with the point of a knife).

Serve with a sauce of your choice, as you would poached salmon. I like this either warm with the Corn Cream (page 80) or at cool room temperature with an herb-flavored mayonnaise. The Salsa Verde (page 74) is excellent with steamed salmon, too.

salmon species

all wild salmon start off life in fresh water, go to the sea to mature, and then return to their freshwater birthplace to spawn and start the process again. There is one species of Atlantic salmon. The five species of Pacific salmon each have their own particular color, flavor, and texture: king (also called Chinook), coho (also called silver), sockeye (also called red), chum (also called silverbright), and pink. The first three command the highest prices, but all can be delicious depending on where and when in their life cycle they are caught and how they are handled. The "sixth salmon," called steelhead, is basically a rainbow trout, a member of the salmonid family. Mainly a freshwater fish, some do go out into the ocean one or more times during their lives and in the process become very salmon-like.

fresh vs. frozen . . .

fresh seafood is usually preferable to frozen—assuming that the fresh has been properly handled. Unfortunately this is not always the case, and in many instances, frozen seafood can be better than fresh, especially if it was caught on a boat many miles out at sea. Flash freezing allows fish to be immediately dressed (cleaned) and then frozen in prime condition. Assuming they are kept that way, they can actually be better than those unfrozen "fresh" fish that take several days to arrive at your local market.

A few years ago in my restaurant, we tried to test whether fresh salmon was better than frozen. Although it was not a scientific study, we bought fresh farmed salmon in the market and compared it to salmon caught and immediately flash frozen in blocks of ice. We cooked them in exactly the same way and then tried them blind on several knowledgeable diners. The vast majority preferred the frozen, caught salmon and commented on its firm texture, sweet flavor, and bright color.

16 shrimp

Fastest Seafood in the West (and East)

Americans
eat more
shrimp
per capita than any other nation. Canned tuna used to reign as America's favorite food from the sea, but it looks now like shrimp is the biggie.

Shrimp belong to the crustacean family along with crab, lobster, crayfish, langoustine, and the like. There are hundreds of species of shrimp around the world. They range from tiny to "gigantic" in size, and their shells come in many colors, from the familiar gray, pink, and white to red, yellow, green, and blue—there are even some with multicolored stripes. Those hundreds of species can be divided into two categories: warm-water species and cold-water. Most of what we consume (80 percent or so) comes from warm waters in the tropics and subtropics. In American markets, basically five types are sold widely:

FROM WARM WATERS

~ **Gulf or Mexican Whites and Pinks:** These are the most expensive, but worth it for their sweet flavor and firm texture. (Whites are herbivorous.) As the name implies, many come

from the Gulf coasts of America and Mexico, but there is also a substantial supply coming to us from Peru, Ecuador, and Chile. Most are wild-caught, but a growing number are being farm-raised, especially in China.

~ **Gulf Browns:** Browns have a somewhat stronger flavor than whites because they are omnivores, feeding on both algae and microscopic animals known as zooplankton. Gulf Browns come from the same areas as the whites and are more plentiful. Most Americans prefer whites, but folks in Texas, among others, often prefer browns.

~ **Tiger Shrimp:** Tiger shrimp shells are marked with a distinctive black or gray stripe. They can be used in the same way as Gulf shrimp, though to my palate, they aren't nearly as good in either flavor or texture. Native to the Pacific and Indian Oceans, most are

farm-raised in Asia and India, and I have serious concerns about how they are cultivated. They survive in fresh or brackish water and some (not all) unscrupulous farmers turn a fast buck by digging a pond, seeding it with these quick-maturing shrimp, harvesting, and starting a new crop again. After the ponds become so polluted that they won't support life anymore,

the farmer moves on, scoops out a new pond, leaving behind the polluted one. I advise you not to buy tigers unless your store can vouch for the fact that they have been *wholesomely and sustainably raised* (an important issue for all our food).

~ **Rock Shrimp:** These have become more available in recent years, especially in restaurants. They come from Florida and the Gulf Coast and, as the name suggests, have shells that are rock hard. This means they must be put through rollers that crush the shells so they can be removed. In the process, the shrimp meat gets a little roughed up, but don't let this dissuade you from buying them—the flavor and texture are delicious. Sometimes described as "poor man's lobster," they do resemble lobster in both flavor and texture. They cook very quickly, so be careful not to overcook them. Rock shrimp are delicious made into cakes, quickly sautéed for pasta or salads, and in stuffings. They come peeled, so they are especially quick to use.

FROM COLD WATERS

~ The icy northern oceans of the world produce several varieties of shrimp, generally quite small (70 to 100 per pound). These are most often sold cooked and peeled and are referred to as "bay" or salad shrimp. Harvested mostly from wild sources, they have a more pronounced iodine flavor. They are ideal for salads, cocktails, and sandwiches. The quality of the little bay shrimp is usually quite good, but can vary depending on the source and supplier.

buying shrimp

Shrimp are usually labeled and priced (at least by the processor and wholesaler) according to their size, which is expressed in number per pound, e.g., "U 10" (under 10 per pound), "10–15" (10–15 per pound), etc. In other words, the higher the number, the smaller the shrimp. Like all fish and shellfish, shrimp should have a clean, fresh, "seaweedy" smell. Any hint of ammonia means that they are old, so don't buy them.

What's the difference between prawns and shrimp?

You've seen both terms. Maybe you've pretended to know the difference. The answer is . . . there is no difference. Basically, it all depends on where you come from. In Britain and former British colonies, all shrimp are called prawns. In the United States, especially in the Northeast, "prawn" was used to describe large (and thus more expensive) shrimp. In a restaurant, you can charge more for "prawns" than "shrimp"! In the South, all shrimp are generally referred to as "shrimp," irrespective of size.

Are fresh shrimp better than frozen?

When it comes to shrimp, don't be fooled by promises of "fresh" and don't be put off by the word "frozen." Unless you are in a place where you can buy shrimp right off the boat, all shrimp have been frozen. Once out of the water, shrimp deteriorate very quickly, and for this reason, they are usually processed and flash frozen. Most shrimp are sold with the head removed because that's the first part to go as they "age."

Before we get to some of my favorite shrimp recipes, let's go over some useful preparation techniques.

~ **Brining:** I almost always brine "green" (uncooked) shrimp before cooking them. It doesn't take long and it adds a succulence and firm, juicy texture that I think is fantastic. You can use a liquid brine made of $1/3$ cup kosher or sea salt and $1/3$ cup brown sugar dissolved in 1 quart of water. Soak the peeled or unpeeled shrimp in it for anywhere from 5 minutes to 1 hour. Or you can use the "dry method" and simply coat peeled, uncooked shrimp with a generous sprinkle of kosher or sea salt and let it sit for up to 10 minutes. With either method, be sure to rinse the shrimp well before you cook them to remove any excess salt. They won't be noticeably saltier, for those of you who are concerned about your salt consumption.

~ **Peeling and deveining:** My recommendation is to always buy your uncooked shrimp with the shell on and peel them yourself. Pre-peeled shrimp are susceptible to freezer burn and are generally less flavorful. Peeling or removing the shell is pretty simple. The vein of the shrimp is actually its intestinal tract and should be removed because it sometimes contains grit and is not necessarily pleasant in taste. To remove the vein from shrimp that are already peeled, simply make a shallow cut down the length of the back with a small sharp knife and pull out the vein. Rinse the shrimp. With unpeeled shrimp, use kitchen shears or sharp scissors to cut the back of the shell down the middle, cutting down the back of the shrimp flesh at the same time. Pull out the vein and rinse. Now you can either peel off the shell or leave it on, as the recipe requires.

save the shrimp shells!

in my classes, I constantly remind students to save the shells from peeling shrimp. Put them in a plastic bag, tie it closed, and keep it in the freezer. When you need a good fish or shellfish stock for a soup, sauce, or stew, all you have to do is simmer the shells for 5 to 10 minutes in a chicken or vegetable stock and then strain them out. The more shells you have, the more flavorful the stock. A classic French cooking technique calls for sautéing or roasting the shells of shrimp or lobster with a little butter or oil and then grinding them up before infusing them in stock. The simpler method is nearly as good and a whole lot faster. I still see recipes today in cookbooks and magazines that call for using bottled clam juice. Ick! Bottled clam juice is often very salty, sometimes bleached to improve its color, and sometimes also includes weird chemical additives like EDTA. Who needs that stuff? This shrimp shell stock is much superior.

perfectly cooked shrimp

FOR ABOUT 2 POUNDS OF LARGE (16–20 SIZE) SHRIMP

The major problem in cooking shrimp is that we generally end up overcooking them, and as a result, they become tough. Restaurants are especially famous for this—even if the cook or chef prepares them perfectly, a few minutes under the hot lamp waiting for pick-up puts them over the top. The objective is to cook shrimp so that they still are a little bit translucent in the center when cooking is finished. The following method, using a version of classic court-bouillon, is a good one that pretty much ensures that the shrimp will be cooked perfectly. Couple this with the brining process laid out above and you'll be in great shape!

2 pounds large (16–20 size) shrimp
1 1/2 cups crisp, light-bodied white wine
1 cup coarsely chopped carrot
1 cup coarsely chopped yellow or white onions

1/2 cup chopped celery
3 large bay leaves
8 whole black peppercorns
1 whole clove
1 tablespoon salt

PEEL AND DEVEIN the shrimp and brine them if you like (see page 271). In a deep saucepan, combine 4 cups of water, the wine, carrot, onions, celery, bay leaves, peppercorns, clove, and salt, bring to a boil over high heat, then lower the heat, cover, and simmer for a few minutes. Add the shrimp, cover, and simmer for 1 minute. Immediately turn off the heat and keep covered. After about 3 minutes, check on the shrimp: if they're nearly opaque but still a little translucent in the center, they're ready. If not, re-cover the pan and wait another minute or two. It should take no longer than 5 minutes off the heat.

Drain, reserving the cooking liquid, and refrigerate the shrimp. Serve cold with your favorite cocktail sauce, or mine—Green and Red Salsa (page 5). In fact, any of the salsas make great cocktail sauces. The shrimp can also be used in any recipe that calls for cooked shrimp. The cooking liquid can be used again: store it in the refrigerator for up to a week or in the freezer indefinitely. You can also strain it, which will then give you the base for a nice stock or sauce. Make it richer in flavor by simmering some shrimp shells in it, as discussed above.

quesadilla marina

I encountered this "open face" quesadilla many years ago at a stand in Mexico, where a guy with a little kerosene stove and a small sauté pan was turning out a quesadilla a minute for an approving line of sun worshippers on a beach near Manzanillo. If you have homemade tortillas, so much the better. Ideally, pan and tortilla should be pretty much the same diameter to facilitate turning it out cleanly. A nonstick pan makes life easier too. Finally, you can also make this in the more traditional way by sandwiching the filling between two tortillas, which is easier to handle, if less exciting to look at.

I regular or whole wheat 6-inch flour
   tortilla
1/2 teaspoon olive oil
1/4 cup sliced red or yellow onions
I teaspoon thinly slivered garlic
Drops of your favorite hot pepper sauce
   to taste
1/2 cup coarsely chopped Perfectly
   Cooked Shrimp (page 273), or any
   cooked shrimp
2 tablespoons coarsely chopped fresh
   cilantro leaves

1/3 cup diced and seeded ripe Roma-
   type tomato
Salt and freshly ground pepper
Fresh lime juice
1/2 cup coarsely grated melting cheese
   such as Sonoma Jack, queso fresco, or
   mozzarella

Accompaniments: fresh guacamole and
   Basic Salsa Fresca or Cruda
   (page 4)

BRIEFLY TOAST THE tortilla in a dry, 6-inch nonstick skillet for a minute or two on each side, and set aside. Add the olive oil, onions, and garlic to the pan and sauté over medium heat until crisp-tender. Add the hot sauce and shrimp, and sauté for 1 minute more. Stir in the cilantro and tomato and season to taste with salt, pepper, and drops of lime juice. Immediately sprinkle the cheese over the shrimp mixture and lay the tortilla on top, gently pressing down to form an even layer. Sauté for 1 minute more to melt the cheese, and then turn over onto a warm plate. Cut into wedges and serve immediately, topped with a little guacamole and salsa, if using.

lettuce cups with thai shrimp and carrot salad

SERVES 6

This make-ahead dish was inspired by a recent trip to Australia. The food scene there has really come of age and though the continent was settled by the British primarily, the food now reflects Australia's proximity to Asia, and Asian flavors and ingredients abound everywhere.

**1 pound Perfectly Cooked Shrimp
(page 273; 21–25 size suggested), or
any cooked shrimp, peeled**
12 crisp iceberg lettuce leaves

Carrot Salad
¼ cup finely chopped unsalted peanuts
⅓ cup fresh cilantro leaves

ARRANGE THE SHRIMP, lettuce, Carrot Salad, peanuts, and cilantro in piles or bowls on a large platter and let guests fill and roll lettuce leaves as they please.

carrot salad

⅓ cup fresh lime juice
2 tablespoons brown sugar
**2 tablespoons Asian fish sauce (see
Glossary and Pantry), or to taste**
**1 teaspoon finely minced serrano chile,
or to taste**

**2 teaspoons peeled and finely minced
fresh ginger**
**1 tablespoon finely minced tender
lemon grass, or 2 teaspoons finely
minced lemon zest**
3 cups finely julienned carrots
1 tablespoon finely slivered garlic

WHISK THE LIME juice, brown sugar, fish sauce, chile, ginger, and lemon grass together in a medium bowl. Taste and adjust the flavor to your liking by adding more of any of those ingredients. (You may want to wait to taste and adjust until after the marinating period.) Add the carrots and garlic, and marinate at least 30 minutes before serving.

MAKES ABOUT 3 CUPS

mini rock shrimp cakes with mango salsa

MAKES ABOUT 12 CAKES

Here is another great little appetizer or hors d'oeuvre. Rock shrimp is not always out on the fishmonger's counter—in parts of the country where it is not as well known, its broken appearance can make it a tough sell—but they can always get if for you, so ask. It's really delicious.

1 tablespoon olive oil

1¼ pounds shelled rock shrimp

1 large egg, beaten

5 tablespoons mayonnaise

½ teaspoon dry mustard

1 tablespoon chopped fresh cilantro
   leaves, plus whole leaves for garnish

3 tablespoons chopped green onions
   (white and green parts)

2 teaspoons white wine worcestershire

Drops of your favorite hot sauce
   to taste

Salt

1½ cups or so coarse dry bread crumbs
   (I like the Japanese-style panko)

Clarified butter or olive oil for sautéing

Mango Salsa

HEAT THE OLIVE oil in a large sauté pan over medium-high heat. Add the shrimp and cook for just 1 minute. The shrimp will start to turn pink, still be translucent and not quite done. Immediately drain the shrimp, and set aside to cool.

In a large bowl, combine the egg, mayonnaise, mustard, cilantro, green onions, Worcestershire, hot sauce, and salt to taste. Chop the sautéed rock shrimp coarsely and fold into the mixture with ½ cup or so of the bread crumbs. Form a small cake and see if the mixture keeps its shape. The goal is to use just enough bread crumbs to hold the cake together. If the mixture is too moist, add slightly more bread crumbs. Form the mixture into 12 mini cakes and lightly coat them with the remaining bread crumbs. At this point, you can go ahead and sauté them or you can hold them in the refrigerator—in a single layer, *uncovered*—for up to 3 hours.

To finish, heat the clarified butter in large sauté pan over medium-high heat, and cook the cakes until lightly browned on both sides. Remove the cakes and drain briefly on paper towels. Top with a little of the Mango Salsa and an herb leaf or two and serve immediately.

mango salsa

1 cup diced firm ripe mango
¼ cup finely diced red onion, soaked
    briefly in ice water and drained
2 tablespoons finely diced red bell
    pepper
3 tablespoons fresh lime juice
1 teaspoon finely minced jalapeño chile,
    or to taste

2 teaspoons peeled and finely minced
    fresh ginger
2 teaspoons olive oil
2 tablespoons coarsely chopped fresh
    cilantro leaves
Salt to taste
Drops of honey to taste

COMBINE ALL THE ingredients and set aside for 30 minutes before serving to let the flavors develop. Store covered in the refrigerator for up to 2 days. MAKES ABOUT 1 ½ CUPS

spicy wok-fried shrimp

SERVES 4 TO 6 AS AN APPETIZER

This is a great party food that requires you to dig in and peel the shrimp, and of course, lick your fingers. Be sure to have lots of paper napkins on hand. I highly recommend seeking out the Sichuan peppercorns (not really pepper) called for. Their fragrant spiciness is really unique. (See Glossary and Pantry for more.) If you can't find them, use any regular pepper.

¾ pound large (16–20 size) shrimp in their shell

1 tablespoon kosher salt

2 teaspoons toasted Sichuan peppercorns, ground

1½ teaspoons sugar

3 tablespoons finely chopped garlic

1 tablespoon peeled and finely chopped fresh ginger

3 tablespoons finely chopped scallions (white and green parts)

1 to 2 teaspoons finely chopped hot red chiles, or to taste

2 tablespoons olive or canola oil

1 teaspoon toasted sesame oil

Garnish if you like with finely chopped fresh cilantro leaves and toasted sesame seeds

CLEAN EACH SHRIMP by cutting through the back with a pair of kitchen shears or a knife and removing the intestinal vein. Leave the shell on but pull off the feathery legs. Brine if you like (see page 271). Bring a large pot of lightly salted water to a boil. Plunge the shrimp into the simmering water for 10 to 15 seconds, and then drain them and run them under cold water to stop any further cooking. Pat dry and set aside.

In a small bowl, combine the salt, peppercorns, and sugar and set aside. In another bowl, combine the garlic, ginger, scallions, and chiles. Heat the olive oil in a wok over high heat. Add the salt mixture and stir-fry for 10 seconds. Add the shrimp and the garlic mixture and continue to stir-fry until the shrimp are just cooked through and the spices coat the shell, about 2 minutes. Stir in the sesame oil and garnish with cilantro and sesame seeds, if desired. Serve immediately.

shrimp with green curry sauce

SERVES 4

This recipe takes advantage of off-the-shelf Thai curry paste, of which there are many varieties. Look for them in Asian markets, in the "ethnic food" aisle, or online. Kaffir lime leaves are also available fresh or frozen in Asian markets or (like me) you can grow your own if you're in a climate that is tolerant of citrus. Galangal is a relative of ginger used extensively in Thai cooking. Its thin skin means it doesn't need to be peeled. You can use this same recipe approach for all kinds of fish, chicken, or pork.

1¼ pounds medium (21–25 size) shrimp
2 cups unsweetened coconut milk, well stirred
1 tablespoon Thai green curry paste, or to taste
4 kaffir lime leaves, or 1 tablespoon finely grated lime zest
1 tablespoon Asian fish sauce (see Glossary and Pantry)
1 tablespoon brown or palm sugar
1 cup lightly packed chopped fresh spinach or romaine lettuce leaves
Fresh lime juice
3 tablespoons olive oil

1 medium white onion, peeled and thinly sliced
1 large red or yellow bell pepper, stemmed, seeded, and thinly sliced
2 tablespoons peeled and finely slivered fresh ginger or galangal
1 tablespoon peeled and finely slivered garlic
1 cup diced and seeded fresh tomato
½ cup fresh tender basil, mint, or cilantro leaves

Accompaniments: steamed aromatic rice, such as jasmine or basmati

PEEL AND DEVEIN the shrimp, brine if you like (see page 271), and set aside. Combine the coconut milk, curry paste, and lime leaves in a saucepan, and bring to a boil. Whisk the mixture to dissolve the curry paste and simmer for 5 minutes or until the sauce is slightly thickened. Discard the lime leaves and stir in the fish sauce, sugar, and spinach. Transfer to a blender and puree. Adjust the hot/salt/sweet/tart elements to your taste with additional curry, fish sauce, sugar, and lime juice. Set aside.

In a sauté pan or wok, heat 2 tablespoons of the olive oil and quickly sauté the onion, pepper, ginger, and garlic over high heat until lightly colored and crisp-tender; add to the curry sauce. Heat the remaining tablespoon of oil in the same pan and sauté the shrimp over high heat until just done. Pour the curry sauce and vegetables into the pan and heat through. Stir in the tomato and the basil leaves. Serve with steamed rice.

grilled shrimp wrapped in soppressata with mango hot mustard sauce

SERVES 4 AS A MAIN COURSE

This is one of those combinations that sounds weird but is a crowd-pleaser. You can serve it as an appetizer or as a main course with steamed jasmine or basmati rice. (Skewer each shrimp individually for a less messy hors d'oeuvre.) Soppressata is a cured Italian sausage similar to salami. It has a wonderful, peppery flavor and is generally available at good delicatessens. Ask for it very thinly sliced—it will stay wrapped around the shrimp better during grilling.

16 small fresh basil leaves

16 large (16–20 size) shrimp, peeled, deveined, and brined, if you like

16 thin slices of soppressata

Mango Hot Mustard Sauce

PREPARE A CHARCOAL fire or preheat a gas or stovetop grill. Place a basil leaf on the side of each shrimp and then wrap the shrimp with a slice of the soppressata. Grill the shrimp until just cooked through. The center should be very slightly translucent—you can check with the point of a small knife. Serve immediately with the sauce spooned over or arranged for dipping.

mango hot mustard sauce

½ cup pureed ripe mango (from 1 medium mango) or canned

¼ cup fresh tangerine or orange juice

¾ teaspoon Chinese hot mustard powder, or to taste

2 teaspoons fresh lime juice

2 teaspoons seasoned rice vinegar

2 tablespoons dry white wine

1 tablespoon canola or other neutral flavored oil

Salt to taste

COMBINE THE MANGO, tangerine juice, mustard powder, lime juice, vinegar, and wine in a blender and pulse 3 or 4 times to puree and combine. Add the canola oil and pulse 3 or 4 times more to make a smooth sauce. Season with salt. Set the sauce aside for at least 2 hours while the flavors marry and build. The sauce can be warmed gently, but do not simmer or boil. Store covered in the refrigerator for up to 3 days.

MAKES ABOUT I CUP

celery, cabbage, and carrot salad with bay shrimp and curry dressing

SERVES 4

This is a crunchy and refreshing salad. Curry powders vary in intensity, so be sure to add it slowly and taste as you go.

FOR THE DRESSING

2/3 cup mayonnaise

1/4 cup buttermilk or unsweetened coconut milk

2 tablespoons fresh lemon or lime juice

1 tablespoon finely chopped sweet pickled ginger (sushi ginger)

2 teaspoons curry powder, or to taste

Salt and freshly ground pepper to taste

1 pound cooked and peeled bay shrimp

1 cup celery sliced on the bias

3 cups very finely sliced green cabbage

1 1/2 cups julienned carrots

2 green onions, cut thinly on the bias (green and white parts)

2 tablespoons chopped fresh mint or cilantro leaves

1/2 cup lightly toasted macadamia nuts or almonds, coarsely chopped

AT LEAST 1 hour before serving, mix all the dressing ingredients together and set aside (in the refrigerator) to let the flavors marry and develop. Taste and adjust the seasoning just before using. Can be made up to 2 days ahead and stored covered in the refrigerator.

In a large bowl, mix the shrimp, celery, cabbage, carrots, onions, herbs, and nuts together. Toss with the dressing and serve on chilled plates.

shrimp with vinegar cream

SERVES 4

This Vinegar Cream sauce goes equally well on anything quickly sautéed, such as chicken breast, pork tenderloin medallions, or vegetables. Try experimenting with different fruit vinegars; it's fun to add some of the same fresh fruit that flavors the vinegar. Note that vinegars differ in strength, so you will want to adjust the amount to your taste.

1 pound large (16–20 size) shrimp
3 tablespoons butter
2 tablespoons olive oil
1/4 cup minced shallots or green onion (green and white parts)
1/2 cup fragrant fruit vinegar, such as pear, plum, or apple (see Note)
2 cups homemade chicken stock or your favorite canned broth

2/3 cup heavy cream or crème fraîche
1/4 cup diced fresh fruit, such as pears, or whatever the vinegar is flavored with (optional)
2 teaspoons finely chopped fresh herbs of your choice
Salt and freshly ground pepper

PEEL AND DEVEIN the shrimp (reserving the shells) and brine if desired. Drain the shrimp, rinse, and set aside.

In a heavy sauté pan, heat 2 tablespoons of the butter and 1 tablespoon of the olive oil over medium-high heat. Coarsely chop the reserved shells and add to the pan, along with the shallots, and stir until lightly colored. Add the vinegar and stock and reduce over high heat until the sauce thickens slightly, about 4 minutes. Strain, pressing down on the solids, and return the liquid to the pan. Add the cream. Reduce again to a light sauce consistency. Stir in the fruit, if using, and herbs, and season to taste with salt and pepper. Set aside and keep warm.

Wipe out the pan, add the remaining butter and oil, and quickly sauté the shrimp until pink and barely cooked through. Arrange on warm plates, and spoon on the warm sauce. Serve immediately.

NOTE: Fruit vinegars are available at gourmet stores. Depending on the strength/flavor of the vinegar you can whisk a little more into the sauce just before serving for a more piquant finish.

paella with chicken, clams, and shrimp

SERVES 6 TO 8

This classic saffron-scented dish from Spain is similar to risotto, but with its own distinctive flavors and traditions. It is often made outside on the grill, ideally over a wood fire. In Spain they use a special round, often copper, pan that is fairly shallow, to allow the smoke to roll over it and flavor the food as it cooks. You can do it however you like—on the stovetop or even in the oven. Paella can contain a variety of meats, including sausages, as well as fish, shellfish, and vegetables, depending on the whim and budget of the cook. The base, however, is the rice. A variety called Valencia is traditional. Any medium-grain rice, such as Arborio, can substitute nicely.

¼ cup olive oil

2 pounds boned and skinless chicken thighs, cut in half

Salt and freshly ground pepper

2 cups (1 large) white onion, chopped

2 tablespoons sliced garlic

1 cup diced poblano or other green chile

2 cups Valencia or other medium-grain rice

½ cup dry white wine

4 cups hot homemade chicken stock or your favorite canned broth

¼ teaspoon saffron threads, or to taste

1 cup diced fresh or drained canned tomatoes

3 or 4 fresh thyme sprigs or 2 teaspoons dried

1 teaspoon fennel seeds

2 pounds fresh Manila or littleneck clams, well scrubbed

1 pound large (16–20 size) shrimp, peeled and deveined

2 cups cooked fresh or frozen giant lima or fava beans

HEAT THE OLIVE oil in a large, shallow pan over medium-high heat. Season the chicken well with salt and pepper, and lightly brown it in the pan on all sides, about 5 minutes. Add the onions, garlic, and chile and stir for another 2 minutes or until the vegetables just begin to color. Add the rice and stir for a minute to coat the grains.

Add the wine, stock, saffron, tomatoes, thyme, and fennel, and stir gently. Bring to a boil and nestle the clams down into the rice mixture. Cover the pan with its lid or with foil if you're cooking outside and cook until the clams open (discard any that don't) and the rice is tender, about 15 minutes. Nestle the shrimp into the rice mixture, cover, and cook for another minute or so, until the shrimp are pink (they will continue to cook as they sit in the mixture). Remove from the heat, stir in the beans, taste and season with salt and pepper, and serve.

17 soy foods

Tofu, Miso, and Tempeh

Only in recent times have Americans in any significant numbers begun to consider eating soy in its many forms, which is fascinating because American farmers produce more than half of the world's supply of soybeans. The bulk of these are used for animal feed, processed into "vegetable" oil (most vegetable oil is soybean oil), or exported to Asia, where they've been an important part of the diet for about three thousand years. The Chinese, who were probably the first to use soybeans, also mashed and strained them for soy milk and tofu, sprouted them, and pressed them for cooking oil.

If you're a longtime vegetarian or if you're of Chinese or Japanese descent and you've been eating tofu your whole life, you may be looking for new ways to use this versatile food. But most likely, you fall under the heading of "informed, but squeamish": you've heard about the tremendous nutritional value of soy and its purported health benefits, but you're not sure if it can taste good or how to begin to prepare it. In this lesson, we'll begin to explore the vast world of soybean products, with a focus on tofu. This is just a little "taster" to get you started.

Part of the recent interest in soy products has come from the understanding that in addition to being very nutritious, soybeans are rich in phyto (plant) chemicals. Soybeans provide a complete protein source: half a cup of cooked soybeans contains about the same amount of protein as 4 ounces of ground beef, but with none of the saturated fat and cholesterol. We are just beginning to understand and identify the unique properties of these chemical compounds. A group called isoflavones, which are found in high concentrations almost exclusively in soybeans, has been shown to help reduce the risk of heart disease, stroke, diabetes, breast cancer, as well as osteoporosis and menopausal symptoms. Pretty impressive, but then I have always believed that food is the first doctor. There are a number of great resources for finding out more about the health benefits of soy products.

But what about eating soybean foods for pleasure? While you're focusing on all these headline-making health claims, you may not have realized that the cultures that have eaten these foods for centuries have done so because they are delicious in so many different preparations. The most familiar soy food to most of us is one eaten purely for pleasure—soy sauce. The best soy sauces are fermented and aged in wood for a year or more. Traditional Japanese soy sauce, called *shoyu*, is made with a combination of wheat and soybeans. You'll also see bottles labeled *tamari*, which is Japanese soy sauce from soybeans only, with no wheat. My favorite soy sauces are those made in Japan, which I think have a more elegant and complex flavor than their Chinese counterparts, but like everything else, use what *you* like. As with vinegars, olive oils, or any other canned or bottled staple, I encourage you to do some taste-tests: buy several bottles (they're cheap enough), pour out a little, smell it, taste it plain, try it on a little rice or some noodles. Then stick with the ones you like best.

Soy is also used to make "milk," oil, flour, and meat and dairy analogues, especially cheeses, yogurts, and sour creams that are great for the lactose-intolerant. For our exploration here, I'm going to focus primarily on tofu (it can be delicious, trust me!), and also try a little miso and tempeh.

Tofu

The great virtue of tofu is that it can be transformed into an almost limitless variety of dishes. In the same sitting, you can have it as part of a delicious creamy dressing on a salad, then go on to serve it roasted, braised, or sautéed for the main course, and finally end with it incorporated into a rich, satisfying dessert. Tofu has been called the cheese of Asia and in fact it's made somewhat like cheese. Soaked soybeans are ground, added to water, and boiled. They are then strained to remove the skins and fiber; what's left is soymilk, which is coagulated with a natural mineral coagulant like calcium sulfate. Very quickly curds form, which are removed from the liquid whey and pressed. The basic differences between various types of tofu are the size of the curd and the length of the pressing time.

SELECTING AND BUYING TOFU

For the sake of understanding the varieties that are out there, I divide tofu into two basic types—Chinese-style and Japanese or silken—each of which is made in soft, firm, and extra firm styles.

The Chinese style is dense, solid, and meaty and keeps its shape. It comes in three types:

EXTRA FIRM TOFU contains a low amount of water. It is very dense and maintains its shape very well. It is ideal for stir-fried dishes, frying, broiling, and grilling. Extra firm tofu contains the most protein and fat. It can be frozen and thawed, then used as a meat replacement.

FIRM TOFU is not as dense, though it also holds its shape for slicing, cubing, frying, and crumbling into salads. Firm tofu works well in any recipe when you are in doubt of the firmness needed.

SOFT TOFU is much less dense and is ideal for blending into drinks, dips, dressings, sauces, and cheesecake. Because of its higher water content, soft tofu also is lower in both protein and fat.

These descriptors are only general guides. Brands can differ dramatically, both in taste (some are much "beanier" than others) and in texture (some are spongier, some smoother), so experiment and find one you like. Chinese-style tofus are all sold refrigerated, both packed in water and vacuum-packed without water. The latter has a significantly longer shelf life unopened. Once opened, tofu should be stored in water that is changed daily and used within 5 days. Always check the expiration date on the package to make sure it is as fresh as possible. Tofu has an almost sweet smell when fresh. If there is any hint of sour or off-aromas, or if it begins to darken around the edges, then it's time to toss it.

Japanese or silken tofu also comes in a range from extra firm to soft; the basic difference is that even the extra firm Japanese tofu is much more delicate, smooth, and custard-like than the Chinese. Silken tofu is best used diced in delicate soups, blended into sauces and dressings, or as a cream substitute. Any silken tofu purees well. Silken tofu is readily available in aseptic cartons that don't need refrigeration until opened. The brand I see most often is Mori-Nu from Japan.

PREPARING TOFU

Tofu, like cheese, is a fresh food that needs no cooking to make it edible. Making it interesting, however, is another matter.

PRESSING TOFU: For dishes where you want to retain the shape of the tofu, pressing is an essential step. (Pressing is for Chinese-style tofus. The silken style is generally too fragile.) All you have to do is to wrap the tofu in clean kitchen towels and gently weight the top of it with a small bag of dry beans or whatever you have on hand. In a pinch, I often just set the block of tofu on a small cutting board that has one end raised so that the liquid will drain away into the sink, and I place a dinner plate on top to press out water. Doing this gives you a denser product that will brown more easily and hold its shape better.

FREEZING TOFU: Freezing Chinese-style tofu dramatically changes the texture, making it firmer and chewier. Frozen and thawed tofu (at left, below) acts more like a sponge, absorbing whatever marinades or sauces you surround it with. Simply leave the unopened water or vacuum-packed tofu in the freezer until frozen solid. You can store it there for up to 4 months. Defrost it in the refrigerator (or if you're in a hurry, place the unopened package under cold running water), drain it, and use as directed in your recipe. It's been my experience that people who don't particularly like tofu can be seduced by a dish made from frozen tofu.

tofu mayonnaise

MAKES ABOUT 2 CUPS

This is a much lower-fat "mayonnaise" with no saturated fat at all. I much prefer it to any of the commercially made "low-fat" or "no-fat" versions (which are usually pretty awful).

16 ounces drained soft or silken tofu
2 tablespoons fresh lemon juice
1 tablespoon Dijon mustard, or to taste

1 teaspoon honey
2 tablespoons extra virgin olive oil
Salt and freshly ground pepper

COMBINE THE TOFU, lemon juice, mustard, and honey in a blender and blend at medium speed until smooth. Add the olive oil and salt and pepper to taste, and pulse to combine. Store covered in the refrigerator for up to 5 days.

variations   Add a tablespoon or two of roasted garlic, drained chopped capers, or chopped fresh herbs.

tofu caesar salad dressing

MAKES ABOUT 1 3/4 CUPS

I like this as much as the traditional Caesar dressing—honestly! If you don't tell, no one will know the difference. It's best made a day or two in advance so that the flavors can marry. It keeps refrigerated and covered for up to 2 weeks, so I often make a double batch. That way, I have it ready to top romaine lettuce hearts garnished with whatever other crunchy vegetable or sprouts I have on hand.

6 ounces silken tofu (1/2 traditional block)
2 teaspoons chopped fresh garlic
1/2 cup freshly grated Parmesan cheese
1 tablespoon Dijon mustard
6 to 8 anchovy fillets packed in oil, drained
2 teaspoons white wine or cider vinegar

1 tablespoon or so fresh lemon juice
1 tablespoon finely grated lemon zest
1/4 cup homemade vegetable or chicken stock or your favorite canned broth, or water
1 1/2 tablespoons olive oil
Salt and freshly ground pepper to taste

COMBINE ALL THE ingredients in a blender and blend until smooth. Taste and season with additional salt, pepper, lemon juice, or anchovy, if you think it needs it. It's a good idea to let the flavors develop for a while before you decide it needs stronger seasoning.

tofu-spinach "tapenade"

MAKES ABOUT 1 1/2 CUPS

Okay, so this isn't really tapenade, but I needed to call it something other than a "dip" or "spread." It's really delicious, and I find it appeals to even those who claim they don't like tofu. Use it like you use other dips and spreads—on crackers, or with vegetable crudités. A key ingredient is the cooked rice. I think it works best when you use a short-grain, sushi-style rice. If you cook the rice in clear vegetable stock rather than just water, the tapenade will have even better flavor. If you're in an Asian mood, substitute seaweed, like dulse flakes or reconstituted chopped wakame, for the spinach.

1 cup softly cooked white rice,
    preferably a short-grain type, warm
    or at room temperature
8 ounces soft or silken tofu
1 tablespoon white balsamic or
    champagne vinegar
1 1/2 tablespoons olive oil
2 tablespoons fresh lemon juice

1 teaspoon chopped poached garlic
1/3 cup chopped green onions (white
    and some green parts)
1/4 teaspoon hot pepper sesame oil, or
    to taste
1/3 cup chopped blanched spinach
Salt and freshly ground pepper to taste

PLACE THE RICE in a food processor and process briefly to puree. Add a tablespoon or two of vegetable stock or water if the rice is too dry to puree. Add the tofu, vinegar, olive oil, lemon juice, garlic, green onions, and hot pepper sesame oil, and process briefly so that the mixture is well combined but still has a bit of texture. Add the spinach and pulse once or twice to combine. Taste and season with salt and pepper. I think this is best eaten the day it is made, but it can be stored covered in the refrigerator for up to 3 days.

tofu baked with a spicy peanut sauce

SERVES 4

This simple preparation was the first tofu that I could get my kids to eat when they were young. If yours can't tolerate any "heat" at all, you can leave out the hot pepper sesame oil. It works well with either pressed fresh tofu or frozen tofu that has been well drained. The other great thing about this recipe is that you can throw the peanut coating together in a couple of minutes, and then the tofu can marinate in it all day or as long as overnight.

3 tablespoons natural peanut butter, excess oil drained away

1 tablespoon chopped garlic

2 teaspoons hot pepper sesame oil, or to taste

2 tablespoons maple syrup or honey

2 tablespoons soy sauce

1 tablespoon rice vinegar

12 ounces firm or extra firm tofu, pressed or frozen, well drained, and cut into 4 slices or fingers

COMBINE THE PEANUT butter, garlic, hot pepper sesame oil, maple syrup, soy sauce, and vinegar in a blender or food processor and puree with enough water to make a thick sauce (¼ to ⅓ cup). In a shallow bowl, coat the tofu well, and marinate for at least 2 hours and as long as overnight, refrigerated. Be sure to turn the slices a few times.

Preheat the oven to 400°F. Lightly oil a baking sheet or line it with a silicone mat. Arrange the tofu on it and bake for 15 to 18 minutes or until the peanut coating has firmed. Serve warm or at room temperature.

~ This tofu is great sliced and served warm on top of a crisp salad, lightly dressed. Grapefruit Vinaigrette (page 26) would be great, as would Spicy Sesame Ginger Vinaigrette (page 28).

~ Try it with shredded carrots and bean sprouts in a warm pita. If you're not opposed, crisp bacon is a fantastic addition.

~ Prepare as bite-size fingers for healthy little hors d'oeuvres.

tofu and noodle salad with peanut sauce

SERVES 4

I serve this at room temperature. Feel free to substitute or add any other any salad ingredients you like, such as cucumbers, finely sliced raw cabbage, etc. Though the daikon and carrot matchsticks give a lovely effect, you can just shred them for ease if you prefer.

1 pound firm tofu, drained

⅓ cup soy sauce, preferably salt-reduced

⅓ cup mirin (sweet rice wine)

2 teaspoons peeled and finely chopped ginger

8 ounces soba or other thin noodles

6 ounces daikon or other radish, cut into long matchstick shapes

2 cups or so fresh pea shoots

1 cup carrots, cut into fine matchstick shapes

Coconut Peanut Sauce (page 198)

SLICE THE TOFU into 4 equal pieces. Combine the soy sauce, mirin, and ginger. Marinate the tofu in this mixture in the refrigerator for at least 30 minutes and up to 4 hours. Turn it occasionally. Remove it from the marinade and gently wipe off any solids.

Preheat the oven to 400°F. Lightly oil a baking sheet or line it with a silicone mat. Arrange the tofu on it and bake for 20 to 25 minutes. Remove and set aside.

Bring a large pot of lightly salted water to a boil, and cook the soba noodles until al dente, 4 minutes or so. Drain the noodles and rinse them well with cold water to stop the cooking and rinse off the surface starch. Place in a bowl and toss with the radish, pea shoots, and carrots along with about half of the peanut sauce, or more if you think it needs it. Divide the mixture among 4 plates or shallow bowls, top with the pieces of tofu, and drizzle with a bit more of the sauce.

spicy tofu omelet

SERVES 4 AS AN APPETIZER OR 2 AS A MAIN COURSE

This is my variation of a popular street snack sold in Indonesia. Ketjap manis is a delicious condiment used widely in Southeast Asia. (Does the word "ketjap" ring a bell? Ketjap manis is the exotic ancestor of our own dear ketchup.) It's delicious as a "drizzle" and as an addition to marinades, sauces, and stir-fries. You can buy it bottled in Asian markets. The key to cooking the shallot chips is to do it slowly, making sure they don't burn.

2 ounces fresh bean sprouts

4 eggs

1/2 teaspoon salt

6 ounces Chinese tofu, drained and cut into 1/4-inch dice

1 teaspoon vegetable oil

2 fresh red or green chiles, seeds removed, finely sliced

2 tablespoons bottled or homemade Ketjap Manis or sweet soy sauce

1 tablespoon white vinegar

2 to 3 tablespoons crushed roasted peanuts

3 tablespoons Fried Shallot or Garlic Chips

1 tablespoon fresh parsley leaves

BLANCH THE BEAN sprouts in boiling water for 15 seconds. Drain and run some cold water over them to refresh them. Drain well and set aside. In a medium bowl, lightly beat the eggs with the salt and add the tofu.

Heat the safflower oil in a 10-inch nonstick skillet or heavy cast iron frying pan, then use a wadded-up paper towel to spread the oil over the whole pan bottom. Add half the egg mixture (make sure half the tofu comes with it), tilting the pan to make a thin omelet. Cook over medium heat, until the egg is set and the underside is lightly browned. Carefully turn over the omelet (usually a spatula and tongs together works best). As soon as it's set, remove and place on a large heated plate. Repeat to make the second omelet.

Scatter the bean sprouts and chiles over each omelet. Combine Ketjap Manis and vinegar, and drizzle over the omelets. Garnish with peanuts, Fried Shallot or Garlic Chips, and parsley leaves. To serve, cut into wedges.

fried shallot or garlic chips

ADD A QUARTER inch or so of peanut or vegetable oil to a skillet, along with very thinly sliced shallots or garlic. Cook over medium-low heat for 3 to 5 minutes, stirring gently to allow the chips to brown slowly and evenly. When just golden brown, use a slotted spoon to remove them from the oil and drain on paper towels until cool. They will turn darker brown as they stand.

ketjap manis

2/3 cup packed dark or light brown
  sugar
2/3 cup unsulfured molasses
1 cup dark soy sauce
1 teaspoon five-spice powder

2 tablespoons fresh lime juice, or to
  taste
1 teaspoon Asian chili-garlic sauce (see
  Glossary and Pantry), or to taste

COMBINE THE SUGAR with 1/3 cup water in a saucepan, and bring to a simmer over medium heat, stirring to dissolve the sugar. Add the molasses, soy sauce, and five-spice powder, and simmer for 5 minutes or until lightly thickened. Remove from the heat and stir in the lime juice and chili-garlic sauce. Store covered in the refrigerator for up to a month.

MAKES ABOUT 2 CUPS

soy-roasted tofu with asian greens

SERVES 4

Here, I'm starting the tofu on top of the stove and finishing it in a hot oven, a technique often used in restaurants for meat and fish. You can also prepare it on the grill, or solely on the stovetop, but you'll need to watch it carefully, as the sugar in the marinade can burn. The greens are available in Asian markets and in many large supermarkets. You can certainly substitute other greens, but try these if you can find them. The Garlic Stock is very little effort for great flavor. It's best if you start with a good homemade Vegetable Stock (page 94).

1 block firm tofu

MARINADE
¼ cup soy sauce
¼ cup sake or dry white wine
¼ cup mirin (sweet rice wine)
2 tablespoons sugar
3 tablespoons chopped green onion (white and green parts)
3 tablespoons peeled and chopped fresh ginger
1 small lemon, thinly sliced

4 tablespoons olive oil
1 pound baby bok choy (also known as Shanghai bok choy), washed and cut diagonally

1 cup shelled, blanched fresh soybeans (edamame), either fresh or fresh frozen
1 pound washed fresh pea shoots or pea leaves
Garlic Stock
Sea salt
Hot pepper sesame oil

Garnish if you like with toasted sesame seeds and fresh daikon radish sprouts or onion sprouts

WRAP AND PRESS the tofu to remove excess water. Slice into 4 rectangles and set aside.

Combine the marinade ingredients, except the lemon slices, in a small saucepan and bring to a boil. Remove from the heat and cool to room temperature. Add the lemon slices, pour the cooled marinade over the tofu, and marinate in the refrigerator for at least 2 hours and up to 8, depending on your preference and schedule. (The longer it sits, the stronger the flavor will be.) Turn the tofu occasionally so that the pieces absorb the marinade evenly.

When ready to serve, preheat the oven to 450°F. Heat 2 tablespoons of the olive oil in an ovenproof sauté pan (preferably nonstick) over medium-high heat. Remove the tofu from the marinade and quickly sauté the slices on one side until lightly browned and "lacquered" looking. Turn the tofu over and place the pan in the oven for 3 to 4 minutes or until the tofu is just warmed through and nicely colored. Be careful not to burn.

While the tofu is cooking, in another skillet, heat the remaining 2 tablespoons of oil over medium-high heat. Add the bok choy and soybeans and stir-fry for a minute or two. Add the pea shoots and stir-fry for a minute longer. Add 1 cup stock and bring to a boil, stirring the whole time. Season the vegetables to taste with salt and a few drops of hot pepper sesame oil.

Place the vegetables and broth in the center of shallow warm bowls and top with the tofu. Garnish with sesame seeds and sprouts, if desired, and serve immediately.

garlic stock

SQUEEZE OUT THE GARLIC from two whole heads of roasted garlic and mash as well as you can. Stir this into 1 quart of vegetable stock, along with a few coins of fresh ginger, if desired, and simmer for a few minutes to develop the flavor.

NOTE: See Glossary and Pantry for information on roasting garlic.

Miso

Miso is a rich paste made from fermented soybeans or soybeans and other grains such as rice, barley, or wheat. Contemporary versions also add flavorings like ginger and seaweed. It is commonly used to make broth for soups (see Miso Soup, page 99). In my kitchen it is "fast food"—I can make a flavorful broth almost instantly by dissolving a tablespoon or so in a cup of hot water. (Note: Asians never boil miso broth because they say it destroys the beneficial bacteria and enzymes. Miso is believed to have many unique medicinal properties, including the ability to buffer the effects of radiation!) It is sold both pasteurized (which many believe also destroys its beneficial properties) in shelf-stable pouches and refrigerated. It should always be refrigerated after opening and has a long shelf life, at least a year in most cases. Color indicates intensity of flavor. White misos are mild and sweet; darker misos are more robust and salty. Here are a couple of recipes to acquaint you with miso beyond broth . . .

miso walnut chutney boats

MAKES ABOUT I CUP

I first had this in Japan. Delicious! Try it also on slices of raw daikon or on rice crackers.

½ cup miso (white if you like it milder, red if you like it stronger)
¼ cup mirin (see Glossary and Pantry)
2 tablespoons sugar

3 tablespoons sake
⅔ cup toasted walnuts, finely chopped
Hot pepper sesame oil
I English or Armenian cucumber

IN A SMALL saucepan, combine the miso, mirin, sugar, and sake and cook over low heat for 3 to 4 minutes, stirring constantly to dissolve the sugar and drive the alcohol off the mirin and sake. Remove from the heat and stir in the walnuts and drops of hot pepper sesame oil to taste (about ¼ teaspoon or so).

Split the cucumber in half and scoop out the seeds with the point of a teaspoon. Cut into 2-inch sections and spoon a little of the chutney into each. Top with a walnut piece or half, if you want to get fancy.

crisp tofu and eggplant with miso glaze

SERVES 4 AS A MAIN COURSE

This brings together two different soy products, tofu and miso. I'm using pea shoots here, but if you can't find them, tender spinach works just as well.

1 12-to-16-ounce block of firm regular or silken tofu

¾ cup sake

4 tablespoons mirin (sweet rice wine)

1¼ cups red or white miso, or a combination

⅓ cup sugar

Canola or other vegetable oil for frying

Flour (preferably rice flour; see page 240) lightly seasoned with salt and cayenne pepper, for dredging

4 small Japanese eggplants, stemmed and cut into thick coins or lengthwise, about ¼ inch thick

8 ounces fresh pea shoots or baby spinach

3 tablespoons soy sauce

2 teaspoons toasted sesame oil

1 teaspoon peeled and finely minced fresh ginger

Garnish if you like with toasted white sesame seeds

GENTLY PRESS AND drain the tofu on paper towels for at least 15 minutes. Cut the tofu into 8 crosswise slices and again place on paper towels to absorb moisture. Meanwhile, combine the sake and mirin in a small saucepan and bring to a boil. Add the miso and sugar and stir over medium heat, without boiling, until smooth. Set aside.

Preheat the oven to 225°F. Heat about ¼ inch of vegetable oil in a large sauté pan. Dust the tofu with the seasoned flour, shake off any excess, and shallow-fry until golden brown on each side. Keep warm on paper-towel-lined baking sheets in the oven.

Dredge the eggplant in the seasoned flour as above, and cook it, in batches if necessary, until golden on both sides. (It's perfectly okay to use the same oil in the same pan from the tofu.) Drain it on paper towels and keep warm. Pour out the oil and wipe out the pan.

Toss the pea shoots with the soy sauce, sesame oil, and ginger, and quickly stir-fry in a hot pan until the shoots just barely begin to wilt, about 2 minutes.

Arrange the eggplant slices on warm plates. Top with the pea shoots and then the tofu. Spread the miso sauce over the tofu and sprinkle with toasted sesame seeds. Serve immediately.

Tempeh

Tempeh is a firm, meaty cake made from hulled, cracked, and fermented soybeans and often other ingredients. It has all kinds of uses. Tempeh originated in Indonesia, where it is the most popular soy-based food. It is highly nutritious and, because of the fermentation that breaks down the indigestible sugars found in beans, it's very easy to digest. It has a distinctive nutty, mushroomy flavor. Like tofu, it readily takes on flavors from marinades and sauces. Many Westerners who don't like tofu fall in love with tempeh, so it's worth a try. I like it best when it's been sautéed first and then added to stir-fries or braised dishes. You can find it in Asian and natural foods stores in both the refrigerator and the freezer cases.

curried tempeh

SERVES 4

8 ounces tempeh, plain or flavored
3 tablespoons olive oil
Salt
½ cup slivered shallots
1 tablespoon slivered garlic
2 teaspoons Thai red curry paste
3 tablespoons peeled and finely julienned
    galangal root or fresh ginger
¼ cup lightly packed fresh mint leaves

1 tablespoon grated lime zest
1½ cups coconut milk
Asian fish sauce (see Glossary and
    Pantry) or soy sauce to taste
¼ cup toasted cashews or macadamias,
    coarsely chopped

Accompaniments: plain steamed rice
    and fresh cilantro leaves

CUT THE TEMPEH into ½-inch cubes. Heat 2 tablespoons of the olive oil in a sauté pan or wok over medium-high heat and stir-fry until the tempeh is crisp and golden brown. Season to taste with salt and set aside to drain on paper towels.

Add the remaining tablespoon of oil to the pan and stir-fry the shallots, garlic, and curry paste for a minute or so over medium heat. Add the galangal, mint, and lime zest and stir-fry for 30 seconds more. Add the coconut milk and tempeh and bring to a simmer. Lower the heat, cover, and slowly simmer for 6 to 8 minutes. Season to your taste with fish sauce or soy sauce. Sprinkle with nuts and serve with plain rice garnished with cilantro leaves, if desired.

18

simple, sophisticated desserts

According to nature writer Michael Pollan, a taste for sweetness is a fundamental human desire, the basis, in all likelihood, for all other desires. Fruit is a universal food, eaten by all peoples in all times; honey is eaten wherever there are bees. We may not need dessert to live, but we need it to be happy. All over the world, dessert is an expression of and occasion for indulgence and celebration.

Getting that sweetness at the end of the meal makes sense. Unlike salty foods, which tend to pique the appetite, sweet foods tend to shut it down.

This lesson is about simple desserts. This is not about complicated, towering restaurant creations that require special tools, talent, and ingredients. Unlike the other lessons in this book, it doesn't focus on a single technique (I promise—no flambéing), or flavor-maker, or main ingredient, though there are recipes that fit those categories. My goal here is pretty straightforward: to reintroduce you to the idea of making dessert. After all, desserts are the first thing that most people, as children, try to cook themselves—chocolate chip cookies or brownies, Jell-O and pudding out of a box, a birthday cake—but for many grown-up Americans, dessert comes out of their grocer's freezer. Happily, there is good ice cream to be had in supermarkets, but sometimes it's nice to make something. I'd like to give you a few dessert options you may not have considered, desserts as sophisticated and interesting as the rest of your menu. I've tried to keep them on the healthy side, as well—many of these recipes are very low in fat—though I would not be doing my job if I didn't include one big, blow-out chocolate dessert.

I've given several examples of the most basic of the dessert building blocks: sauces. If you know how to make a couple of simple sauces, then good store-bought ice cream and pound cake or even a fruit salad can be turned into something very special, very easily.

raspberry sauce

MAKES ABOUT 1 CUP

Sweetened fruit purees, the restaurant-plate-decorating darlings of recent years, are among the easiest sauces you can make. They are wildly versatile, complementing everything from lemon sorbet to rich chocolate cake, adding flavor, color, and textural interest to old stand-bys. They also freeze well. Whole berries frozen without sugar (known as IQF— individually quick frozen—in the trade) are a fine year-round substitute for fresh.

3 cups fresh or frozen raspberries (preferably IQF), thawed

1 tablespoon fresh lemon juice
2 tablespoons sugar, or to taste

COMBINE ALL THE ingredients in a blender and puree. Strain through a fine mesh strainer to remove the seeds if they bother you, and add drops of lemon juice or more sugar to your taste. Store covered in the refrigerator for up to 5 days, or in the freezer for up to 3 months.

rosy apple syrup

MAKES ABOUT 2 CUPS

My grandmother's Scotch-Irish-German sensibility never let her waste anything. Apple skins have lots of flavor and also tannins, which give that little "bite" to an apple's flavor. I think she's right—it'd be a shame to throw that away. (The wine is my improvement to her recipe. She used a combination of apple juice and water.) Try this drizzled on any fresh fruit or over a creamy blue cheese served with fresh sliced apples. The syrup stores almost indefinitely.

2 cups crisp, light-bodied white wine
2 cups sugar
Peelings from 4 or 5 large red apples

1 2-inch cinnamon stick or 1 whole star anise

COMBINE THE WINE and sugar in a heavy saucepan, and bring to a simmer, stirring to dissolve the sugar. Add the peels and cinnamon, and continue to simmer uncovered until the syrup is thickened, about 15 minutes. Let the syrup cool for safety while pouring, then pour it through a strainer, pressing down on the solids. Refrigerate in a tightly sealed jar.

simple chocolate sauce

MAKES ABOUT 2 CUPS

To get the very best chocolate sauce, use the very best chocolate you can find. What makes it "the best"? If you want to get technical, better chocolate has a lot of chocolate mass with a minimum of cocoa butter and other stuff—even natural stuff. Scharffen Berger, Valrhôna, Callebaut, and Ghirardelli brands are all wonderful. If you have enough dessert-making experience to know that chocolate can be tricky to work with, relax: the key is to heat the chocolate gently so that the mass doesn't separate from the cocoa butter. Use a heavy-bottomed pot and work over low heat. If you have a double boiler, now's the time to use it. The microwave also works well if you do it in short bursts, stirring in between.

8 ounces bittersweet or semisweet chocolate, depending on your taste
6 tablespoons unsalted butter
¼ teaspoon salt
2 teaspoons vanilla or ¼ cup dark rum, brandy, or coffee liqueur

½ cup light corn syrup
2 teaspoons finely grated orange or lemon zest (optional)
¾ cup heavy cream

CHOP THE CHOCOLATE into coarse pieces and combine it in a saucepan or microwave-safe bowl with the butter, salt, vanilla, corn syrup, and optional zest. Over low heat, gently warm the ingredients until the chocolate softens but has not completely melted. (You can test this by poking at it. Particularly in the microwave, chunks of chocolate may still look solid when they are in fact almost melted.) Whisk until the mixture is smooth, then whisk in the cream. Serve slightly warm or at room temperature.

Store covered in the refrigerator for up to 2 weeks. Warm very gently to return to its sauce consistency, either by placing the bowl in a pan of simmering water or by microwaving uncovered in a microwave on medium power.

sweet fritters with red wine and star anise sauce

SERVES 4 TO 6

Many home cooks shy away from deep frying both because it is a little intimidating and because it can be messy. Neither need be the case. The key to deep frying is making sure that the oil is always in what I call the "magic range" of 350 to 375°F. This requires that you get yourself a deep fry thermometer—one that clips right on the side of the pot so that you can easily monitor temperature. Don't drop anything in until the temperature is in the magic range; stop adding ingredients when it falls to 350°F. It's when you let the temperature drop that oil is absorbed and the food gets leaden and heavy. And above 375°F., the oil is too hot and the food browns or burns before it is cooked through. Foods fried in the magic range, whether sweet or savory, come out crisp, light, and not greasy. As to the mess factor, you don't need all that much oil to deep fry most things. About an inch of oil in a big pot minimizes splatter and makes cleanup easy. Discard the oil after using it.

You can also serve these fritters alone or with any of the dessert sauces above. All of the sauces can be made a long time ahead. The fritters, however, need to be deep fried right at serving time.

4 tablespoons butter, cut into small pieces	Vegetable oil for frying
2/3 cup flour	Red Wine and Star Anise Sauce or other sauce of your choice
1 tablespoon fresh lemon juice	1 cup sliced fresh strawberries
1 teaspoon grated lemon zest	
1/2 teaspoon vanilla extract	Garnish if you like with powdered sugar
3 large eggs	

PLACE THE BUTTER in a saucepan with 1/2 cup of water and bring to a boil. Remove the pan from the heat, dump in the flour all at once, and with a wooden spoon or an electric mixer, beat in the flour to form a smooth paste. Beat in the lemon juice, zest, and vanilla. Then beat in the eggs, one at a time. Be sure to thoroughly incorporate each egg before adding the next.

Preheat the oven to 225°F. Heat 1 inch of oil in a deep skillet or wok to 360°F. Working in batches, drop rounded tablespoons of dough into the oil and fry until golden brown, about 1½ minutes on each side. Be careful not to crowd the fritters. Drain on paper towels and keep warm on a baking sheet in the oven for up to 20 minutes.

To serve, place a shallow pool of warm sauce in individual serving bowls. Place 3 or 4 fritters on top. Scatter on sliced berries and dust with powdered sugar, if desired. Serve immediately.

red wine and star anise sauce

¾ cup sugar
1 cup medium- or full-bodied red wine
1 cup water

2 teaspoons cornstarch
3 whole star anise
1 × 3-inch strip of orange zest

COMBINE ALL THE ingredients in a saucepan, stir to dissolve the cornstarch, and bring to a boil. Immediately reduce the heat and simmer slowly, uncovered, for 5 minutes. Let the syrup cool for safety while pouring, and then pour it through a strainer, pressing down on the solids. Store covered in the refrigerator for up to 3 weeks.

MAKES ABOUT 2½ CUPS

vanilla baked peaches and blueberries

SERVES 6

This recipe would work with any good stone fruit such as nectarines, apricots, or even pears and apples. You can also substitute any berry. If ripe fresh berries are available, by all means use them, but IQF (individually quick frozen without sugar) berries in the supermarket often have a better flavor because they are picked dead ripe and then immediately frozen. You can also decide when to add them to the peaches—maybe you'll decide they shouldn't be cooked at all. It's up to you.

1 cup sugar

½ cup crisp, light-bodied white wine

2 3 × ½-inch strips of orange zest

1 small cinnamon stick broken in half

1 3-inch vanilla bean, or 2 teaspoons vanilla extract

6 large ripe peaches, halved and pitted

4 small (1-inch) fresh rosemary sprigs (optional)

2 cups fresh or IQF whole blueberries

Accompaniments: crème fraîche, yogurt, or ice cream (vanilla and coconut are my favorites with this)

PREHEAT THE OVEN to 375°F. In a saucepan, combine the sugar, wine, orange zest, and cinnamon stick. Split the vanilla bean lengthwise, scrape its seeds into the saucepan, then add the bean (or add vanilla extract, if using). Over medium heat, bring the mixture to a boil, and then reduce the heat and simmer for 2 minutes or so. Remove the pan from the heat.

Place the peaches cut side up in a baking dish just large enough to hold them in a single layer. Tuck rosemary sprigs, if using, in between the peaches and pour the sugar syrup over them. Bake for 30 to 35 minutes, basting frequently, or until the peaches are cooked through but still maintain their shape. After 20 minutes, you can sprinkle the blueberries around the peaches to let them soften just a little and infuse the peaches and syrup with their flavor. (If you put them in sooner, they'll cook to mush. If you put them in later, they won't really cook at all. Whatever you like is fine.)

Spoon the fruits and syrup into bowls and serve warm or at room temperature with crème fraîche, yogurt, or ice cream.

orange ricotta cake with strawberries

MAKES ONE 8-INCH CAKE; SERVES 6 TO 8

The key to this cake is to use good, whole milk ricotta. A lot of what we see in the supermarket is part skim milk and usually pretty tasteless. My favorite where I live is from Bellwether Farms, who make both a cow and a sheep milk version. A cheese store or Italian delicatessen will have good ricotta, and it makes all the difference in the world. I've suggested fresh strawberries here, but you can use any fruit or fruit sauce that you like or even a scoop of good ice cream.

FOR THE CAKE

2¹⁄₂ pounds whole milk ricotta
5 whole eggs
¹⁄₂ cup sugar
¹⁄₃ cup orange marmalade
¹⁄₄ cup dark rum
¹⁄₃ cup cake flour or all-purpose flour
2 tablespoons finely grated orange zest

FOR THE STRAWBERRIES

1 pint fresh ripe strawberries
¹⁄₃ cup sugar, or to taste
¹⁄₄ cup fresh orange juice

PREHEAT THE OVEN to 325°F. Lightly butter and flour an 8-inch springform pan. Combine the ricotta, eggs, sugar, and marmalade in a food processor, and process until the mixture is smooth. Add the rum, flour, and zest, and process again in short bursts until smooth.

Pour the mixture into the pan and bake for 1 hour. The center will still be soft (and look jiggly) at this point. Turn the oven off and leave the cake in the oven with the door very slightly ajar for about 20 minutes. Remove the cake from the oven, let cool completely, and then refrigerate at least 2 hours before serving.

Remove the cake from the refrigerator and let it return to room temperature. Meanwhile, hull, wash, and slice the berries. Toss them gently with the sugar and orange juice and set aside.

To serve, remove the sides from the pan and slice the cake. Serve each piece with some strawberries on top or on the side. The cake can be made a day ahead and stored refrigerated in its pan, wrapped with plastic.

buttermilk panna cotta

SERVES 6

Gelatin desserts have gotten a bad rap among sophisticated eaters because of our experience with Jell-O. But gelatin has a history that predates the little box by centuries, and it can be the basis for some very contemporary desserts. This panna cotta is one of my favorites. In Italian, panna cotta translates to "cooked cream." In this version, buttermilk lightens the texture and adds an interesting tang. Look for a quality buttermilk with good flavor. The tip-off for me are those labeled Russian- or Bulgarian-style. This is fabulous with the Raspberry Sauce (page 306).

2 teaspoons unflavored gelatin (less than 1 envelope)
½ cup sugar
½ cup heavy cream

2 teaspoons finely grated lemon zest
2 cups buttermilk
Raspberry Sauce (page 306)

POUR ⅓ CUP water into a small saucepan and sprinkle in the gelatin. Set aside for 5 minutes while the gelatin softens. Add the sugar, cream, and zest, and heat slowly, until it just begins to steam. Do not simmer or boil. Stir constantly to dissolve the sugar. This will take about 4 minutes. Remove from the heat and stir in the buttermilk.

Pour the mixture through a fine mesh strainer, then transfer it to a 3-cup decorative mold or ring-shaped cake pan or into six ½-cup molds. Cover the mold(s) with plastic wrap and refrigerate until the dessert is firm and chilled, at least 2 hours. Panna cottas can be made a day ahead and then unmolded at serving time.

To serve, dip the mold(s) into hot water for a few seconds and then invert the panna cotta onto a serving plate or individual plates. Gently shake to loosen, and then remove the mold(s). Serve with Raspberry Sauce.

individual molten chocolate truffle cakes

SERVES 8

Most restaurants today seem to have some version of a "molten" chocolate cake. So here's one for you to wow family and friends with. This is a showy, elegant recipe that is really pretty easy. You don't need to be an experienced baker or have "great hands" or a delicate touch; it just works. This recipe also has a dividend—the chocolate truffles, which can be served just as they are. You will need 4-ounce custard cups or ramekins in which to bake the cakes. Parchment paper is usually available in the supermarket alongside the waxed paper and aluminum foil.

FOR THE TRUFFLES

4 ounces bittersweet or semisweet chocolate, chopped very finely
3 tablespoons heavy cream
1 tablespoon unsalted butter
2 tablespoons liqueur of choice (Chambord, cassis, or framboise is nice if you're going to garnish with raspberries or serve with a berry puree, but any flavor that goes with chocolate will work great)

FOR THE CAKE

5 ounces bittersweet chocolate, chopped very finely
5 ounces (1¼ sticks) unsalted butter, cut into small pieces
3 eggs, at room temperature
3 egg yolks, at room temperature
½ cup sugar
5 tablespoons plus 1 teaspoon all-purpose flour
Powdered sugar for dusting (optional)

Garnish if you like with whipped cream, fresh raspberries, and mint sprigs

TO MAKE THE TRUFFLES: Combine the chocolate, cream, and butter in a small, heatproof bowl set over simmering water to gently warm. When the chocolate is almost melted (test by poking it), remove the bowl from the heat and stir the mixture until smooth. Stir in the liqueur and refrigerate the mixture, stirring occasionally, until it is thick enough to mound on a spoon, about 30 minutes.

Line a baking tray with waxed or parchment paper. Using 2 spoons, form 8 round truffles (alternatively, scrape the chocolate mixture into a pastry bag fitted with a #3 plain tip and pipe 8 truffles onto the prepared tray). Refrigerate until firm, at least 15 minutes. Can be made a day ahead and stored covered in the refrigerator.

TO MAKE THE CAKE AND FINISH THE DESSERT: Preheat the oven to 350°F. Cut circles of parchment paper to fit inside eight 4-ounce custard cups or ramekins (they don't have to fit exactly). Generously butter the cups and line the bottoms with the parchment rounds (see Note). Set aside.

In the top of a double boiler or in a small heatproof bowl set over simmering water, melt the chocolate and butter together. Set aside to cool slightly.

Meanwhile, in the large bowl of an electric mixer, beat the eggs, egg yolks, and sugar on high speed until tripled in volume, about 5 minutes. Scrape in the chocolate mixture and, on low speed, beat just until combined. Remove the bowl from the mixer (or the mixer from the bowl, if you're using a hand-held) and fold in the flour, using a rubber spatula. Spoon a little of the batter into each of the prepared cups, top with 1 truffle, and cover the truffle with the remaining batter.

Arrange the cups on a baking tray and bake until the edges of the cakes begin to pull away from the sides of the cups, 12 to 13 minutes. Remove from the oven and let cool for 10 minutes. Invert onto individual dessert plates and carefully peel off the parchment circle. Dust with powdered sugar, if desired. Serve warm, garnished with whipped cream, berries, and mint, if you like.

NOTE: The cups need to be heavily buttered and don't skip the parchment or the cakes will stick!

nut oil cake

Among my favorite flavor secrets are good nut oils. Like great olive oils, they are often drizzled on as a condiment just before serving, but their rich and subtle flavor makes them a versatile ingredient in all kinds of dishes. Traditionally, the most fragrant, flavor-concentrated oils came from Europe, and particularly France. A domestic producer in the Napa Valley that I like a lot is California Press. They make wonderful oils from walnuts, almonds, filberts (also called hazelnuts), pecans, and pistachios. Any good nut oil matched to the same chopped nut would be great in this simple cake. My favorite is pecans with pecan oil. It makes a light and tender cake, which I like to bake in small loaves, cut thickly, and serve either as the base for a fresh fruit dessert or to accompany good coffee or tea.

⅓ cup toasted nut oil, plus additional
    for oiling pans
3 eggs
1 cup sugar
⅓ cup fresh orange juice

1½ cups all-purpose flour
2 teaspoons baking powder
⅛ teaspoon salt
½ cup toasted and finely chopped nuts

PREHEAT THE OVEN to 350°F. Using a little nut oil, lightly oil an 8-inch round cake pan or 2 mini loaf pans and set aside.

In a large bowl, beat the eggs with an electric mixer and then gradually add the sugar and beat until the mixture is light and fluffy, about 5 minutes. Slowly add the toasted nut oil and orange juice and continue to beat for another minute or so. In a separate bowl, whisk together the flour, baking powder, and salt. Gently beat the flour mixture into the egg mixture until smooth. Gently fold in the nuts. Pour the batter into the pan(s) and bake for 25 minutes for the mini loaves or 40 minutes for the round cakes or until the center is firm and a toothpick inserted into the center pulls out clean (or with only crumbs clinging).

Let the cake cool in the pan for a few minutes, then turn out onto a cooling rack to cool completely. To store, wrap in plastic and store at room temperature for up to 3 days.

lemon zabaglione

SERVES 6

Zabaglione (Italian) or sabayon (French) is an impressive and unusual but *easy-to-do* dessert that can be made at the very last minute if necessary. This version can be made 30 minutes or so ahead. Zabaglione is like a soufflé without the dish . . . or the beaten egg whites . . . or the baking. I like to serve it with fresh fruits spooned on the side. For a more dramatic presentation, arrange fresh fruits in a shallow heatproof dish, spoon the zabaglione on top, and quickly brown it with a propane torch (if you've gone nuts) or under a hot broiler.

2 large whole eggs
4 large egg yolks
¾ cup sugar
Finely grated zest and juice of 2 medium
  lemons (about ¼ cup juice)

⅓ cup white port, muscat, Sauternes, or
  other sweet dessert wine

COMBINE ALL THE ingredients in the top of a double boiler and set aside. Fill the bottom of the pot with water and bring it to a simmer. Whisk the mixture until it is light and thick. Place the mixture over the simmering water and whisk vigorously until it has tripled in volume (just eyeball this) and is thick and even lighter in color. Total cooking and whisking time will be 6 to 8 minutes. Remove the top of the pot from the heat and whisk to cool slightly (this keeps the egg yolks from scrambling).

Serve immediately or set aside and cover loosely with plastic wrap. Use within 2 hours.

wine

An Important Flavor-Maker

As someone who has spent most of his adult life in the wine country of California, learning and writing and teaching about wine as well as food, I'm amazed that most Americans still rarely, if ever, drink or cook with wine. Setting aside those who simply don't like it and those who have religious objections or other concerns about alcohol consumption, there is still a big bunch of you who don't partake, and I'd just like to say bluntly: I think you're missing something great.

For me, a glass of wine *is* food. It's another flavor—often many flavors in one sip—to be enjoyed along with the other foods that I'm eating at a meal. More than any other beverage, wine has the ability to complement and enhance other flavors. Though you hardly ever hear any chef or food authority say this, the simplest possible technique for adding flavor interest to any meal is to drink a glass of wine alongside it. Try it sometime with even a slice of pizza and see how many more flavors you taste in that ordinary, familiar dish.

In addition, wine can make an important culinary contribution to many dishes, whether savory or sweet. As you've no doubt noticed, wine is an important ingredient in recipes throughout this book. Both chefs and home cooks will tell you that adding wine to sauces, marinades, risottos, braises, ragus, broths, or just the stuck-on browned bits in a sauté pan (see Simple Savory Sauces, page 70), enhances flavor. If you ask why, they may tell you that it's because of the wine's fruity character or its acidity. But there's more to wine than just fruit and acidity. As a cooking agent, wine and other alcoholic beverages work harder than you may think, thanks to alcohol's amazing ability to extract flavors that would otherwise remain trapped in food.

Wine has its own wonderful flavors from the grape as well as those that it develops from fermentation. During the fermentation of grape juice, large, bland molecules break down into smaller, more flavorful compounds, producing dramatic changes in flavor. Enzymes break big carbohydrates into sugars. Then yeast and other microorganisms ingest these sugars, plus sugars originally present in the grape juice, and give off carbon dioxide, alcohol, and all sorts of flavorful by-products, including organic acids from acetic acid and lactic acid to amino acids. The acidity causes more molecular breakdowns, until eventually the amount of alcohol in the wine reduces the activity of these little microorganisms. At some point, the winemaker decides that the wine has the desired flavors and it's bottled. So whether you're drinking it or cooking with it, wine offers a complex mixture of flavorful compounds.

But the *alcohol* itself in wine helps to create flavor in food. Different flavor components in foods dissolve in different mediums. Some dissolve in water, and some dissolve in fat. One of the reasons that fat-free foods often taste so boring is that the fat-soluble flavors in the dish remain locked in the food. Even a tiny bit of fat can dissolve and carry flavors, making a dish much more flavorful than if it were totally fat-free. Alcohol, be it wine, beer, or hard liquor like vodka and bourbon, is a powerful flavor extractor too. It dissolves not only water and fat-soluble flavors but also flavor components that neither water nor fat can dissolve. For example, we use alcohol to extract flavor from vanilla beans, and the reward is vanilla extract. It just wouldn't work if we used water or fat. This ability of alcohol to extract and carry flavors makes it a great asset for cooks. When you splash a few tablespoons of wine into a skillet that was used to sauté meat or vegetables, you usually scrape up the stuck-on bits of food so they'll dissolve in the wine. By doing this, you're not only getting the flavors of the wine and of the caramelized browned bits in your dish, you're also getting some extra flavors that only alcohol can extract. This may be why vodka, which is relatively weak on flavor but high in alcohol, makes an occasional appearance in sauces. Why would a tomato sauce spiked with vodka have so much more flavor even though the sauce simmers long enough to boil off most of the alcohol? There must be a key flavor component in tomatoes that dissolves in alcohol. Once the alcohol dissolves that flavor component and releases it into the sauce, its job is done, so it doesn't matter that most of it boils off.

Does the alcohol in wine evaporate in cooking?

Some people have concerns about alcohol, and the conventional wisdom is that when you cook wine or any other spirit, the alcohol is evaporated by the heat of cooking. It's true that alcohol boils at a lower temperature than water, so you'd think that the alcohol would completely evaporate before the water, but this doesn't happen. Some of the alcohol and water combine to form an inseparable mixture called an azeotrope. So even after lengthy boiling, some alcohol remains bound with water. Not surprisingly, the cooking method and cooking time also influence how much alcohol evaporates. Flambéing removes about 25 percent of the original alcohol. Simmering on the stovetop for thirty minutes evaporates about 65 percent. And two and a half hours of simmering removes about 95 percent. So if you have religious or other personal concerns about consuming or serving alcohol, then cooking with wine is clearly not an option for you.

You might ask then if there is a substitute for wine in recipes. To replace the fruity flavor of the wine itself, you can use grape or other fruit juices or something called verjus (unfermented and unripe grape juice), but without the alcohol to do its flavor-extraction magic, you won't get as much complexity. To draw out as much flavor as possible without alcohol, include a little water and fat to dissolve and carry both the water and fat-soluble flavors. You can also boost flavor with things like citrus zest, vinegar, fresh herbs, salt, sugar, pepper, and other spices.

What wine should I use in cooking?

This may be the question I'm asked more than any other. The answer I give is to be sure to use a wine that you would be willing to drink at that moment. Some people have the idea that an inferior wine or maybe one that you opened and didn't like and stuck in the refrigerator door for three weeks can be used for cooking. I say if you wouldn't drink it, then don't cook with it.

There are no hard rules as to when to use white or red. My basic rule of thumb is that if the dish is a hearty one, like Basic Beef Pot Roast (see page 132), then the wine should also be hearty, which suggests a big red like Cabernet Sauvignon. For a more delicate dish, like Salmon Fillet Roasted in Lemon Butter (see page 257), a more delicate wine seems desirable, preferably a white that won't "stain" the food, like Sauvignon Blanc. In the recipes, I've often suggested a wine varietal, but don't feel you have to go out and buy that particular one. I've tried to describe the style ("light," "fruity," "off-dry," "hearty") to help you if you're getting a recommendation at the wine store or choosing from the bottles you have at home.

What's a wine style?

A wine style is a flavor profile—a category that tells you how the wine tastes. Though even the wine-phobic have become comfortable with buying or ordering varietal wines (wines named by the dominant grape variety in them), the grape variety doesn't tell you anything about how the wine actually *tastes!* Chardonnay, for example, can vary widely in style and flavor from crisp/clean/green appley to rich/thick/oaky/buttery/toasty. And many of the world's wines are identified not by their dominant grape but by where they were made. So here's my attempt to simplify. I've organized white wines into four categories and red wines into three. In addition, I've also briefly commented on sparkling wines and sweet dessert wines. Once you know the style you like, you won't be disappointed even if you are unfamiliar with the grape variety, the region or country the wine came from, or any of those other confusing and confounding details. It will also give you a starting place for a conversation with your wine merchant.

white wine styles

White wines need to have bright, refreshing acidity to taste good, but this very quality can make them seem sour when tasted without food. With food, however, the acidity can become an advantage, perking up food in the same way that a squeeze of lemon would. White wines can be divided into four styles.

CRISP, CLEAN, LIGHT-BODIED WHITES Other terms typically used to describe these are *refreshing, brisk, racy, zesty,* and *acidic.* They are typically pale in color, slightly lower in alcohol, and have spent little or no time aging in oak barrels. Typical aromas and flavors in these wines are green apple, lemon, grapefruit, melon, pineapple, citrus blossoms, herbs, and minerals. Popular varieties made in this style include Sauvignon Blanc,

Chardonnay, Pinot Blanc, Pinot Gris (Pinot Grigio), Semillon blends (in Bordeaux and California with Sauvignon Blanc, in Australia with Chardonnay).

SMOOTH, ROUND, MEDIUM-BODIED WHITES Other terms used to describe these are *silky, fruity, creamy, elegant, ripe,* and *easy-drinking.* They typically have a little more golden color and slightly more alcohol (13 percent or so). They also often have some oak aging. Typical aromas and flavors are apple (green and sweet), citrus, banana, and, if aged in oak, toasty, spicy, vanilla, nutty, and clove. Popular varieties made in this style are Chardonnay, Sauvignon/Fume Blanc, Pinot Blanc, and Pinot Gris.

RICH, FULL-BODIED WHITES Terms like *creamy, buttery, mouth-filling, ripe, full fruit, toasty,* and *smoky* are used to describe these wines. They are usually deeper in color, from straw to deep gold, and a bit higher still in alcohol (13 to 14 percent). These wines have almost always spent some time in oak, both during fermentation and aging, which contributes the toasty/vanilla flavors. Malolactic fermentation and aging on the lees produces great texture and softens acidity. Popular varieties made in this style include Chardonnay (again), some Sauvignon Blancs, often identified as "Fume Blanc," Viognier, and Pinot Blanc.

AROMATIC DRY OR OFF-DRY WHITES These can be made in either a dry or off-dry (slightly sweet) style. Their distinguishing characteristic, however, is their pronounced floral and fruit aromas. Terms like *apricot, peach, ripe melon,* the whole range of tropical fruits (*mango, passion fruit, litchi*), flowers like *honeysuckle* and *gardenia,* and sweet spices like *cinnamon* and *clove* are often used to describe them. They vary in color from almost clear to straw and light golden. Generally, the sweeter the wine, the more golden it is. Alcohol levels can be as low as 8 percent for the sweeter, off-dry whites to 13 percent for bone dry. All typically have a good acid balance to go along with their rich flavors. Popular varieties include Rieslings, Gewürtztraminers, muscats, Viognier, Chenin Blanc, and Malvasia Bianca.

red wine styles

Red wines can be divided into three styles.

FRUITY LIGHT-BODIED REDS These can also be described as *fresh, lively, juicy, clean, straightforward, soft* wines. They are usually light, vibrant, and translucent red in color, lower in alcohol than other reds, with little or no oak or tannins. (Tannins are the astringent compounds that give you that "dry mouth" feeling—think strong black tea.) Typical aromas and flavors include cherry, strawberry, raspberry, rose, and "soda pop." Popular varieties made in this style include Gamay, Pinot Noir, Grenache, Merlot, Zinfandel, and often blends of two or more grapes. The popular French Beaujolais Nouveau, whose release every November has become a wine-marketing event, is a fruity, light-bodied red.

SMOOTH, MEDIUM-BODIED REDS Other terms used to describe these reds are *round, juicy, balanced,* and *silky.* They are usually darker red in color, tending toward ruby and garnet, and a bit higher in alcohol (12.5 to 13.5 percent). Their flavors and aromas can be described as blackberry, raspberry, cherry, plum, mint, eucalyptus, coffee, bittersweet chocolate, mushrooms, and, because of moderate oak aging, toasty, vanilla, and sweet spice. Popular varieties in this style include Merlot, Pinot Noir, some Cabernets, Sangiovese, and Syrah/Shiraz (two names for the same grape).

RICH, HEARTY, FULL-BODIED REDS These are often described as *big, meaty, chewy, intense fruit, complex, tannic, powerful* wines. They are typically very deep red in color, often almost black. They have high alcohol content (13.5 to 15 percent). Varieties made in this style include Cabernet, Merlot, Syrah/Shiraz, Nebbiolo, Zinfandel, Petit Sirah, and big proprietary blends (belonging to individual winerys), often referred to as "meritage" blends in America.

dessert wines and sparkling wines

Two other categories of wines also made in a variety of styles and flavors should be mentioned here.

DESSERT WINES As the name suggests, dessert wines usually range from gently to intensely sweet. Some, like port, are fortified with additional alcohol to give them a special character, but their use is generally restricted to the end of the meal. In my view, dessert wines are best consumed by themselves, not with dessert but as dessert.

SPARKLING WINES AND CHAMPAGNES These are made in styles ranging from crisp and bone-dry to sweet. There are many sparkling wines from all over the world—prosecco, cava, cremant, for example—that are not technically Champagne, a term that can only legally be used to describe wines made in France's Champagne region according to a traditional method. It's unfortunate that sparkling wines are perceived as a cocktail or apéritif beverage or only appropriate for special occasion toasts, because I think they offer great opportunities for matching to food.

Fear of wine—or fear of feeling stupid around wine—is one of the qualities that divide Americans from the rest of the world. All over the globe, from Argentina to Greece to South Africa to France, wine is a drink. Like fruit juice. Or beer. Or tea. Just like with those everyday beverages, people drink the wine that's available, that they like, or that they can afford. Many of these countries also have wine experts, but that doesn't interfere with the enjoyment of wine as a beverage. It's cool to know a lot about wine. It's a rich subject. But you don't need to *know* wine to enjoy it any more than you need an advanced degree in botany to appreciate the daffodils in your own front yard.

glossary and pantry

ASIAN CHILI-GARLIC SAUCE

Every Asian cuisine has some variation on this condiment, which is a blend of hot chiles, garlic, vinegar, and sometimes other spices. Asian chili-garlic sauce is a staple in my pantry and I find I use it as much as I use salt and pepper. It's generally sold in glass jars; the Lee Kum Kee brand made in Hong Kong is one of my favorites and widely available. Try several and pick the one you like best (you can give the others to your neighbors!).

ASIAN FISH SAUCE

Fish sauce is a pungent, salty liquid made from salted, fermented fish. Tasting it straight or even smelling it is too intense an experience for most people, but a small quantity adds immeasurably to the flavor of many dishes. It is a key ingredient in Thai and Vietnamese cooking and popular throughout Asia. Like chili-garlic sauce, each Asian cuisine has its own version and they vary in intensity. Look for those that are golden in color and relatively clear; they tend to be a little less salty and fishy. If you're concerned about a particular sauce's strength, add half of what the recipe calls for—you can always add more to taste. Fish sauce is increasingly available in supermarkets and always in Asian markets. The name may differ according to country of origin (*nam pla* in Thailand, *nuoc mam* in Vietnam, *patis* in the Philippines, *shottsuru* in Japan), but they are interchangeable. Fish sauce is also referred to as fish gravy.

BOIL

Technically, the point at which a liquid changes into a gas (or vapor) is its boiling point. For cooking purposes, liquid has come to a boil when bubbles form uniformly across the surface; when the bubbles are so vigorous they cannot be stirred down, it is called a hard, rolling boil. Reduction sauces, pasta, and crisp cooked vegetables, for example, are always cooked at a hard, rolling boil.

CHILES
Chiles, Fresh

There are innumerable chile varieties, but the following are generally the most readily available in the United States and the ones that I call for in this book. You can use them interchangeably—just remember that they vary in heat intensity, so if you're preparing a dish for someone who is sensitive to chile heat, start by using half the amount called for and then adding to your own taste. Also remember that even within a single variety, fresh chiles can vary dramatically in their heat level, depending on origin, the time of year, and so on. The only way you can be really sure of the heat is to taste a bit. *With all chiles, be sure to wash your hands thoroughly with soap and water after removing the seeds and inner ribs, where the heat from the active ingredient, capsaicin, is located.*

HABANERO While the habanero chile has a distinctive flavor, it is one of the hottest chiles. This small lantern-shaped chile ranges in color from light green to bright orange and may have originated in Cuba, as its name suggests (think "Havana").

JALAPEÑO This smooth, oval dark green chile is named after Jalapa, the capital of Veracruz, Mexico. It is about 1 inch in diameter and 2 inches long. The chile can be very hot if the seeds are not removed, but without the seeds it is much milder. The jalapeño is one of the most popular chiles used in the United States.

POBLANO Probably best known for its role in the Mexican dish chiles rellenos, the poblano is a very dark green to reddish-brown chile with a mild, rich, almost smoky flavor. I use it in place of green bell peppers in recipes since I think it has a deeper, meatier taste I prefer. Dried, it is known as the ancho chile.

SERRANO The serrano is a small (about 1 1/2 inches long), medium-hot green chile, with a little more fire than a jalapeño. It has an acidic flavor, which makes it very popular to add to salsas.

Chiles, Dried and Powdered

The world of dried chiles is vast. Several dried chiles are used in the book and each has its own unique flavor. Chile powder is also called for in several recipes. The most important thing to note is that I'm referring to pure chile powder with no other seasonings added to it. Supermarket "chili" powders or chili seasonings include a blend of spices and seasonings. Pure ground chile is exactly what it sounds like—dried chile peppers, ground to a powder.

ANCHO My favorite all-purpose pure chile powder is made from the ancho chile. It's a medium-hot chile with a rich, round, almost sweet fruity flavor. In Mexico, fresh chiles have different names than their dried counterparts. A dried ancho is made from a fresh poblano.

CALIFORNIA California chile powder is milder than ancho. It's often a blend of several different chile varieties, but nevertheless, it is still a pure chile powder because it contains nothing but powdered dried chile peppers. It is readily available in Hispanic markets.

CHIMAYO The Chimayo chile is grown in the Chimayo area of New Mexico near Santa Fe. It's not as readily available as the ancho chile but very delicious.

GUAJILLO The dried guajillo (little gourd) chile is so named because the seeds within its dried pod rattle. This flavorful chile can be quite hot and is used in stews and sauces. In its fresh state it is referred to as miraso.

Chipotle Chiles in Adobo

Chipotle chiles are jalapeños that have been both dried and smoked. When you cook with them, you get the double hit of hot spice and smoke. They can also be purchased canned as chipotles in adobo, packed in a sauce of tomatoes, garlic, vinegar, and other spices that I find irresistible. Canned chipotles in adobo are readily available in Mexican markets and often in the Mexican section of many supermarkets. Chipotles are pretty powerful, so if you have a low threshold for heat, add a little less than the recipe calls for. You can always add more. If you're like me, however, you'll soon be using them in everything. The leftovers freeze well.

CHINESE FIVE-SPICE POWDER

An all-purpose powdered seasoning made from five (or more) ground spices: star anise, fennel, cinnamon, cloves, and Sichuan peppercorns or sometimes ginger. Sold in tins and bottles.

GALANGAL

A member of the ginger family, galangal is similar in its flavor and pungency but has a decidedly more peppery flavor, making it too hot to eat by itself. You can find it fresh in Asian markets. It has a very thin, translucent skin. It's also available dried but it's not nearly as interesting and aromatic as when it's fresh. Interestingly, galangal was popular in European cooking during the Middle Ages but was then "lost" and has only recently been rediscovered through interest in the cooking of Southeast Asia.

GARLIC
Poached Garlic

To poach garlic, separate the cloves but don't peel them. Place them in a small saucepan, cover them with at least ½ inch of cold water, and bring to a boil over high heat. As soon as the water boils, drain it off, cover the garlic again with ½ inch of cold water, and bring to a boil. Rinse the cloves to cool. Remove the husks from the poached garlic and store tightly covered in the refrigerator for up to 10 days.

Roasted Garlic

Preheat the oven to 375°F. With a large, sharp knife, cut off the top of a whole head of garlic to expose the very top of the cloves. Drizzle with a little olive oil and season with salt and pepper. Wrap each head loosely in foil and roast for 45 minutes or until the head is soft when gently squeezed. Open the foil and roast for another 5 to 10 minutes to lightly brown and caramelize the garlic. Remove from the oven, let cool, and squeeze the garlic out of the husks—like squeezing toothpaste out of a tube. Store tightly covered in the refrigerator for up to 10 days.

Toasted Garlic

To toast garlic, separate the cloves but don't peel them. In a dry (oil-free) sauté pan, toast the garlic over moderate heat for 3 or 4 minutes or until they have brown spots on all sides. The husk will now slip off very easily. Toasting adds a rich, nutty flavor and moderates the harshness of the raw garlic. Store tightly covered in the refrigerator for up to 10 days.

JICAMA

A native of Central and South America, jicama is now grown widely throughout the Pacific Rim. It is a fleshy, crisp, sweet root that ranges in size from less than a pound to 5 pounds or more. I think it is best eaten raw, although some Chinese dishes call for it to be steamed or stir-fried. It does need to be peeled. It makes a great addition to salads and has an excellent affinity for tart-sweet vinaigrettes. Jicama is the best alternative to fresh water chestnuts in Chinese cuisine, as it has a similar sweet, crunchy flavor and texture. It is generally available year-round, especially in Latin American and Chinese markets. Look for jicama that are very firm with no dark spots.

MIRIN

Mirin from Japan is a sweet, syrupy, clear fermented rice product with added distilled alcohol that is used in cooking only. It has an alcohol content around 12 percent and a high sugar content, and the combination of the two gives mirin its distinctive flavor and sweetness—and also provides it with two particularly prized characteristics: the ability to mask strong fish and meat odors and the sheen it imparts to food, most noticeably in teriyaki. Mirin is almost always sold in clear glass bottles and is commonly used in grilled and simmered dishes, dipping sauces, and broths.

MISO

Miso, a rich, salty paste made from fermented soybeans and other grains, is available in the refrigerator section of most health and natural foods stores and certainly in Asian (especially Japanese) markets. See page 301 for a description of various types. If it comes in a nonresealable container, transfer the leftovers to a clean glass jar with a tight-fitting lid. Miso should be refrigerated; it will keep indefinitely.

NUT OILS

As the name suggests, these are oils made from pressing nuts of various types. The best nut oils come from nuts that have been lightly toasted before pressing, giving them a richer, nuttier flavor. Up until recent times the best nut oils came from France, which has a long tradition of their use. In the last few years, however, American producers have come to the fore, especially in California, where most of the nation's nuts are grown. Two sources that I like are California Press (www.californiapress.com) and Spectrum Naturals (www.spectrumorganic.com). Gourmet food stores such as Sur La Table and Williams-Sonoma also carry good nut oils as do many natural foods stores.

The most popular nut oils are made from walnuts, almonds, filberts (hazelnuts), pecans, and pistachios. The best are simply cold-pressed and unrefined, though as a result they have a finite shelf-life. Like all unrefined oils, their enemies are light and heat. They should always come in either a tin or a dark glass bottle. You really should use them within 3 months after opening. I store mine in the refrigerator, which seems to preserve them longer.

NUTS, TOASTING

For me, the flavor and aromatic quality of toasted nuts are well worth the little extra effort. It's a simple process, but it requires some attention to avoid over-toasting the nuts, which makes them bitter. Though it's certainly possible to toast nuts on top of the stove in a dry pan over moderate heat, I think the safest and surest method is to use the oven. Spread the nuts out in a loose single layer on a baking sheet and put them in a preheated 375°F. oven. Depending on their size, they'll take just a few minutes. Start checking after 4 minutes. You're looking to add just a slight amount of color. The better indicator is the aroma. As soon as you smell the toasty, nutty aroma, remove the pan from the oven and get the nuts off the baking sheet to cool them. Store in an air-tight container. If you are storing for a long time, put them in a jar with a tight-fitting lid in the freezer. My rule is that anytime nuts are used in a recipe I lightly toast them first.

PANKO

Panko are Japanese bread crumbs that have a lighter and coarser texture—almost more like a flake—than the commercial dried bread crumbs we're familiar with. They're perfect for breaded and fried food, since they brown and crisp quickly and keep their crunchy texture even after sitting for a while. Panko is widely available in Asian markets and increasingly in supermarkets because in recent years American chefs have talked about it so much.

PEPPER

To me, freshly ground pepper is one of the greatest and most underappreciated flavor enhancers around. The Egg Drop Soup on page 92 is a great example of a low-key dish elevated to real flavor excitement by plenty of fresh ground pepper. The emphasis is on "fresh ground." Please don't buy preground pepper. Like many spices, peppercorns lose much of their wonderful aroma within a few minutes after grinding. Black peppercorns are, of course, the most common; when white pepper is specified, it's for the look of the finished dish. The many varieties of peppercorns do taste different, but you can use any kind in any recipe. Black peppercorns are the immature fruit of a tropical vine native to India and Indonesia that have been dried in the sun to develop their pungent flavor. White peppercorns come from the mature berry, left on the vine until fairly ripe and red in color. The red skin is removed by soaking and rubbing and then the peppercorns are dried. Pink peppercorns are not a true peppercorn, but rather the dried berries of the Baies rose plant, or the pepper rose, grown in Madagascar. Chinese Sichuan pepper also is not a true pepper but comes from a shrub related to the prickly ash tree. It has a sharp tingly taste with a spicy, lemony fragrance. If you have the interest and the counter space, buy several pepper mills, fill them with different peppercorns, and experiment. At home, I use a mixture of peppers in my pepper mill to create a complex marriage of aromas and flavors. Try using a heavier hand with the pepper than you're used to. I promise: real flavor excitement, not just sneezing, awaits.

ROASTED PEPPERS

To roast bell peppers, use a long-handled fork and char them over an open flame until they are blackened all over. The burner on a gas range is fine. Or you can place them under a preheated broiler about two inches from the heat and turn occasionally until they are well blackened. An even simpler way is to cut the pepper down one side, remove the seeds and stem, and flatten it on a baking sheet, skin side up. Place it under the broiler until charred—you don't even have to turn it. Place the blackened peppers in a bowl, cover them with plastic wrap, and let them steam for a few minutes. With your fingers or the point of a knife, remove the blackened skin. *Do not* wash the peppers as some books advise—you'll wash away the juices and all of that lovely toasty flavor that's developed from the charring.

If you haven't already, cut off the tops and discard the stem and seeds. Roasted and peeled peppers freeze well (flatten, place a layer of wax paper in between each, and wrap well in foil) and are also delicious covered in olive oil and stored in the refrigerator for up to 3 weeks. Don't forget to use the flavorful oil when the peppers are gone.

PUREE

To puree is to finely mash any food to a smooth consistency until no identifiable pieces or chunks are left. A puree can be thick or thin, depending on what's being pureed. The best way to puree any food is in a food processor or blender. Just dump it in and run the machine until the solids are all pulverized—no need for pulsing or checking. We often puree soups and sauces to achieve a smooth, velvety texture. Purees of fruits and vegetables are also used to make salad dressings and to act as thickeners for sauces and stocks.

RICE

There are thousands of varieties of rice. Some estimates put the number at more than 100,000, with at least 8,000 currently or in recent times having been cultivated for food. Rice is grown on every continent except Antarctica and has an amazing ability to adapt to a broad range of growing conditions. In America we consume somewhere around 20 pounds of rice per person per year. This seems like a lot until you compare it to parts of Southeast Asia where average consumption tops 500 pounds a year.

With rices and recipes of the world available to us, it is easy to be confused by the way rice is identified on packages and in print. Let me shed some light: Rice can be described by its *size*, such as long grain, medium grain, and short grain; by its *botanical variety*: Arborio, basmati, jasmine, etc.; by the degree of *"stickiness,"* such as "glutinous rice" (a misnomer because rice contains no gluten); by its *color*: brown, red, and white; and by the kind of *processing* it's gone through: instant, parboiled, enriched, polished, and so on. I find the most practical way to describe rice for most American cooks is by its size and then tack on whatever other modifier is helpful. For example, I'll describe a risotto rice as a *"medium grain rice such as Arborio or Carnaroli."*

All three sizes are available in both white and brown versions, and every botanical variety of rice is (theoretically, at least) available both brown and white.

White rice is the rice grain minus the inedible hull and the bran. Brown and other colored rices have had the hull removed but the bran left on. Wild rice, which is unique to North America, is not a true rice but the seed of a wild grass.

RICE WINE AND SHAOXING WINE

The most famous of rice wines in America is no doubt sake, which originated in Japan. There are several sake producers in America now, especially on the West Coast. The other rice wine often called for in Chinese cooking is Shaoxing wine, which originates in the city of Shaoxing in eastern China. It's made from a blend of fermented rice, millet, and yeast and aged for up to 100 years. It has a rich amber color, full-bodied aroma, and an alcohol content similar to dry sherry, which can be used as a substitute.

SALT

Salt has many faces and, believe it or not, many flavors. Most salt sold commercially today is rock salt, which is mined out of the ground from salt deposits left behind by ancient, extinct seas. You can also buy sea salt, which comes from existing seas and is simply seawater that has been evaporated by the sun. There are substantial differences in the flavor of various sea salts depending on origin. Some have a strong mineral taste, while others taste of seaweed, and still others are almost sweet.

Most tasters (including me) prefer sea salt to ordinary table, or mined salt. It simply seems to have a more complex flavor. Also ordinary table salt has additives such as anticaking agents that detract from the flavor, in my opinion. Try a taste test and I think you'll be convinced that good sea salt is superior to ordinary table salt. Some cooks also believe that sea salt is nutritionally superior to rock salt, but there is no truth to this. Any extra minerals that may be found in sea salt occur in such small amounts that they wouldn't make any dietary difference. Kosher salt has large, flaky crystals and dissolves somewhat more slowly than ordinary salt—qualities that are helpful in drawing the blood out of meats before cooking, which is a requirement of Jewish dietary law. I like its large crystals as a garnishing salt, sprinkled on just at serving time. When you do this you often end up using less salt, since the salt flavor is right on top when you bite into the food.

My recommendation, then, is to go with either sea salt or kosher salt. They are interchangeable in cooking, but in some recipes I've specified one or the other, just to encourage you to try using more than one kind in your kitchen!

SALTED BLACK BEANS

Also known as fermented or preserved black beans, these are used widely in Chinese cooking and add a rich "meaty" flavor and salty taste. Salted black beans are typically included in braised, steamed, or stir-fried dishes. They are made by steaming small black beans, then fermenting them with salt and spices, such as ginger. You'll find them in Asian and especially Chinese markets in all kinds of packages, from plastic bags to tins to cardboard containers. The beans should feel soft and not dried out and hard. It's best to store them in a jar that you can tightly close in the refrigerator, where they will last almost indefinitely.

SAUTÉ

This term is used often in the book, since it is one of the most common techniques in the world's repertoire. To sauté anything—whether a bit of chopped garlic or a whole chicken breast—is to cook it in a little fat, such as butter or oil, in a wide, shallow pan over high heat. If you used more fat, we would call it frying. Sauté comes from the French word *sauter*, which means "to jump," suggesting that the food jumps when added to the hot pan. There are two schools of thought about whether the fat should be added to a cold pan or a heated one. The only time I think it makes a difference is when you use butter. If the pan is very hot when you add butter, you run the risk of the butter burning before you can get the food you want to sauté into the pan. My advice: warm the pan before adding the fat and then bring it up to sauté temperature. If you're using butter you can control the tendency to burn by also adding a little oil, such as olive oil, along with the butter. Vegetable oils have a higher smoke or burn point and give that cushion to the butter.

SESAME OIL

Sesame oil is available anywhere Asian groceries are sold, including the ethnic foods aisle of most supermarkets, and comes in a variety of forms. Toasted sesame oil should be in everyone's pantry. Made from seeds that have been toasted before pressing, it is a medium-brown color and has a deep, nutty flavor. If the oil is brown, you can be sure that it is toasted sesame oil, whether or not the label says so. I also love sesame oil that has been infused with chile pepper and use it in several recipes in the book. This oil is generally labeled hot pepper sesame oil or something similar and is bright orange-red. A few drops are a great way to add both nutty flavors from the sesame and spice (heat) to many dishes, but it is not a substitute for toasted sesame oil—it's much too hot. Whatever the variety, only buy brands that are labeled pure and not mixed with other oils, which dilutes the flavor. Like all oils, plan to use it within 6 months after opening.

SHRIMP PASTE

This strong, salty paste made from fermented shrimp is used in many Asian cuisines. It is very pungent, but don't let that put you off. A tiny amount adds incredible flavor. Sometimes I use it to make a simple fish stock by adding just a little to low-salt or unsalted chicken stock. Called *kapi* in Thailand and *mam ruoc* in Vietnam, it is available in Asian markets and comes in plastic and glass containers. You'll see it in various forms, sometimes as a thick pinkish paste and sometimes with oil. I prefer the former. After opening, store it indefinitely in the refrigerator.

SIMMER

To simmer means to cook just below the boiling point, when the surface of the simmering liquid shows occasional bubbles and a little movement but not much. We use this technique for gentle cooking. Recipes that call for simmering often specify whether the pot should be covered or uncovered, or partially covered. This is not as mysterious as it appears: if long simmering is to reduce or thicken and concentrate flavor, then the pot needs to be uncovered so that water can cook off in the form of steam. If the simmering is to cook food or blend flavors without losing liquid, then the pot needs to be completely or partly covered. Grains like rice are simmered in tightly covered pots because the point is to let the grain absorb the liquid and not to let it escape into the air.

STAR ANISE

Easy to recognize, star anise is a dried seed pod about an inch across with 6 to 8 points, which comes from the Chinese magnolia tree. Each point of the star encases a shiny brown seed. It has a rich, spicy licorice flavor and is added to soups, sauces, braises, and poaching liquids where it imparts its unique flavor. Star anise is removed from the finished dish before eating. The Chinese believe that it also aids digestion and freshens the breath. You'll find it in the dried spice section of many supermarkets and certainly in all Asian markets. Be sure to buy star anise that are whole and not broken; the pods begin to lose their flavor when broken. Star anise is one of the spices in Chinese five-spice powder.

THAI CURRY PASTE

Bottled Thai curry pastes may be green, red, yellow, and other colors and are commonly used in Thailand as a convenient substitute for homemade mixtures. The color of the paste comes from the ingredients; it is not an indicator of heat level. Green curry paste, for example, is made from a pureed or pounded blend of fresh green chiles, lemon grass, galangal, oil, and other seasonings. Red curry paste uses dried red chiles, among other similar ingredients. You can buy prepared curry pastes of all descriptions in Asian markets or online. Refrigerate after opening and use them within 3 months or so.

TOMATILLO

From Mexico and Central America, the tomatillo (which means "little tomato") resembles a small green tomato in a papery husk. It is, however, more closely related to other plants such as the ornamental Chinese lantern or the purple ground cherry. It has a bright acid flavor that can be overpowering when raw but mellows in cooking and suggests lime or lemon. Its distinctive flavor makes the tomatillo an essential ingredient in Mexican green sauces or salsas. Add it finely chopped to your next batch of guacamole.

index

Achiote Paste, 163
Achiote-Grilled Sea Bass, 163
Adobo Pork Roast, 138–39
Agrodolce Dressing, 36
Apple Cider Dressing, 121
Apple(s)
    Curry Buttermilk, and Pecans, Poached
      Chicken Breast Salad with, 213
    oven-drying, 116
    Syrup, Rosy, 306
apricots, oven-drying, 116
Artichoke and Olive Sauce with
    Conchiglioni, 187
Artichoke Aïoli, 248
Arugula
    and Cannellini Bean Salad, 228
    Grilled Beef *Tagliata* with Rosemary,
      Capers, and Lemons, 160–61
    Grilled Eggplant and Red Pepper
      Sandwich with Basil-Mint Pesto and,
      157
    Grilled Portabella Sandwich with
      Artichoke Aïoli, 248
    Grilled Tuna with Spicy Sesame Ginger
      Greens, 29
    Melon and Goat Cheese Salad with
      Agrodolce Dressing, 36–37
    White Bean Salad with Salsa Fresca, 8
Ascorbic Dip, 117
Asian Butter Sauce, 218–19
Asian chili-garlic sauce, 326
Asian fish sauce, 326
Asian Marinade, 60
Asian Pesto, 43
Asian Vegetable Soup with Asian Pesto, 46
Asian-Flavored Short Ribs, 136–37
Asparagus with Vinaigrette, 25
Avocado Sauce, Grilled Thin Pork Chops
    with Xnipec and, 13

Balsamic Vinegar
    buying, 21
    -Lemon Glaze, 259
    Marinade, Simple, 57
    Reduced, 161
    Vinaigrette, 25
bananas, oven-drying, 116
Basil
    Asian Pesto, 43
    Green Herb Sauce for Pasta, 193
    -Mint Pesto, 45
    Pesto, Basic, or Pistou, 42
Bean(s), 220–25
    Black, Gazpacho Salad, 228–29
    black, salted, 330
    Cannellini, and Arugula Salad, 228
    cooking, about, 222–25
    Esther's Swedish, Baked, 231

Flageolet, with Mushrooms, Tomatoes,
    and Gremolata, 232
Garbanzo and Blue Cheese Hummus,
    227
Grilled Portabella Mushrooms with
    Lentils and a Spicy Tomato Broth,
    250–51
Okra, and Peppers Stew, 230
White, Mashed, with Roasted Garlic,
    226
White, Salad with Salsa Fresca, 8
Beef
    Asian-Flavored Short Ribs, 136–37
    Basic Red Wine Pan Sauce for
      Hamburgers or Steaks, 78
    Brisket Braised in Coffee, 142–43
    Grilled, *Tagliata* with Rosemary, Capers,
      and Lemons, 160–61
    Herb and Pistachio–Stuffed Veal Pot
      Roast, 144–45
    Mojo-Marinated Skewered, 61
    Oxtails Braised in Red Wine, 140–41
    Pot Roast, Basic, 132–33
    pot-roasting, about, 130–31, 133
    Stew, Slow-Cooked, or Pot Roast,
      134–35
black beans, salted, 330
blueberries, oven-drying, 116
Blueberries and Peaches, Vanilla Baked,
    310
Blue Cheese and Mustard Vinaigrette, 26
braising, defined, 130
Breads
    Calzones, 165
    Flatbread on the Grill, 164–65
    Kulchas, 165
    Pizzas, 165
Broccoli Sauce for Pasta, Laurie's, 188
Broccoli Soufflé, 173
broth, about, 88–89
Buttermilk Panna Cotta, 312

Cabbage
    Asian Vegetable Soup with Asian Pesto,
      46
    Celery, and Carrot Salad with Bay
      Shrimp and Curry Dressing, 282
    oven-drying, 117
    Soy-Roasted Tofu with Asian Greens,
      296–97
Caesar Salad Dressing, Tofu, 291
Cake(s)
    Individual Molten Chocolate Truffle,
      314–15
    Mini Rock Shrimp, with Mango Salsa,
      276–77
    Nut Oil, 316
    Orange Ricotta, with Strawberries, 311

Calzones, 165
Caper Dill Vinaigrette, 25
Capers, Fried, 161
Cardamom Ice Cream, 129
Carrot(s)
    Cabbage, and Celery Salad with Bay
      Shrimp and Curry Dressing, 282
    Cold Cream of Red Bell Pepper Soup
      from the Juicer, 97
    Jus or Sauce, Fresh, 76
    Orange, and Ginger Soup, 95
    Salad, Lettuce Cups with Thai Shrimp
      and, 275
Cauliflower, Oven-Dried, Corn, and Red
    Pepper Risotto, 123
cauliflower, oven-drying, 117
Cheese
    Blue, and Garbanzo Hummus, 227
    Blue, and Mustard Vinaigrette, 26
    Goat, and Melon Salad with Agrodolce
      Dressing, 36–37
    Goat, Soufflés, Twice-Baked, with
      Watercress and Oven-Dried
      Tomatoes, 178–79
    Grilled Tortillas with Fresh Chiles and
      Pickled Red Onions, 156–57
    Grits Soufflé, 175
    Orange Ricotta Cake with Strawberries,
      311
    Parmesan-Pepper Egg Drop Soup, 92
    Pecorino, Couscous Risotto with
      Oven-Dried Mushrooms and
      Tomatoes and, 127
    Soufflé, Basic, 171–73
    Soufflé, variations on, 173–74
    Tofu Caesar Salad Dressing, 291
Chicken, 202–7
    Basic Herb Pan Sauce for, 77
    Breast, Poached, Salad with Curry
      Buttermilk, Apples, and Pecans,
      213
    Breasts, Pan-Roasted, with Asian Butter
      Sauce, 218–19
    Breasts, Poached, 212
    Breasts, Sauté of, with Vinegar, 208
    Breasts, Simple Soy-Marinated and
      Roasted, 209
    Clams, and Shrimp, Paella with, 284
    Cold Noodle Salad with Coconut
      Peanut Sauce, 198
    Ginger-Poached, and Stock, 214
    Grilled Yogurt and Mint, 63
    Kebabs, Grilled Indian-Spiced, 166–67
    Noodle Soup with Laksa, 104–5
    pan-roasting, 218
    poaching, 212
    Pot-Roasted, with Vegetables, 146–47
    Roast, Basic, 210

conversion chart

EQUIVALENT IMPERIAL AND METRIC MEASUREMENTS

American cooks use standard containers, the 8-ounce cup and a tablespoon that takes exactly 16 level fillings to fill that cup level. Measuring by cup makes it very difficult to give weight equivalents, as a cup of densely packed butter will weigh considerably more than a cup of flour. The easiest way therefore to deal with cup measurements in recipes is to take the amount by volume rather than by weight. Thus the equation reads:

1 cup = 240 ml = 8 fl. oz.   ½ cup = 120 ml = 4 fl. oz.

It is possible to buy a set of American cup measures in major stores around the world.

In the States, butter is often measured in sticks. One stick is the equivalent of 8 tablespoons. One tablespoon of butter is therefore the equivalent to ½ ounce/15 grams.

LIQUID MEASURES

Fluid Ounces	U.S.	Imperial	Milliliters
	1 teaspoon	1 teaspoon	5
¼	2 teaspoons	1 dessertspoon	10
½	1 tablespoon	1 tablespoon	14
1	2 tablespoons	2 tablespoons	28
2	¼ cup	4 tablespoons	56
4	½ cup		120
5		¼ pint or 1 gill	140
6	¾ cup		170
8	1 cup		240
9			250, ¼ liter
10	1¼ cups	½ pint	280
12	1½ cups		340
15		¾ pint	420
16	2 cups		450
18	2¼ cups		500, ½ liter
20	2½ cups	1 pint	560
24	3 cups		675
25		1¼ pints	700
27	3½ cups		750
30	3¾ cups	1½ pints	840
32	4 cups or 1 quart		900
35		1¾ pints	980
36	4½ cups		1000, 1 liter
40	5 cups	2 pints or 1 quart	1120

SOLID MEASURES

U.S. and Imperial Measures		Metric Measures	
Ounces	Pounds	Grams	Kilos
1		28	
2		56	
3½		100	
4	¼	112	
5		140	
6		168	
8	½	225	
9		250	¼
12	¾	340	
16	1	450	
18		500	½
20	1¼	560	
24	1½	675	
27		750	¾
28	1¾	780	
32	2	900	
36	2¼	1000	1
40	2½	1100	
48	3	1350	
54		1500	1½

OVEN TEMPERATURE EQUIVALENTS

Fahrenheit	Celsius	Gas Mark	Description
225	110	¼	Cool
250	130	½	
275	140	1	Very Slow
300	150	2	
325	170	3	Slow
350	180	4	Moderate
375	190	5	
400	200	6	Moderately Hot
425	220	7	Fairly Hot
450	230	8	Hot
475	240	9	Very Hot
500	250	10	Extremely Hot

Any broiling recipes can be used with the grill of the oven, but beware of high-temperature grills.

EQUIVALENTS FOR INGREDIENTS

all-purpose flour—plain flour
baking sheet—oven tray
buttermilk—ordinary milk
cheesecloth—muslin
coarse salt—kitchen salt
cornstarch—cornflour
eggplant—aubergine

granulated sugar—caster sugar
half and half—12% fat milk
heavy cream—double cream
light cream—single cream
parchment paper—greaseproof paper
plastic wrap—cling film
scallion—spring onion

shortening—white fat
unbleached flour—strong, white flour
zest—rind
zucchini—courgettes or marrow